ACTION, KNOWLEDGE,
AND WILL

TENK

Thank you veddy much. — LATKA
GRAVAS
"TAXI"

ACTION, KNOWLEDGE, AND WILL

JOHN HYMAN

(handwritten annotations:)

As long as there is coffee in the cupboard have worked would trees being used being be? — Cassandra Clare

No FURNITURE As so charming As Books

"There's many a slip betwixt the cup & the lip."
— English proverb —

"What each man does is based **NOT** ON certain and direct knowledge but ON pictures made by himself or given to him."
— Walter Lippmann —

"Man seeks in society comfort, use & protection."
— FRANCIS BACON —

OXFORD
UNIVERSITY PRESS

OXFORD
UNIVERSITY PRESS

Great Clarendon Street, Oxford, OX2 6DP,
United Kingdom

Oxford University Press is a department of the University of Oxford.
It furthers the University's objective of excellence in research, scholarship,
and education by publishing worldwide. Oxford is a registered trade mark of
Oxford University Press in the UK and in certain other countries

First Edition published in 2015

Impression: 1

Published in the United States of America by Oxford University Press
198 Madison Avenue, New York, NY 10016, United States of America

British Library Cataloguing in Publication Data
Data available

Library of Congress Control Number: 2014949673

ISBN 978–0–19–873577–9

Printed and bound by
CPI Group (UK) Ltd, Croydon, CR0 4YY

For George

Contents

Preface

*unlike b?
knowledge
an ability
or*

The main ideas I shall defend in this book can be summarized quite briefly.

First, human agency has several distinct dimensions, some of which it has in common with the agency of other animals, or other agents more generally, others of which it does not. For we can think about human agency in physical, psychological, intellectual, and ethical terms. And we cannot hope to understand it philosophically unless we understand how these different dimensions of agency are defined, and how they are related.

If we survey the philosophy of action in the modern period, bearing this in mind, it is bound to seem painfully inadequate. Modern philosophy developed a remarkably simplistic theory of action, which eventually enabled philosophers to equate action in general, human action, voluntary action, intentional action, and action done for reasons. It was less an intellectual revolution than an earthquake, and it levelled a complex conceptual structure that enables us to think and reason effectively about the different dimensions of human agency. One aim of the book is to criticize this relentlessly simplifying philosophy and reconstruct the edifice, separating the storeys that were sandwiched together in the collapse.

Second, understanding the intellectual dimension of human agency involves thinking about the relationship between knowledge and rational behaviour in a substantially new way, and this offers the prospect of a new conception of knowledge itself. Many philosophers still think of knowledge as what Ryle sardonically called an élite suburb of belief, true belief with a special accreditation or guarantee. But unlike belief, knowledge is an ability, so if we want to understand what knowledge is, and why we value it, we need to ask what it is an ability to do, instead of asking how it can be certified or acquired. We need to think prospectively not retrospectively, about how knowledge is applied, employed, expressed, in the infinitely varied circumstances of human life. In the last three chapters, I shall make a case for reorienting the theory of knowledge in this way.

Combining these two tasks means in effect realigning the philosophy of action and the theory of knowledge, and reforming received ideas about some of the main structural features of our thought about human action—in particular, about the relationships between voluntary agency, intentional agency, rational agency, and agency as such; about the explanation of intentional action; and about the distinction between activity and passivity in human life. But I do not want to exaggerate how radically I am departing from tradition. Philosophy does sometimes seem incapable of making gradual progress, so that only the most violent attack, with its own kind of excess, can overcome the vested interests of the *ancien régime*, and achieve deep and lasting change. But this is a pity, because philosophical theories are more often exaggerations or simplifications than intellectually worthless 'houses of cards'.

So it is, I believe, with the theories of human action that emerged in the third quarter of the twentieth century, when first Wittgenstein and Anscombe and then Davidson held sway. Their ideas are still dominant, but we have gained sufficient distance from them in recent years to reassess the whole subject, freed by their efforts from the errors they criticized, but also free from the intellectual trap of discipleship.

The philosophy of action takes up most of the book because the range of concepts it involves is large and complex, and the dominant ideas about them are deeply rooted in early modern philosophy. My aim in this part of the book is analytical rather than historical, as it is throughout, but I have included a certain amount of historical material because even the ideas that philosophers imagine they spin out of themselves like spiders have long and complicated histories, and we cannot hope to understand them, or assess them properly, or improve on them, unless we know about their past. Philosophy is not a formal discipline: logical acumen is not enough.

My approach is therefore partly historical, but my aim is to contribute to the development of the philosophy of action, in two main ways: first, by encouraging an approach to the study of human agency that emphasizes the distinctions between its physical, ethical, psychological, and intellectual dimensions; and second by bringing the most general questions in the theory of knowledge within its compass—what knowledge is and why it is of value; why, as Julian 'the Apostate' put it, the serpent was a benefactor rather than a destroyer of the human race.

My plan for this book was always to combine epistemology and the philosophy of action, and I always intended to keep the text close to 100,000 words, in the hope that it might be read as a continuous argument, and not just cited or searched. I therefore knew that I would be unable to discuss some important topics in the philosophy of action, and so it has turned out. There is nothing here, or next to nothing, about the social dimension of human action; about deliberating, deciding, and intending; about trying and attempting; about strength, weakness, and freedom of the will; or about processes and events. And there is nothing about so-called mental acts in general, as opposed to acts of will in particular. Consequently, several interesting and influential studies in the philosophy of action do not receive the attention they would require in a more comprehensive work. But like every author, I hope my work will be judged mainly by what I have written, rather than what I have left out.

I should like to record my thanks to the many friends and colleagues who kindly read and commented on drafts of chapters, especially Maria Alvarez, Alexander Bird, Lesley Brown, Jonathan Dancy, Antony Duff, Víctor Durà-Vilà, James Grant, David Hillel-Ruben, Jennifer Hornsby, Erasmus Mayr, Yuuki Ohta, Christopher Pulman, Joseph Raz, Natalia Waights-Hickman, and the anonymous authors of some very astute reports commissioned by OUP. I am doubly indebted to Sir Anthony Kenny, who read several chapters of the book in draft, and whose own writings on these topics have had a profound influence on my work. (The title of this book is a tribute to his *Action, Emotion and Will*.) Peter Momtchiloff, Emily Brand, and Sarah Dancy have guided and advised me and edited my work with great skill and patience. I am very glad to be able to thank them here as well.

Much of the work on the book was done during my tenure of a Leverhulme Major Research Fellowship, in 2010–12. I am very grateful to the Leverhulme Trust for the award, and to the Governing Body of The Queen's College and the Faculty of Philosophy in the University of Oxford for permitting me to take leave of absence during these two years.

John Hyman
London, June 2014

intellectual trap / discipleship.

And the Lord went before them by day in a pillar of a cloud, to lead them the way; and by night in a pillar of fire, to give them light . . .

Exodus, 13.21

I

Agency and the Will

1.1 Introduction

This chapter, which is in effect a prolegomenon to the main business, is about the modern theory of the will and its incomplete demise. By the modern theory of the will I mean a theory of human action that held sway in philosophy, in several variants, from Descartes in the seventeenth century to Mill in the nineteenth century. It could also be called the empiricist theory of the will, except that Descartes is one of its main sources. The Appendix contains a brief historical digest of the theory and the early dissent from it by Bain, James, and Russell.

The philosophers who defended one variant or another of the modern theory uniformly regarded the will as the source of all voluntary or intentional action, and generally also as the source of human action in general, so that an act cannot be attributed to the agency of an individual at all unless it originates in her will. And since it was widely regarded as axiomatic that only voluntary action can merit praise or blame, or be justly punished, these were also thought to be dependent on the will.[*] Considered in itself, independently of its causes or effects, an act was held to consist in either motion or thought, for example, the motion of your legs when you walk, or your lips when you speak, or the thoughts that occur in your mind when you do mental arithmetic or recite a sonnet in your head. As for the cause of the act, it was thought to be a kind of conscious choosing or willing, usually called a

---

[*] It was controversial whether moral responsibility was contingent on the will's being 'free', and if so what this entailed. But even strict adherence to the principle of utility was held to be consistent with the doctrine that only acts caused by the will ought to be punished. See Bentham, *Introduction to the Principles of Morals and Legislation*, 13.10.

'volition' or 'intention', not merely a wish or desire or appetite or aversion, but a *sui generis* act or operation of the will.

Why did philosophers postulate a *sui generis* act of the will? The reason is simple. The mere fact that I feel hungry clearly isn't sufficient to make me eat, because when I feel hungry, I can still choose not to eat. And feeling hungry isn't necessary to make me eat either, because I can decide to eat despite not feel hungry at all, perhaps because I am ill and have lost appetite. So, it was thought, for me to eat, or at least for my eating to be my own act, and not forced on me, there needs to be a mental act, a choice or decision, which causes my eating. And this is the 'volition' or 'act of will'.[1]

When I say that the modern theory held sway from the time of Descartes to that of Mill, I do not mean to imply that it is now defunct. But in the second half of the nineteenth century, philosophers influenced by the emerging science of experimental psychology began to explain voluntary action without postulating *sui generis* acts of will, as in fact Hobbes had done, writing at the same time as Descartes: first Bain, later James in *The Principles of Psychology*, and then Russell, who followed James closely. Then, in the middle of the twentieth century, the modern theory came under fierce attack, not merely on the grounds that postulating volitions is unnecessary, as James and Russell claimed, but on the more radical grounds that the very idea that a voluntary act is a bodily movement with a mental cause is misconceived. Wittgenstein argued in these terms in his *Brown Book* and *Philosophical Investigations*, drawing on broadly Kantian ideas which he had learned from Schopenhauer, and Ryle did so in *The Concept of Mind*, drawing on ideas that would have been familiar to philosophers in the empiricist tradition, but deploying them with unprecedented destructive energy and panache.

Ryle describes a volition as the means by which a mind gets its ideas translated into facts:

> I think of some state of affairs which I wish to come into existence in the physical world, but, as my thinking and wishing are unexecutive, they require the mediation of a further executive mental process. So I perform a volition which somehow puts my muscles into action. Only when a bodily movement has issued from such a volition can I merit praise or blame for what my hand or tongue has done.[2]

In one of the most brilliant passages in *The Concept of Mind*, Ryle argues that the 'doctrine of volitions' is a myth, 'a causal hypothesis, adopted because it was wrongly supposed that the question, "What makes a bodily movement voluntary?" was a causal question.'[3] Wittgenstein agrees: 'There is a difference', he writes, 'between the voluntary act of getting out of bed and the involuntary rising of my arm. But there is not one common difference between so-called voluntary acts and involuntary ones, viz, the presence or absence of one element, the "act of volition".'[4] A voluntary movement, Wittgenstein suggests with enviable insouciance, may simply be one by which the agent is not surprised.

In the decades that followed, some philosophers criticized the idea that the will is the source of individual human agency in general (e.g. Frankfurt), and others criticized the idea that any act consists in the observable motion we associate with it, such as the motion of a limb (e.g. Hornsby), or in any kind of motion or event at all (e.g. von Wright). For some, the attack by Wittgenstein and Ryle proved that teleological explanations of voluntary or intentional human acts cannot be reduced to explanations in terms of mental causes (e.g. Anscombe). Some argued on the contrary that the idea of a volition or act of will should be discarded, but not the idea that intentional action consists in motion of the agent's body with a particular kind of mental cause (e.g. Davidson). And others defended a purified conception of the will as the *capacity* or *ability* to act intentionally or for reasons (e.g. Kenny and Raz), without postulating any specific kind of mental event as the cause of action of these kinds. Davidson's position is the dominant one today, but it is widely and increasingly contested.

My overall view about the attack on the modern theory of the will in the twentieth century is that it did not go far enough. The elements of the theory singled out for criticism were indeed erroneous or confused. But the critics did not pay sufficient attention to the fact that it was a theory of several quite different things at once: *voluntary* action, *intentional* action, action *as such*—to which we must now add action done for reasons. Whatever details of the modern theory we criticize or reject, the very idea of a will is a standing invitation to participate in this confusion, and we do not gain much by dismissing 'mysterious acts of the will' if, at the same time, we equate voluntary action and intentional action, claim that being intentional (in some respect or 'under some description') is the 'mark of agency', and define intentional action as action that is done for reasons.[5]

As I see it, we think of human action in four different dimensions, by means of four tightly knit families of concepts, although of course the relationships between these concepts are not confined to the family to which they principally belong. In the order in which I shall discuss them in this book, human action has a *physical* dimension, in which the principal concepts are those of agent, power, and causation; an *ethical* dimension, with the concepts of voluntariness and choice; a *psychological* dimension, with the concepts of desire, aim, and intention; and an *intellectual* dimension, with the concepts of reason, knowledge, and belief. The whole point of the philosophy of action is to understand these dimensions of human action, to distinguish between them, and to explain how they are related to each other—not to amalgamate them or equate them, or reduce them in number. Such at least is the main premise of this book.

1.2 Agency and voluntariness

Ryle's readers can form the impression that the modern theory of the will prevailed for three hundred years, unchallenged and unaltered, from Descartes's *The Passions of the Soul* (1649) to *The Concept of Mind* (1949). Of course, this is very far from being the case. Most importantly, Descartes, Locke, Berkeley, Hume, Reid, Bentham, and Mill postulated volitions or intentions—*sui generis* acts of will, distinct from desires and memory-images—whereas Hobbes, Bain, James, and Russell did not. But despite this difference, and the other differences described in the Appendix, philosophical thought about the will was marked by three constant features, which Ryle refers to in the remarks quoted above:

(A) The will was generally seen as *both* the source of voluntary action, which was considered to be apt for praise or blame and punishment or reward, *and* the source of individual human agency as such, so that the bodily movements we ourselves cause personally originate in our wills, whereas the bodily movements we do not cause personally have another cause, whether exogenous, as when one person moves another person's limb, or endogenous, as when our pupils dilate or our hearts contract.

(B) A specific kind of conscious thought was held to cause every voluntary act. Even James and Russell, who anticipated Ryle's claim that the traditional doctrine of volitions is a myth, never doubted that the question, 'What makes a bodily movement voluntary?' is a causal question. They simply held that an idea of a movement or a kinaesthetic image is generally sufficient to cause motion in our bodies, without what James called a 'super-added "will-force"'.[6]

(C) Considered in itself, independently of its causes and effects, an act was held to be a bodily movement, such as the movement of a limb, or, as the influence of physiology on the theory of the will grew in the nineteenth century, a muscular contraction.

Ryle and Wittgenstein were mainly interested in (B), and I shall discuss their views about it in 1.4 and 1.5. I shall comment on (C) in 1.4.3 and 3.1. But my immediate concern is with (A), the idea that the will is the source of *both* voluntary action *and* individual human agency in general.

Agency is a highly abstract physical concept, of the same order as the concepts of substance, causation, and event, whereas voluntariness is an ethical concept. An act is done voluntarily if it is *not* due to ignorance or compulsion, and the point of saying that an act is not due to ignorance or compulsion is that these are both normally exculpations, factors which excuse someone from blame (see 4.1). But the operation of the will was widely held to explain *both* agency *and* voluntariness, *both* the difference between active and passive movements of the body or operations of the mind *and* the difference between the kinds of conduct that can and cannot merit punishment or reward, gratitude or resentment, praise or blame.

I shall criticize the doctrine that will or intention is the mark of agency in the next chapter, and examine the idea of voluntariness per se in Chapter 4. For the moment, I am interested in the relationship between agency and voluntariness, and the principal point I want to make is simply that it is one thing to explain the difference between activity and passivity—e.g. eating and being eaten or kissing and being kissed—and another quite different thing to explain the difference between choice and compulsion—e.g. being kissed consensually and being kissed against one's will. One task belongs to the theory of agency, while the other belongs to the theory of voluntariness. The ideas of agency and voluntariness refer to different aspects of human action and they cannot be equated.

Has this ever been in doubt? Stated in these terms, perhaps not. But both the proponents and the opponents of the modern theory of the will have tended to confuse the ideas of agency and voluntariness. For example, consider the following passage from Reid's *Essays on the Active Powers of Man*:

In morals, it is self-evident that no man can be object either of approbation or of blame for what he did not. But how shall we know whether it is his doing or not? If the action depended upon his will, and if he intended and willed it, it is his action in the judgment of all mankind. But if it was done without his knowledge, or without his will and intention, it is as certain that he did it not, and that it ought not to be imputed to him as the agent.[7]

Every sentence in this passage, bar the question, is untrue. First, a man can be praised or blamed for what he did not do, as well as for what he did; or for what others did or did not do, for instance if he coerced them, or if they were in his charge or under his command. Our moral responsibility extends beyond our deeds in both these ways. Second, in the latter case, an action may depend on one man's 'will', and be intended by that man, but still be the action of another. Third, many acts, including ones with serious consequences, are done without the agent's knowledge or intention.

How could Reid have gone so badly wrong? The answer seems to be that he thought of 'will and intention' as the single cause that *both* makes action qualify as voluntary *and* makes it imputable to an individual as the agent, and he confused or equated the ideas of voluntariness and agency as a result. He thought of agency as being negated by ignorance, and as a condition on which moral responsibility depends, because these things are true, or approximately true, of voluntariness.

In the nineteenth century, the confusion between voluntariness and agency was imported into jurisprudence, and in the twentieth century it was perpetuated even by philosophers who opposed the modern theory of the will. As a result, each concept was made out to be more like the other than it really is: the concept of agency was invested with an ethical character it does not have, and the concept of voluntariness was divested of the ethical character it does have. Hart makes the first mistake:

> The difference between 'His body moved in violent contact with another's' and 'He did it' (*e.g.*, 'He hit her') [cannot] be explained without reference to [...] sentences by which liabilities or responsibility are ascribed.[8]

And Ryle makes the second mistake. For example, the following passage is from his chapter on the will in *The Concept of Mind*:

> Very often we oppose things done voluntarily to things suffered under compulsion. Some soldiers are volunteers, other are conscripts; some yachtsmen go out to sea voluntarily, others are carried out to sea by the wind and tide. [...] So sometimes the question 'Voluntary or involuntary?' means 'Did the person do it or was it done to him?'[9]

This is no more plausible than saying that we sometimes oppose things done happily to things suffered unhappily, so sometimes the question 'Happy or unhappy?' means 'Did the person do it or was it done to him?' Ryle is confusing the distinction between active and passive and the distinction between voluntary and involuntary, or rather, he is stating the confusion as a positive claim.

Similarly, in *Elbow Room*, which is dedicated to his teacher Ryle, Dennett asks 'Are decisions voluntary? Or are they things that happen to us?'[10] But these are quite different questions. *Are* decisions voluntary? Some are, some are not. 'Did he decide to hide the gun, make the broadcast, perjure himself...voluntarily?' These are practical questions, and the answers can be yes or no. Are decisions things that happen to us? In other words, are they passive or active operations of the mind? This is a theoretical question, and the answer cannot vary from case to case, although of course some decisions are spontaneous, perhaps automatic, perhaps unconscious, whereas others are carefully thought through in advance. 'Did he decide voluntarily or did the decision happen to him?' makes as much sense as 'Did he pay up voluntarily or was he paid?'

1.3 Voluntary passivity and involuntary activity

1.3.1 Terminology

Agency and voluntariness are different phenomena, and the distinctions between active and passive and between voluntary and involuntary cut across each other, since activity can be either voluntary or involuntary and so can passivity. But the confusion between agency and voluntariness encouraged philosophers to ignore two of these possibilities. They thought about voluntary activity, but they ignored voluntary passivity, or in some cases denied that it exists. And they equated activity and voluntary activity, as if activity were always voluntary. I shall comment on voluntary passivity and involuntary activity in turn. But I shall begin with some brief comments about terminology.

The use by philosophers and jurists of terms such as 'voluntary act', 'voluntary movement', and 'willed movement' has tended to conflate the ideas of voluntariness and intention. Very roughly, an act is voluntary if it is due to choice as opposed to ignorance or compulsion (see 4.1), and an act is intentional if the agent does it because she wants to do it or values doing it for its own sake, or because it seems conducive to something else she wants or values (see 5.2).* But if we want to understand what writers who accept or are influenced by the modern theory *mean*, including writers who oppose it, we need to bear in mind that when they describe an act as 'voluntary', they commonly do not mean one of these things rather than the other, or even both things at once, because they do not distinguish clearly between them. And the reason why they do not distinguish between them, at least part of the reason, is that their thought about human action, and therefore their use of terms as well, is influenced by a *picture*: desire—or the 'uneasiness' of desire, as Locke described the feeling of wanting something—causing the mental act of willing or choosing, and the mental act causing the motion of a limb. It is this process that is supposed to make the act (i.e. the motion) qualify as 'voluntary', 'intentional', or 'willed'.

Naturally, the use of the term 'involuntary' is also affected, and it is commonly reserved for thoughts or changes in the body which the agent is unable to control, e.g. 'an involuntary concurrence of ideas', 'the involuntary running of urine', or 'the involuntary closing of the eyelids when the surface of the eye is touched' (all three examples are taken from the OED). If we define 'involuntary' in this way, it is clearly not equivalent to 'not voluntary'. For example, a man who hands over his wallet because he is threatened with physical violence does not hand it over voluntarily, but he does not hand it over involuntarily either, in this sense, because he does not lose physical control.

But although the use of the terms 'involuntary' and 'not voluntary' match this convention to some extent, it also deviates from it in many cases, especially but not exclusively in the law. For example, 'involuntary manslaughter' means *unintentional* manslaughter, where death results from recklessness, criminal negligence, or an unlawful act, without a specific intent to kill; 'involuntary euthanasia' means euthanasia *without consent*; and the term 'involuntary servitude' in American law refers to labour that is *coerced*. 'Involuntary' is evidently not used in these cases in the narrow sense explained in the last paragraph. We therefore have a choice. I shall use 'involuntary' as the negation of 'voluntary', which is how it is generally defined in dictionaries. The difference between an act the agent is unable to control and an act

---

* The difference between voluntariness and intention affects the meaning of passive constructions. For example, as it would normally be meant and understood, 'He was killed voluntarily' implies that he chose to be killed, whereas 'He was killed intentionally' refers to the intention of the killer rather than the victim. If we want to attribute intention to the victim, we use the active voice: 'He submitted intentionally', 'He allowed himself to be killed intentionally', etc.

elicited by coercion is obviously important, and I shall discuss it in detail in Chapter 4, but we do not need to mark it lexically in this way.

The terms 'active' and 'passive' also require comment. Basically, the term 'active' refers to the exercise of an active power, that is, an ability to cause change, while 'passive' refers to the exercise of a passive power, a liability to undergo change. But, confusingly, 'passive' is also commonly used to mean inactive, quiescent, or unresponsive. I shall avoid using 'passive' in this way. As I shall use them, 'inactive' is the *negation* of 'active'—it simply means not active—whereas 'passive' is the *converse* of 'active', as 'child' is the converse of 'parent' and 'buy' is the converse of 'sell'.

So much for terminology. I said that the distinctions between active and passive and between voluntary and involuntary cut across each other. So it is a mistake to imagine that activity is always voluntary, that there is no involuntary activity; equally, it is a mistake to think that voluntariness can only be attributed to acts—or only to acts and failures to act, positive and negative acts, as Bentham called them, or only to the things a person does, as opposed to the things that are done to him—because it can be attributed to passivity as well, in other words, to the reception, and not only the performance, of an act. I shall comment on voluntary passivity first and involuntary activity after that.

1.3.2 Voluntary passivity

Aquinas certainly understood that both activity and passivity can be voluntary. In the *Summa Theologiae*, he states:

> An action is termed voluntary in two ways. First with respect to action, or acting upon, as when one wills to do something. Second, with respect to passion, or being acted upon, as when one wills to receive another's action.[11]

By contrast, the proponents of the modern theory of the will, and even its opponents, almost without exception, ignore voluntary passivity, or else deny explicitly that it exists.* In the whole corpus of his writings,

---

* The same is not true of voluntary inactivity. The idea of a sin of omission was too salient to be ignored, the very phrase having been in use since the beginning of the fifteenth century. But since Hobbes and Locke, philosophers have typically regarded voluntary inactivity as a kind of activity—Bentham's 'negative act' or 'act of omission', Davidson's 'standing fast'. So their acknowledgement of voluntary inactivity is not a sign that they understood that voluntariness and activity do not coincide. Exceptionally, Anscombe acknowledges voluntary passivity, following Aquinas. See below 2.3.1 and 4.6.

Wittgenstein mentions voluntary *in*activity in a solitary remark from 1947 about Wundt's theory that voluntary actions are caused by feelings of innervation,[12] and as far as I know he does not mention voluntary passivity even once. Ryle maintains that the terms 'voluntary' and 'involuntary' apply exclusively to acts.[13] And White, who developed Wittgenstein's and Ryle's ideas about the will, and applied them in jurisprudence, claims that 'something may not be voluntary because it is not an act at all, as when a man is carried bodily on to another's land'.[14]

White's example refers to the seventeenth-century legal case *Smith* v. *Stone*, in which the report states:

> A. brought an action of trespass against B. pedibus ambulando; the defendant *pleads* this special plea in justification, viz. *that he was carried upon the land* of the plaintiff *by force* and violence *of others*, and was not there voluntarily, which is the same trespass for which the plaintiff brings his action.[15]

But White misinterprets the case. It is true that the man was not carried onto the plaintiff's land voluntarily, but the reason for this is not that being carried cannot be voluntary, since it is not an act, but rather that he was carried 'by force and violence of others', against his will. A man *can* be carried voluntarily, for example, a wounded man on a stretcher or Anchises escaping from Troy on his son Aeneas's back. If not being an act prevented something from being voluntary, there would be no sins of omission or voluntary deaths.

As it happens, the OED's entry for 'voluntary' begins with voluntary thoughts and feelings, and then proceeds to voluntary acts; and if we turn to the entry for 'voluntarily', we find several quotations in which the word qualifies something passive. For example, the first and the eighth are as follows:

> **c1374** CHAUCER *Boeth.* III. pr. xii. (1868) 103 Ther may no man douten, that thei ne ben gouerned uoluntariely. [...] **1663** BP. PATRICK *Parab. Pilgr.* xiii. (1687) 87 At last he voluntarily, and without any compulsion but that of his Love, died upon a Cross.

The fact is that the distinction between voluntary and involuntary applies to passivity and inactivity in exactly the same way as it applies to activity. Children can be kissed and put to bed voluntarily, and they sometimes sit still voluntarily in front of the TV. For their part, adults undergo surgical procedures voluntarily, they are sometimes voluntarily unemployed, and they may die voluntarily, as Bishop Patrick says Christ did, and as people suffering from painful illnesses do every day. There is no reason to deny that voluntariness can be attributed equally to all of these things; or to think that it is a different attribute, depending on which of them we have in mind.

Roughly, voluntariness is about choice as opposed to ignorance or compulsion, and both children and adults sometimes choose whether or not to be kissed or carried, just as they sometimes choose whether to kiss or carry someone or something else. So the question whether it was voluntary or involuntary can arise in the passive case just as it can in the active case. Again, a man can allow himself to fall in love with a woman in the knowledge that he could avoid falling in love with her if he chose to, or allow himself to fall asleep in the knowledge that he could avoid falling asleep if chose to; or alternatively he can fall in love willy-nilly, or fall asleep despite trying to remain awake. In the first case, he falls in love or falls asleep voluntarily, in the second case not. But falling in love and falling asleep are not acts, any more than falling in battle or falling downstairs.

1.3.3 Involuntary activity

It is a mistake to imagine that activity is always voluntary. But proponents of the modern theory of the will commonly assumed that it is, and by the nineteenth century, the assumption sometimes took the form of a definition. John Austin (not J.L. Austin, but Bentham's disciple and the first Professor of Jurisprudence in the University of London) introduced the definition into jurisprudence, and it has been repeated by British and American jurists ever since.

Austin defines an act as follows: 'A voluntary movement of my body, or a movement which follows a volition, is an act.' The American jurist and Supreme Court justice Oliver Wendell Holmes writes: 'An act is always a voluntary muscular contraction and nothing else [...] An act implies a choice.' The English jurist D.A. Stroud defines a 'simple' act as 'a voluntary movement of the body', and a complex act as 'a series [...] of simple acts and their consequences.' Glanville Williams defines an act as 'a willed bodily movement', adding, 'Since every act is by definition willed, there is no need to call it voluntary.' R.W.M. Dias defines an act as a 'voluntary bodily movement', adding that voluntariness is 'a criterion of responsibility and connotes controllability of the action in question.' Michael S. Moore defines an act in the same way as Glanville Williams, as a 'willed bodily movement', and states (now following Mill) that 'human acts are themselves a compound of other events, consisting of a volition causing a bodily movement.'[16]

When we read these definitions, we need to bear in mind that the use of the terms 'voluntary movement' and 'willed movement' often conflated the ideas of voluntariness and intention. Nevertheless, none of these definitions can be right. Some acts are voluntary; others are not. Equally, some are intentional; others are not. Putting out one's hands to break a fall is often neither voluntary nor intentional, and the same is true of licking one's lips absent-mindedly, smiling with pleasure, frowning with concentration, laughing when one is tickled, or crying out involuntarily with pain; speaking or changing one's posture in one's sleep; acts caused by hypnotic suggestion or by abnormal or pathological conditions, such as panic or psychosis; and acts done without knowledge or foresight, such as involuntary manslaughter, which was mentioned above.

These are preliminary remarks, to be substantiated in later chapters of this book. And I have so far ignored the assumption, which is made explicitly by all the jurists quoted above, that physical acts are bodily movements or muscular contractions (see 1.4.3 and 3.1). But it should already be clear that the confusion between agency and voluntariness has permeated modern philosophy, at least from the eighteenth century on. And the reason should be clear as well. The modern theory represented voluntary action, intentional action, and action as such—i.e. action that can be imputed to an individual as the agent—by means of a single picture: desire (or the 'uneasiness' of desire) causes the mental act of volition, which in turn causes motion in our limbs.

Some philosophers and psychologists in the second half of the nineteenth century and the first half of the twentieth century modified this picture, substituting ideas of movements or kinaesthetic images for acts of will, and explicitly adding muscular contractions to the sequence of events. Then, in the 1930s and 1940s, Wittgenstein and Ryle both argued (in Ryle's words) that 'the doctrine of volitions is a causal hypothesis, adopted because it was wrongly supposed that the question, "What makes a bodily movement voluntary?" was a causal question.' But, as we shall see now, not even this radical departure from empiricism was enough to overcome the confusion between voluntariness and agency, because for that we need to disaggregate the physical, psychological, and ethical dimensions of human action, which neither Wittgenstein nor Ryle quite did.*

---

* In recent decades, some neuroscientists have criticized the modern theory of the will, but generally in less radical terms than Wittgenstein and Ryle, preferring epiphenomenalism to the latter's eliminativism about volitions. For example, Wegner agrees with them that voluntary

1.4 Wittgenstein on the will

1.4.1 Against empiricism

Wittgenstein wrote about the will in every phase of his career. The earliest remarks are in the notebooks that record the development of the ideas eventually published in the *Tractatus,* and the last are in a typescript composed in 1947.[17] The constant theme of the material he wrote in the 1930s and 1940s is stated in the following remarks, which date from 1935 and 1947:

> There is not one common difference between so-called voluntary acts and involuntary ones, viz, the presence or absence of one element, the 'act of volition'. (BB pp. 151*f*)
>
> Voluntary movements are certain movements with their normal *surroundings* of intention, learning, trying, acting. (RPP I §776)

The main influence on Wittgenstein's ideas on this topic was Schopenhauer's Kantian theory of the will, which Wittgenstein seems to have fully accepted in 1916, and which still influenced his thinking in 1947. Schopenhauer had argued, against the empiricists, that an act of will cannot be an impression or thought, because impressions and thoughts are mere phenomena: they are occurrences we can experience or be aware of—for example, we can be conscious of a sensation or a wish—but considered in themselves they are motionless and inert, whereas the will is an active principle if it is anything at all. Schopenhauer's own view was that the act of will and the act willed—the action of the body, as he called it—are one and the same thing, 'perceived and apprehended in a twofold manner':

> What makes itself known to *inner* apprehension or perception (self-consciousness) as real *act of will,* exhibits itself at once in *outer* perception, in which the body stands out *objectively,* as the *action* of the body.[18]

In Wittgenstein's *Notebooks,* these ideas are repeated: 'The act of will is not the cause of the action but is the action itself.' 'Wishing is not acting. But willing is acting.' 'The act of will is not an experience' (NB, pp. 87–89).

---

action is not caused by acts or experiences of willing. But he maintains that all the same there is such a thing as a 'feeling of voluntariness' or 'feeling of doing', whose function is to 'label events as our personal actions' (*The Illusion of Conscious Will,* pp. 3 and 325).

And in the *Philosophical Investigations*, he presents the same self-consciously Schopenhauerian ideas in quotes:

> 'Willing, if it is not to be a sort of wishing, must be the action itself. It cannot be allowed to stop anywhere short of the action'. (PI §615)

The quotes are not there because Wittgenstein proposes to contest this. He is still convinced that willing and acting are one and the same thing. But he now wants to insist on a way of understanding this idea that discards the Kantian mythology in which Schopenhauer had clothed it, the idea of an event that presents two different faces to 'interior' and 'exterior' perception. So he replies to the claim in quotation marks, as follows. If willing *is* the action, then it is so 'in the ordinary sense of the word': 'so it is speaking, writing, walking, lifting a thing, imagining something. But it is also trying, attempting, making an effort,—to speak, to write, to lift a thing, to imagine something etc.' (PI §615). These are all things we normally do 'at will', and as such they are all that willing can possibly consist in. There is no additional internal psychic push—no 'will force', as James called it. The act of will has vanished altogether, leaving the 'action of the body' that it was postulated to explain. It is true that there is willing without acting: trying to lift a heavy weight is an exercise of the will, whether or not the attempt succeeds. But we should not imagine that every act is preceded by an effort or attempt: 'When I raise my arm,' he writes, 'I do not usually *try* to raise it' (PI §622). So 'trying' is not the vernacular name for a volition or act of will.

Wittgenstein also rejects the doctrine, which James and Russell had defended, that voluntary movements are caused by memory-images of the kinaesthetic feelings that make us aware of the movements we perform. They maintained that beginning in infancy, involuntary movements produce these kinaesthetic feelings, and images of the feelings are stored in the memory. As a result, we eventually possess a repertoire of ideas of possible movements, each one composed of the memory-images of the kinaesthetic feelings that occurred when we performed the movement in the past, and these ideas are the only mental antecedents needed for voluntary action (see the Appendix).

Wittgenstein's attack on this theory is radical and astute. For he rejects the very idea that kinaesthetic feelings make me aware or 'advise me' (*belehren mich*) of the movement and position of my limbs. It is true, of course, that I can normally feel how my limbs are disposed and how they move. But it does not follow that I am normally aware of feelings—'certain queer feelings in my muscles and joints' (PI §624), as Wittgenstein puts it—which advise me of these things. And as a matter of fact, I am not normally aware of such feelings: 'I let my index finger make an easy pendulum movement of small amplitude. I either hardly feel it, or don't feel it at all. Perhaps a little in the tip of the finger, as a slight tension' (PI p. 185). Perhaps we postulate these feelings because there seems to be no other way of explaining how I know what my limbs are doing: 'But after all,' Wittgenstein imagines his inter-locutor saying, 'you must feel it, otherwise you wouldn't know (without looking) how your finger was moving' (PI p. 185). To this he replies:

> But 'knowing' it only means: being able to describe it.—I may be able to tell the direction from which a sound comes only because it affects one ear more strongly than the other, but I don't feel this in my ears; yet it has its effect: I *know* the direction from which the sound comes; for instance, I look in that direction. (PI p. 185)

This remark is not convincing in detail. Knowing something does not only mean being able to describe it; and I can tell where a sound is coming from because of the phase difference between the sounds that reach my ears rather than because of a difference in volume. But the substance of Wittgenstein's remark is true: whatever physiological mechanism enables me to know where a sound is coming from, there is no need to postulate a sensation corresponding to the direction. Similarly, whatever mechanism enables me to know how my finger is moving, there is no need to postulate a kinaes-thetic sensation corresponding to the movement of my finger either. Memory, Wittgenstein points out, provides another analogous example. I know I had toast for breakfast, but not because a feeling of pastness is associated with my thought of eating toast.

Finally, Wittgenstein considers the idea that willing to raise my arm is deciding to raise it:

> Examine the following description of a voluntary action: 'I form the decision to pull the bell at 5 o'clock, and when it strikes 5, my arm makes this movement.'—Is that the correct description, and not *this* one: '...and when it strikes 5, I raise my arm'?—One would like to supplement the first description: 'and see! my arm goes up when it strikes 5.' And this 'and see!' is precisely what doesn't belong here. I do *not* say 'See, my arm is going up!' when I raise it. (PI §627)

Wittgenstein's thought here is influenced by Schopenhauer again. It is, in effect, that if willing were deciding, the so-called act it is supposed to cause could not be an act at all: it could only be a phenomenon I observe. If willing were 'something different from the action of the body, and the two connected by the bond of causality', then whether it was wishing, wanting, or deciding, a kinaesthetic feeling or a memory image of a kinaesthetic feeling, it could not make the motion of my arm qualify as my act.[19]

1.4.2 The normal surroundings of voluntary movements

Turning now to Wittgenstein's positive remarks in *Philosophical Investigations* about how voluntariness should be defined, we find that he begins by returning to an idea mentioned half a dozen pages earlier, where the topic is what he calls 'a false picture of the processes called "recognizing"'—a picture according to which one recognizes an object by comparing the impression of it with a memory-image, and identifying the object in this way. There he writes:

> Asked 'Did you recognize your desk when you entered your room this morning?'—I should no doubt say 'Certainly!' And yet it would be misleading to say that an act of recognition had taken place. Of course the desk was not strange to me; I was not surprised to see it, as I should have been if another one had been standing there, or some unfamiliar kind of object. (PI §602)

Thus recognizing something need not involve an 'act of recognition' or a memory image of the object: it may involve no more than seeing the things in a familiar place, without feeling surprised. (Presumably, it may also involve being able to confirm that this is the desk one would have expected to see had one thought about it, and similar things.)

Equally, Wittgenstein now suggests, voluntary action need not involve an 'act of volition'—to use his phrase from *The Brown Book*—or a memory image of a kinaesthetic feeling: it too may involve no more than behaving in a familiar sort of way, without feeling surprised. Following on from the last sentence of §627—'I do *not* say "See, my arm is going up!" when I raise it.'—he makes the following suggestion: 'So one might say: voluntary movement is marked by the absence of surprise' (PI §628).[20] Clearly, this is not a plausible *definition* of voluntary action. (Wittgenstein himself seems to think of the absence of surprise as part of a 'family of phenomena' that are characteristic of voluntary action (BB p. 152).) It is true that I am not normally surprised by the movements of my body that are under my control, just as I am not normally surprised by a car's change of speed or direction when I am driving it myself. One sign is that I can maintain my posture more easily than when someone else is driving. But this does not seem to be an important clue to how voluntary action should be defined. For, on the one hand, a high-jumper may be surprised when she clears an exceptionally high bar, and I may be surprised when I succeed in wiggling my ears for the first time, and, on the other, we commonly find our involuntary movements and reactions unsurprising. For example, I am not surprised when I find myself panting at the end of a strenuous run.

But the idea that voluntary action is marked by the absence of surprise is interesting, because it signals Wittgenstein's determination to reject the doctrine that voluntary action is action with a particular kind of cause, without embracing the mysterious idea that 'the nexus of the will corresponds [...] to that between the inner and the outer', or anything similar. Perhaps the most telling remark is §615. Here it is again:

> 'Willing, if it is not to be a sort of wishing, must be the action itself. It cannot be allowed to stop anywhere short of the action.' If it is the action, then it is so in the ordinary sense of the word; so it is speaking, writing, walking, lifting a thing, imagining something. But it is also trying, attempting, making an effort,—to speak, to write, to lift a thing, to imagine something etc. (PI §615)

The interlocutor here is Wittgenstein's earlier self, the author of the remarks in the *Notebooks* quoted above: 'The act of will is not the cause of the action but is the action itself.' 'Wishing is not acting. But willing is acting.' Wittgenstein does not deny that what the interlocutor says is true. He merely points out what we are bound to acknowledge it implies, if we refuse to mystify the will.

Wittgenstein's conclusions flow naturally from this point. For if a volition is not the cause of an act, or an aspect of it that is revealed to 'inner apprehension', whatever exactly this means, perhaps it is the context of action that makes it voluntary—'its character and its surroundings'—including, in most cases, the absence of surprise (Z §587). Here is the 1947 remark again: 'Voluntary movements are certain movements with their normal *surroundings* of intention, learning, trying, acting.' For example, we regard the behaviour of a child playing with a doll as voluntary, but not because we assume that volitions or kinaesthetic images are causing her movements. It is because we know she has learned how to make these movements, they are coordinated and purposeful, she is not alarmed or surprised or distressed by them, she attends to what she is doing, and so on. If we feel the need to postulate a

If we turn to the postulate Gesture later

hidden cause, it is because we ignore these features of a movement and its context, which are for the most part in plain view.

1.4.3 Assessment

Voluntary action is *not* action caused by a certain kind of thought or sensation. On this point I believe Wittgenstein was dead right. On the contrary, it is action that is *not* due to ignorance and compulsion, so it is defined causally, but in negative not positive causal terms (see 4.1 and 4.7). But there are also serious weaknesses in Wittgenstein's treatment of this subject, even if we set aside his failure to develop his ideas adequately and the obscurity of many of his remarks, because he fails to make a sufficiently radical break with the past.

(A) First, he inherits the failure to distinguish between voluntariness and agency from the tradition from which he was trying to break loose. Ostensibly, his topic is 'voluntary action', but he is really interested in the difference between the motion in our bodies that we impute to ourselves as agents, such as when we get out of bed, and the motion that we do not impute to ourselves as agents, such as when one presses the back of one's hand against the wall, then steps away from the wall and let one's arm rise 'of its own accord'. That is why he returns repeatedly to the differences between raising one's arm or moving a finger, and coughing or sneezing or the beating of the heart (RPP I §806; cf. Z §579; PI §612).

The fact that Wittgenstein was mainly interested in theories about how we move our bodies explains (borrowing his own telling phrase) his one-sided diet of examples. Arms are raised, fingers are moved, but few other kinds of action get a mention, and then only in passing. He does mention speaking, eating, and walking, but he does not compare speaking with crying out (involuntarily), eating a salad with eating the bug in the salad (inadvertently), walking with walking into a lamppost (accidentally) or being frogmarched (against one's will), presumably because in all these cases, one is active rather than passive, even though one does not do the act voluntarily.

one-sided diet of examples!

The same preoccupation also explain the following remark: 'How do I know whether the child eats, drinks, walks, etc. voluntarily or not [*willkürlich oder nicht willkürlich*]? Do I ask the child what it feels? No; eating, as anyone does eat, is voluntary' (RPP I §763). If we are using the word 'voluntary' as it is normally used (and how else are we supposed to use it?)

then eating, drinking, and walking by children is not always voluntary by any means. Wittgenstein ignores the difference between eating ice-cream, which is normally voluntary, and eating green vegetables, which is often not. Nor is eating always intentional. One can eat a bug in a salad without intending to, and eat nuts automatically, without even being aware of what one is doing. Children often eat the snot from their noses this way. Presumably, the reason why Wittgenstein ignores these kinds of examples is, again, that he is interested in defining bodily motion that is attributable to the agency of the person whose body moves—motion, as Reid puts it, that can be 'imputed to him as the agent'. For even when it is not voluntary and not intentional, eating is active as opposed to passive, something that a boy chewing cabbage under protest or eating nuts mindlessly *does and not* something that he *undergoes*.

As a result, some of the remarks in the *Investigations* are ostensibly about voluntariness or intention—in particular, the ones that are directed against the theory that what makes an act 'voluntary' is a special kind of mental cause, such as a kinaesthetic feeling—while others are explicitly about agency; for example, the famous question 'What is left over if I subtract the fact that my arm goes up from the fact that I raise my arm?', which has exactly the same meaning and exactly the same answer whether I raise my arm voluntarily or intentionally or not. But there is no sign that Wittgenstein is conscious of the difference between these topics.[*]

(B) The second main weakness in Wittgenstein's remarks on voluntary action is his failure to distinguish between action and motion. For example, suppose I raise my arm. How are my action, my raising of my arm, and the motion of my arm related? He does not claim explicitly that they are identical, as several philosophers did in the 1960s and 1970s, but like many of his predecessors, including Schopenhauer, he makes this assumption.

This comes out clearly in the passage leading to the idea about the absence of surprise. Thus, in §627, he points out that we could describe a voluntary act (*einer willkürlichen Handlung*) by saying 'I raise my arm', but not 'My arm makes this movement' or 'See, my arm is going up!' And from this he infers: 'So one might say: voluntary movement [*die willkürliche Bewegung*]

---

[*] There is a change in Wittgenstein's approach in 1947. The focus of his attention broadens, he considers acts that do not merely consist in someone raising an arm or moving a finger (*RPP I*, §§762ff, §902), he notices that inactivity as well as activity can be voluntary (§845), and he makes the connection between voluntariness and awareness (§§761, 844, 902).

is marked by the absence of surprise' (PI §628). Evidently, he thinks the reason why I do not describe my action by saying 'See, my arm is going up!' is that I am not surprised, and that what is wrong with the description 'See, my arm is going up!', what prevents it from being a satisfactory description of a voluntary act, is the word 'See ... !', the expression of surprise, rather than the phrase 'My arm is going up'. It does not occur to him that 'My arm is going up' describes the motion of my arm, and that the act and the motion—the *Handlung* and the *Bewegung*—are different things, as different (as we shall see in 3.1) as a killing and a death.[21]

Similarly, in the passage from the *Brown Book* quoted above, Wittgenstein fails to notice that getting out of bed is an act, whereas the rising of his arm is not an act, whether it is voluntary or not. He may be right in saying that there is not one common difference between voluntary and involuntary acts; but the difference between his getting out of bed and the rising of his arm is the difference between action and motion, that is, causing motion and motion caused, and not the difference between two kinds of act. (Of course, the claim that action and motion need to be distinguished must be argued in detail. The argument is in 3.1.)

In summary, in his mature thought about action and the will, Wittgenstein discards the idealist mythology he had once accepted, but he retains Schopenhauer's idea that willing—unlike wishing, wanting, or deciding—is not distinct from the act willed. This is one reason for his opposition to the modern theory of the will. His attack on James and Russell is also part of the anti-sensationalist argument that runs through the *Investigations*, and it is both radical and convincing, in my view. But he does not succeed in offering a plausible alternative to the empiricist ideas he attacks, mainly because he inherited both the confusion between agency and voluntariness and the confusion between action and motion from Schopenhauer, and therefore indirectly from the empiricist tradition he opposed.

1.5 Ryle on volitions

Ryle is the most trenchant and influential critic of the doctrine that voluntary acts are caused by *sui generis* acts of will. He offers two main arguments.

The first argument is that we cannot answer a variety of questions about volitions that we should be able to answer without difficulty if the modern theory of the will were right: 'Can they be sudden or gradual, strong or weak, difficult or easy, enjoyable or disagreeable? [...] Can we take lessons in executing them? Are they fatiguing or distracting?'[22] But this argument is unconvincing. It is true that few, if any, of Ryle's volley of questions about volitions have straightforward answers, and as he points out it is hard to say anything sensible about their 'frequency, duration or strength'. But the same can be said about other mental operations whose reality is not in doubt. For example, how often do I acquire a belief in the course of a day? How many beliefs do I acquire when I walk into an unfamiliar room? How long do they last? How strong are they? Can we take lessons in acquiring beliefs? And is acquiring them a fatiguing or distracting business? These questions are no easier to answer than the ones about volitions, but this is not a convincing reason to accept eliminativism about beliefs. It is true that volitions were traditionally supposed to be conscious mental acts, and we can acquire beliefs without doing so consciously. But the essence of the modern theory of the will would not be jeopardized by the admission that volitions can also be unconscious.

Ryle's best-known objection to the modern theory of the will is that it leads to an insoluble dilemma:

> Some mental processes [...] can, according to the theory, issue from volitions. So what of the volitions themselves? Are they voluntary or involuntary acts of mind? Clearly either answer leads to absurdities. If I cannot help willing to pull the trigger, it would be absurd to describe my pulling it as 'voluntary'. But if my volition to pull the trigger is voluntary, in the sense assumed by the theory, then it must issue from a prior volition and that from another *ad infinitum*.[23]

This argument has been extensively discussed. But is it fatal to the theory of volitions? The answer, I suggest, depends on whether we regard the theory of volitions as a theory of voluntariness or as a theory of agency.

(A) Assume first that it is a theory of voluntariness. On this way of understanding the theory, it clearly implies that if a volition is voluntary then it must have been caused by another volition. Hence, if the regress is to be avoided, the original volition which causes a voluntary act cannot be voluntary itself. (Both Locke and Reid concede this.) What about the other horn of the dilemma? If I cannot help willing to pull the trigger, *would* it be absurd to describe my pulling it as 'voluntary'?

The answer is not obvious, because in some cases the involuntariness of a thought makes its effects involuntary, but in other cases it does not.

On the one hand, blushes are commonly caused by thoughts. For example, suppose an unbidden thought about Juliet makes Romeo blush. If the thought is involuntary, the blush must be involuntary as well. It makes no difference if the thought is a sudden desire to kiss Juliet, and therefore has the kind of content a volition is supposed to have.[24] In order for a blush to be voluntary, the thought that causes it must be voluntary as well, as it would be, for example, if Romeo thought about Juliet on purpose to make himself blush. But if Romeo couldn't help having the thought about Juliet that made him blush, then it *would* be absurd to describe the blush as voluntary.

On the other hand, many voluntary acts are caused by involuntary thoughts. The sudden thought that I forgot to take my keys out of the front door causes me to get up and fetch them; hearing my phone ring causes me to reach across the table and pick it up; and so on. We can be *caused* to do an act by hearing, feeling, or thinking something without being *compelled* to do it (see 4.6). So if I cannot help remembering about my keys or hearing the phone, and this causes me to act, it would *not* be absurd to describe the act as voluntary.

What is the difference between the two examples, and which does a volition causing an act resemble in the relevant respect? Both thoughts are involuntary, but the difference between the cases is that if Romeo has the thought about Juliet, he cannot stop himself from blushing, whereas if I have the thought about the keys, I *can* stop myself from fetching them from the door. But if we recall what volitions are supposed to be, they must resemble the thought that made Romeo blush in this respect, and Ryle must be right in saying that if I cannot help willing to pull the trigger, it would be absurd to describe my pulling it as 'voluntary'.

Beginning with Locke, empiricist philosophers regularly concede that it is difficult to find the right words to describe a volition (see the Appendix). In his *Essay Concerning Human Understanding*, Locke describes it as 'a thought or preference of the mind ordering, or, as it were, commanding the doing or not doing such or such a particular action' (2.21.5). But he admits that the words 'preferring', 'ordering', and 'commanding' do not capture the phenomenon precisely, because once I have preferred, ordered, or commanded, I still have to do the act, and I can refrain from doing it instead; whereas the volition is the final and irrevocable commitment to the act, and once I have performed it, I have done all I can to make the act occur. So while I can will and fail, and can even *ensure* that my willing fails, as Odysseus did, when he had himself strapped to the mast, I cannot *both* will *and* refrain. But it follows that if I cannot help willing to pull the trigger, then I *cannot* refrain from pulling it, and, as Ryle says, 'it would be absurd to describe my pulling it as "voluntary"'.

One qualification should be mentioned. I can voluntarily put myself in a situation where I cannot help doing something, or at least trying to do it. For instance, Wittgenstein ingeniously suggested that I can make myself will to swim by jumping in the water (PI §613), and it is debatable whether my swimming would be voluntary in these circumstances. This is comparable to a case where someone is compelled to do an act by a threat to which he voluntarily laid himself open, to which I shall return in 4.1. But setting this special kind of case aside, Ryle's claim is confirmed.

(B) Ryle's dilemma is therefore a fatal objection to the theory of volitions considered as a theory of voluntariness. But volitions were not always postulated to explain voluntariness. Descartes in particular, Ryle's main target, postulated volitions to explain how we set our bodies in motion, not to explain when our acts are voluntary and when not. According to Descartes, voluntariness is due to the *freedom* of the will, the control we have over our volitions, and there is no reason why Descartes should be obliged to explain *this* by postulating further volitions. But Ryle's dilemma is powerless against the theory of volitions considered as a theory of agency.

On the one hand, the volition that causes my finger to move would not need to be caused by another volition, and so on ad infinitum. For if the motion of my finger can be imputed to me as agent when it is caused by a specific kind of thought, this thought can itself be caused in various different ways—by sensations, memories, emotions, feelings of discomfort, and so on. The variety of causes does not disqualify the volition from making its effect attributable to my agency. And, on the other hand, if I cannot help willing to pull the trigger, it certainly does *not* follow that it would be absurd to describe my pulling it as my act.

If we distinguish in this way between postulating volitions to explain agency and postulating them to explain voluntariness, we can see why some philosophers have accepted Ryle's dilemma argument and some have rejected it. Of course, there are few ideas in philosophy on which everyone is agreed, but the explanation of *this* disagreement is that Ryle's argument seems convincing to those who regard the modern theory of the will as a theory of voluntariness, and unconvincing to those who regard it as a theory of agency. For example, Kenny regards it as a theory of voluntariness, and describes Ryle's argument as 'decisive';[25] whereas Hornsby claims that Ryle is attacking a theory in which volitions are postulated 'to distinguish between "mere bodily movements" and the voluntary movements *that are actions'* (Hornsby's emphasis). She comments:

> [Ryle's] *reductio* tells at most against an account that identifies [volitions] both with causes of actions and with actions themselves. For the fundamental step is: whenever there is one action, there are two actions; and the conclusion is: there are infinitely many actions.[26]

If we regard the theory of volitions as a theory of agency, this is a plausible defence, since active movements can have passive causes. So, considered as a theory of agency, the theory does *not* imply that whenever there is one action there are two. But if we regard it as a theory of voluntariness, Hornsby's rebuttal of Ryle's dilemma fails. For if it is claimed that being caused by a volition is what makes something *voluntary*, it *does* follow that volitions must be voluntary themselves, as we have seen. So, understood this way, the theory *does* imply that whenever there is one voluntary act there are two.

1.6 Conclusion

Wittgenstein's attack on James and Russell is compelling, and Ryle's dilemma argument is an effective refutation of the modern theory of the will considered as a theory of voluntariness. But neither Wittgenstein nor Ryle attacked the modern theory of the will with unqualified success, particularly because they both failed to keep the concepts of agency and voluntariness firmly apart. The main lesson of the various arguments and ideas considered in this chapter is that a convincing philosophy of human action needs to disaggregate the different dimensions of human action, and that is how I shall proceed. I shall examine the *physical* dimension of action in Chapters 2 and 3, and its *ethical* dimension in Chapter 4. The *psychological* and *intellectual* dimensions of action will occupy Chapters 5 and 6. In the final chapters, building on the preceding material, I shall defend the theory that knowledge is an ability that is exercised in rational thought and behaviour, and explain why knowledge is a better guide to acting the right way than true belief.

2

Action and Integration

2.1 Locke on the idea of active power

What is the difference between the movements in my body I cause personally myself, such as the movements of my lips when I speak or the contraction of my fist when I clench it, and the movements I do not cause personally, such as the growth of my toenails or the contraction of my heart? The orthodox answer to this question is that will or intention makes the difference. Only 'voluntary' motion, motion initiated by the will, is imputed to the whole person as the agent. So every act a person does is intentional or willed at some stage or in some respect. I reject this view root and branch. In order to define human action, we need to think of human beings in more abstract terms, purely as complex agents with functionally differentiated parts. As with other such agents, including machines, institutions, and super-organisms, the mark of individual human agency is functional integration.

I shall begin with the origin of the orthodox doctrine.

In modern philosophy, the idea that every act an individual does origin-ates in her will is not primarily due to a theory of human action: it is rooted in the deeper soil of metaphysics. In fact, it mainly stems from the difficulty philosophers from Hobbes and Descartes onwards experienced in accom-modating the activity of matter within the emerging scientific picture of the physical world. This difficulty, and the way it led to the elimination of involuntary action, appears especially clearly in Locke's discussion about the source of our idea of active power—in other words, the observations or experiences that enable us to form this idea in our minds.

According to Locke, the idea of power is indispensible in science, because it is, he says, 'a principal ingredient in our complex ideas of substances' (2.21.3).[1] For example, the liability of gold to be melted in a fire and to dissolve in *aqua regia* (which is a mixture of nitric and hydrochloric acids) is no less essential to our idea of gold than its colour and weight. And even colour and weight, Locke claims, also turn out to be powers when we consider their nature carefully. But if all the materials of reasoning and knowledge—all our ideas—are ultimately derived from experience, as Locke insists they are, what are the sources in experience of the idea of power?

Locke's answer depends on distinguishing between two complementary kinds of powers: active powers, that is, abilities to produce change; and passive powers, liabilities to undergo change. Action, he explains, is the exercise of an active power, whereas passion is the exercise of a passive power. The origin of our idea of passive power is, he thinks, quite clear. Bodies produce this idea in us, because we cannot avoid perceiving the changes that they undergo, 'and therefore with reason we look on them as *liable* still to the same change'. But he claims that we cannot observe the *production* of a change in the same way. For example, when we see one ball strike another ball, and set it in motion,

> [the first ball] only communicates the motion it had received from another, and loses in itself so much, as the other received; which gives us but a very obscure idea of an *active power* of moving in body, whilst we observe it only to transfer, but not produce any motion. (2.21.4)

Observing interactions between bodies cannot therefore be the source of our idea of active power. Rather, Locke claims,

> we have [this idea] only from reflection on what passes in ourselves, where we find by experience, that barely by willing it, barely by a thought of the mind, we can move the parts of our bodies, which were before at rest. (2.21.4)

So according to Locke, our idea of active power is drawn from our experience of producing motion voluntarily ourselves. Passive power is an idea of sensation, like shape and solidity, whereas active power is an idea of reflection, like pleasure and pain. This is his answer to the question about the sources in experience of the idea of power. But (as Reid saw clearly) it follows that, strictly speaking, voluntary action is the only action there is.[2] For when bodies interact, motion is communicated, but it is not produced; and action, Locke insists, is the *production* of motion, or some other kind of change. The mere transfer of motion does not amount to action. All real action is therefore voluntary action, consciously effected by the mind.

(Remember, 'voluntary' action here means action that originates in the will: voluntary action and intentional action are not sharply distinguished. See 1.3.1.)

Locke's elimination of involuntary action belongs, as I have said, to an emerging scientific picture of the world which could not accommodate the activity of matter. The elimination is already implicit in Descartes's conception of matter as *res extensa*, because nothing dynamic—in other words, no action, no exercise of active power—is included in the ideas of shape, size, motion, and division into parts. It is explicitly advanced by Berkeley, who rules out any efficient cause but Spirit: 'when we talk of unthinking agents,' he writes, 'or of exciting ideas exclusive of volition, we only amuse ourselves with words.'[3] And the picture is fully realized in Hume's *Treatise*, where causation is regarded purely as a relation between events; science is seen as a system of laws that describe the regular sequences in which events belonging to specific kinds occur; and terms such as 'agency', 'efficacy', 'power', and 'force'—Hume dismissively describes them as 'nearly synonymous'—are held to be of purely subjective, psychological import.[4]

Unlike Descartes, Berkeley, and Hume, Locke wanted to retain the Aristotelian model of natural kinds of substance with their characteristic active and passive powers, for example, gold with its (active) ability to produce the idea of yellowness and its (passive) liability to melt. But at the same time, he regarded the basic mechanical transaction between bodies as a bare sequence of events—motion, impact, motion—to which the Aristotelian concepts cannot be applied. This is the fundamental inconsistency in his conception of matter, and it underlies two mistakes. First, the distinction between transferring and producing motion is specious. Second, Locke fails to see that if his argument were sound, voluntary action by human beings would be excluded, no less than involuntary action by billiard balls. I shall explain these two points in turn.

There is certainly a difference between producing and transferring or transporting people or goods. For example, manufacturers produce goods, whereas exporters transport goods from one place to another, and parents produce children, whereas bus-drivers transport them from one place to another. Now, if a bus-driver transports children from a school to a playing-field, the same children who embark at the school disembark at the playing-field. Not just the same number of children, but the very same children. That generally matters quite a lot to their parents. But suppose one ball strikes another similar ball, sets it in motion, and decelerates appreciably itself. Has motion been transferred or produced? How are we to decide? We cannot ask whether the second ball acquires the very same motion—not merely the same *quantity* of motion but, as it were, the very same *package* of motion—that the first ball loses, because motion is not a kind of stuff, which can be packaged and then either handed over or withheld.

But if, as Locke says, the first ball loses the same quantity of motion as the second ball gains, is this not a reason for denying that motion has been produced? One tempting answer to this question is to point out that even if Locke is right about this particular case, it does not follow that we *never* observe the production of motion. For example, when a cannon is fired, motion is not transferred from the powder to the ball. But this is a superficial answer. For it is easy to reply on Locke's behalf that although we would find his argument more persuasive today if it were based on the conservation of energy instead of motion, his basic point is sound. The right answer is that there is no reason why the production of motion—that is, action—should be in breach of *any* conservation laws.

This is the crux of the matter. Locke denies that the first ball produces motion in the second ball because it 'loses in itself so much, as the other received'—in other words, because the interaction between the balls conserves the total quantity of motion distributed between them. But it follows that he can only acknowledge that the production of motion— that is, action—has occurred if the total quantity of motion is *not* conserved. An action must therefore be a breach of, or an exception to, the laws of nature, in other words a miracle, an interference in the natural course of events by a being with the *super*natural ability to inject motion into the natural world, rather than merely transferring or communicating it to something else.

Compare wealth. We distinguish between producing and transferring wealth in the way Locke wants to distinguish between producing and transferring motion. The rich man who leaves his money to his son merely transfers wealth from one person to another, but the entrepreneur (we say) actually creates wealth. We are able to think about wealth in this way because there are no conservation laws in economics—something we have reason to be grateful for most of the time—so businesses do not need to work miracles to succeed. But there *are* conservation laws in physics, and it follows that Locke's conclusion, that we are acquainted with action by 'reflection on what passes in ourselves', is unsustainable, because human beings do not have supernatural powers. If his argument were sound, it would really establish that, miracles aside, action does not occur at all.

Reflecting on Locke's argument from our present vantage point, it is not difficult for us to see this, because we understand that the conservation of energy—one of great discoveries of nineteenth-century physics—applies to human behaviour no less than to the behaviour of billiard balls. Since we understand this, we can see that his argument is really eliminativist in tendency. It does not confine action to the mind. It excludes it entirely from the natural world.

To summarize: in Locke's thought, and in the empiricist tradition stemming from Locke, the idea that all action is voluntary did not arise from a theory of the will. It was generated by a combination of two ideas: first, the doctrine that matter is inert, never a source of motion in its own right; and second, a not yet fully naturalized conception of human beings—that is, a conception in which human beings, or in some philosophical systems living beings, are not constrained in their behaviour by the same conservation laws as the rest of the natural world. The first idea encouraged Locke to eliminate action, while the second held him back. The point of equilibrium was the confused idea that all action is voluntary, consciously executed by the mind.

But if we reject the doctrine that matter is inert, things look very different. We are now free to acknowledge that action occurs throughout the world, some of it voluntary and some of it not, some of it by human beings and some of it not, some of it by living beings and some of it not, and there is no reason to accept that we are acquainted with action by 'reflection on what passes in ourselves' when we move 'the parts of our bodies which were before at rest'. On the contrary, we observe action whenever we observe the 'beginning', as Locke calls it—in other words, the bringing about or causing—of motion or of any other kind of change. And we observe this whenever we see someone walking or speaking, when we see birds building their nests or ants carrying fragments of food in their mandibles, when we feel the sun warming our skin or ice cooling our tongue, and when we see one ball set another ball in motion.

2.2 Chauvinism about action

Our common-sense concept of agency does not include the idea that matter is inert, and is not confined to human beings. For example, beavers build dams and wasps make nests, and we think of them as being active when they do so, no less than people building houses or making cars. We also describe inanimate materials as agents of one sort or another, with their own distinctive active powers. For instance, soap is a detergent, i.e. a cleansing agent, cortisone is an anti-inflammatory agent, oxalic acid is a precipitating agent, and so on.

So we say. But philosophers commonly claim or assume that human beings are the only real agents that exist, so when a man pumps water from a well or melts some butter in a pan, these are genuine examples of agency, but when his heart pumps blood around his body or the sun melts some butter on the kitchen table, these are not. In *Intention*, Anscombe says that the word 'acting' can be uttered with 'special emphasis' to convey the idea of acting for a reason, but philosophers have become so used to the emphasis that they forget that an abnormally restricted concept of action is then in play.[5]

The difference between these two ideas of agency—the one confined to human beings, the other including every substance capable of causing change—is not merely a difference in the use of words. Philosophers sometimes use phrases like 'full-blooded agency', or 'agency in the strict sense'. But although these sorts of phrases are typically used in philosophy to introduce stipulations, the philosophers who talk about 'agency in the strict sense' do not believe that this is what they are doing. They do not think of themselves as introducing a special, technical sense of the word 'agency', with a narrower scope than it has in its usual, non-technical sense. On the contrary, they think of themselves as using the word in its non-technical sense, but with a heightened degree of intellectual circumspection. And for their part, non-philosophers do not think of themselves as using the word 'agent' metaphorically when they are not talking about human beings.

So why does the difference between these two ideas of agency exist? Does the influence of the empiricist tradition still persist? Or are our usual ways of speaking and thinking careless, or informed by a false conception of the way non-human beings behave? For example, it is sometimes said that an anthropomorphic tendency, deeply rooted in human nature, makes us inclined to endow animals, plants, and even mountains, rivers, and the wind with thoughts and intentions. Is this the right explanation?

I do not believe it is. If action necessarily involved thought or intention, a verb that refers to a kind of action would include the idea of thought or intention in its meaning. For example, 'build' would attribute thought or intention to the one that builds, and 'cook' would attribute thought or

intention to the one that cooks. So these verbs could not be used unam-
biguously to refer to action, on the one hand, and to the behaviour of
animals incapable of thought, or to bodily organs, on the other. But of
course they can. 'Grind' has exactly the same meaning, whether it refers to a
cook grinding meat or a bird's gizzard grinding seeds; 'bend' has the same
meaning whether it describes a blacksmith or the wind; and 'build' means
the same in the sentences 'The man built a shed' and 'The wasps built
a nest'.

But if we were told that a man had built a shed, we would assume that
thought and intention were involved; whereas if we were told that a swarm
of wasps had built a nest, we would not, or at least should not, make the
same assumption. True. But this is not because 'build' is ambiguous,
involving the idea of thought or intention in one meaning and not the
other; it is because human beings do not build things without thought and
intention, whereas wasps do. Similarly, if we were told that the Pope
walked across St. Peter's Square, we would assume that he was wearing
clothes, whereas we would not make this assumption if we were told that a
cat walked across the garden. But this is not because 'walk' is ambiguous,
involving the idea of clothing in one meaning and not the other; it is
because Catholic clergymen do not walk in public places in the nude.
The fact is that non-human animals engage in many basic kinds of activity
thoughtlessly—feeding, copulating, communicating, caring for young, and
so on—although the same kinds of activity do involve thought in the case of
human beings. So attributing active powers to them need not involve any
kind of anthropomorphism. And the same applies to plants and inanimate
agents, although of course the modes of activity they have in common with
human beings are different from the ones just mentioned.

I do not mean to deny that we think anthropomorphically about many
things: no doubt we do. Strawson comments that if we see a boulder roll
down a mountainside and flatten a wooden hut in its path, '[we may] in
some barely coherent way, identify with the hut (if we are one kind of
person) or with the boulder (if we are another): putting ourselves imagina-
tively in the place of one or the other'. But, he adds, our tendency to do this,
if we have such a tendency, has no bearing whatever on our rationale for
thinking of the boulder's flattening the hut as action on a par with vastly
many other instances of action and interaction, which, 'whether entered
into by animate or inanimate beings [. . .] supply wholly satisfactory explanations of their outcomes'.[6]

Some kinds of action do necessarily involve thought or intention, and some verbs of action therefore do include the idea of thought or intention in their meaning. For example, the verb 'murder' means kill wickedly or unlawfully. So if we describe a shark as murderous, either we are using the word metaphorically or we are confused. But reflecting on this kind of case should help us to see that there is nothing either metaphorical or confused in the thought that sharks kill, as opposed to murder, that wasps build nests, that a tree sucks up moisture from the ground, or that the wind bends the tree's branches. These thoughts do not involve the idea that sharks, wasps, trees, or the wind have intentions, purposes, or plans. They do of course involve the idea that these things do not merely undergo changes, but actually cause changes. But an agent's causing a change is not intentional or purposeful as such.

Our willingness to think of non-human beings as agents is not careless or anthropomorphic. On the contrary, restricting agency to human beings is absurdly chauvinistic. It is at least as egregious a case of human exception-alism as Descartes's claim that only human beings are conscious and feel sensations, perhaps more so, since consciousness inhabits a much smaller part of the natural world than agency does. Of course, we can confine our use of the *words* 'agent' and 'act' to human agents, if we wish. But in reality we have just as much reason to confine them to adults and exclude children, or to Gentiles and exclude Jews. Our principal philosophical interest may be in human action, but we can only hope to understand it properly if we acknowledge that action is a highly abstract concept, of the same order as substance, power, process, and event, and if we ask what is distinctive about human agency once the broader category has been defined.

2.3 Action and causation

The concepts of agency and action are highly abstract, and by no means confined in their application to human beings. But we can still approach a general definition of action by reflecting on the way we think about it in the context of human life. This approach has the advantage that it is more likely to seem persuasive to philosophers who find the chauvinist position tempting, and it is how I shall proceed.

2.3.1 Action, agency, and active power

Our thought about action in human life is shaped by three main comparisons. First, we contrast action with thought when we compare an active life and a contemplative life, or when we state the legal doctrine that a crime requires an act. Second, we compare action with speech when we say that actions speak louder than words, although it is also true that speech is a kind of action, and may qualify as sedition, conspiracy, or incitement. Third, we contrast action with passion, by which I do not mean intense feeling, but enduring or undergoing—in an antiquated use of the word, suffering—change.

All these comparisons point to the same idea. To act is to intervene, to make a difference, to make something happen, to cause some kind of change. The change may be momentous or trivial, it may be a process or an event, it may be a kind of motion, as when someone opens or closes a door or throws a ball, or another kind of change may be involved, as when one burns some toast. What runs like a thread through our thought about action is the simple idea of an agent's causing change.

Broader definitions of action are possible, most obviously, by counting *preventing* change as action as well as *causing* change. This is a natural extension of the definition proposed here, since preventing change, like causing change, is a way of influencing the course of events. But the more restrictive definition seems to me preferable, because of a combination of two points. First, preventing change is always achieved *by* action or *by* inaction of some kind, as when one prevents someone from leaving a room by locking the door or by not unlocking it. But second, the idea that inaction is a kind of action—i.e. that there are 'negative' as well as 'positive' acts—seems to me no more plausible than the idea that poverty is a kind of wealth, or that unemployment is a (badly paid) kind of job. Inaction can of course be voluntary—as poverty and unemployment can—but it is not a kind of action, any more than continuity is a kind of change.[7] The platitude (or is it a tautology?) that *not* doing something is not *doing* something seems to me incontrovertible.[*]

---

[*] Cf. Bach, 'Refraining, Omitting and Negative Acts'. Is it possible to *cause* change by inaction, e.g. to burn a sauce by leaving it unattended on the hob? If we distinguish between causing and allowing, i.e. not preventing, then we should say no, although of course one can let a sauce burn deliberately in this way.

The combination of these two points suggests that, at most, prevention should be counted as active when it is achieved by means of action. Ensuring that something doesn't change by not changing something may be as consequential as an act, but it is not an act, even though not doing something can be deliberate and voluntary, and one can try not to do something, such as bite one's nails, and either succeed in the attempt or fail.[8] But if preventing cannot be active *as such*, because it inherits its status as active or inactive from the means by which it is achieved, it seems preferable not to include it in a definition of action. Such at least is how I shall proceed.

The concept of action is correlative with the concept of agency, because action is by agents, and agents act.[9] Agency is expressed in activities, such as knitting or playing chess, and in acts, such as making a purl-stitch or taking a pawn, the difference between them being that in the case of activities, but not in the case of acts, if 'A is ϕing' is true at all times between t_1 and t_2, it follows that A ϕs between t_1 and t_2.[10] For example, swimming is an activity, whereas swimming the Hellespont is an act. If it was true at all times between eleven and noon that Byron was swimming, it follows that Byron swam between eleven and noon; but if it was true at all times between eleven and noon that Byron was swimming the Hellespont, it does not follow that Byron swam the Hellespont between eleven and noon, because he may not have reached the opposite shore until a quarter past, and may not have reached it at all. I shall concentrate on acts here, although much of what I shall say applies equally to activities.[*]

Just as we contrast action with passion, we contrast agents with patients, and active powers with passive powers. Agents bring about or cause change, whereas patients undergo or suffer change; active powers are abilities to cause change, whereas passive powers are liabilities to undergo change. For example, when Paul melts a knob of butter in a pan, Paul is the agent and the knob of butter is the patient. Paul exercises his ability to bring about the change the butter undergoes, and the butter realizes its liability to undergo the change Paul brings about. If we use the verb in the active voice to report

---

[*] The fact that one can fail to complete an act is sometimes thought to require a qualification of the idea that to act is to cause a certain kind of change. Varying the example, one can be engaged for a time in drying a plate without completing the task. But it is argued that one cannot properly be said to be engaged in causing (as opposed to attempting to cause) a plate to become dry unless this result occurs. If that is right, we cannot infer from the fact that *to do* an act of a certain kind is *to cause* a change of the corresponding kind, that *to be doing* an act of the same kind is *to be causing* a change of the corresponding kind. (See Szabó, 'On the Progressive and the Perfective'.)

the act—'Paul melted the butter'—the subject refers to the agent and the object refers to patient. If we use the verb in the passive voice—'The butter was melted by Paul'—the subject refers to the patient and the agent is referred to in the complement 'by Paul'.

But we cannot simply divide the world into agents and patients—for example, we cannot say that human beings are agents whereas knobs of butter are patients—because one is an agent or a patient only in relation to a particular act. For example, a boxer is an agent in relation to a punch he lands on his opponent, but he is a patient in relation to a punch his opponent lands on him. It is even possible to be both agent and patient in relation to a single act, as Descartes and Bentham both point out.[11] For example, a man who commits suicide is both agent and patient: as the one who kills, he is an agent; as the one who dies, he is a patient. The words 'agent' and 'patient', we may say, do not refer to kinds of beings, but to roles.

2.3.2 Causative/mutative alternation

The class of verbs used to report action is vast and varied, because agents cause a vast number of different kinds of change, and because many of the verbs and verb phrases we use to report action do more than merely identify the kind of change the agent caused. For example, to kill something is to cause its death. (A few writers have denied this, but their reasons for doing so are weak. I shall address them shortly.) So 'Cain killed Abel' simply means that Cain caused Abel's death. The verb does not tell us whether he did it knowingly or unknowingly, quickly or slowly, with a stone or with a knife. By contrast, 'Cain murdered Abel' means that Cain killed Abel wickedly or unlawfully; and 'Cain assassinated Abel' means that Cain killed Abel with treacherous violence.

Even these last two examples are straightforward illustrations of the idea that to act is to cause some kind of change, because we can paraphrase the sentences 'Cain murdered Abel' and 'Cain assassinated Abel' in the form 'Cain caused Abel's death {adverb/adverbial phrase}'. But English is not always so cooperative, and the claim that to act is to cause some kind of change does not imply that every sentence used to report an act can be paraphrased in this way. For example, 'Byron swam the Hellespont' reports an act, but we cannot paraphrase the sentence in a way that brings out its causative meaning simply by substituting a dictionary definition of the verb 'swam'. Even so, to swim the Hellespont *is* to cross the Hellespont by swimming, and therefore by moving—i.e. causing movements of—one's limbs.

We use a vast range of verbs to report action: some refer implicitly to legal, moral, or psychological dimensions of an act, while others do not; and some are easy to paraphrase in a form which says explicitly that the agent caused a certain kind of change, while others take more lexical knowledge and more verbal dexterity to explain. Still, there is no shortage of verbs whose causative meaning is obvious. We have 'open', 'close', 'raise', 'lower', 'melt', 'burn', 'twist', and 'tear', and so on, derived from intransitive verbs, and 'slow', 'still', 'wet', 'dry', 'anger', 'calm', and so on, derived from adjectives. It would not be difficult to extend the list. In each case we find the same pattern. To open or close something is to cause it to open or close; to wet or dry something is to cause it to become wet or dry; and so on. This is true whether one opens or closes a door or one's fist, and whether one dries the dishes or one's hair, and regardless of the means by which the act is performed.*

In many cases the same verb can occur transitively or intransitively—i.e. with a grammatical object or without one—sometimes with a modification, as with 'fell' and 'fall'. When it occurs transitively, it is described as causative because it refers to a kind of action; when it occurs intransitively, it is described as mutative because it refers to the corresponding kind of change. The existence of the two forms is called causative/mutative alternation. Note that the range of verbs from which causatives can be formed is wider in some languages than in others. For example, in Hebrew it includes transitive verbs: *lamadh* (to learn), *limmadh* (to teach); *'akhal* (to eat), *he'ekhil* (to cause to eat); *shakkah* (to forget), *shikkah* or *hishkiah* (to cause to forget); and so on. There are some English examples, but not many. For instance, 'learn' was commonly used to mean teach until at least the eighteenth century, although the OED describes this use today as vulgar.

2.3.3 Direct and indirect causation

I say that to raise, move, wet, dry, kill, etc., something is to cause it to rise, move, become wet, become dry, die, etc., regardless of identities of the

---

* In each case, the *to*-infinitive complement identifies the kind of change that results from the kind of act we report with the causative verb. An expression referring to the change caused in doing an act can always be derived from a sentence that uses this kind of construction—viz. 'X caused Y to φ'—by nominalizing the object + *to*-infinitive complement clause, e.g. 'the door's opening', 'her hair's becoming dry', etc.

agent and the patient and regardless of how the act is done. But it has been objected that only the causative verb (e.g. 'raise' or 'move') can be used in cases where an agent moves part of her own body, and only the verb phrase (e.g. 'cause to rise' or 'cause to move') can be used in cases where causation is indirect. Hence, for example, when we move our hands in the way we normally move them, we do not cause our hands to move; and if one causes a man's death by hiring an assassin, one does not kill the man oneself. But the objection is unconvincing. I shall reply to it by commenting on these two examples in turn.

Concerning the first example, it is uncontroversial that if someone moves her left hand with her right hand, or with a pulley, she causes her left hand to move. It is also uncontroversial that whether she moves her left hand indirectly, as in these cases, or directly, in the normal way, she moves her left hand. The controversial question is whether she causes her hand to move when she moves it directly, in other words, without doing so by moving something else. If we equate moving with causing to move, we are bound to say that she does. But this is sometimes denied, on the grounds that we would not normally *say* 'She caused her hand to move' in the direct case, and it could be misleading if we did say it.[12]

The standard reply to this argument is due to Grice. Grice pointed out that we cannot infer from the fact that we would not normally say something, or that it would be misleading or wrong to say it, that it is not true. For example, if we knew that someone had finished his dinner, we would not normally answer the question whether he has begun his dinner with a simple 'Yes'. But it would not be untrue to say this. For if someone has finished his dinner, then he must have begun it. Again, the remark 'Marcus may be a banker, but he's an honest man' is objectionable if in fact most bankers are honest. But if Marcus is in fact an honest banker, describing the remark as untrue is not the right way to capture what is wrong with making it. So although we would not normally describe someone as causing her hand to move, and although it would normally be confusing or misleading if we did, it does not follow that it would be untrue.

This is a defensive reply to the argument. But the main reason for insisting that to move (raise, open, close, etc.) something is to cause it to move (rise, open, close, etc.) is simply that this is the most plausible way of explaining what these verbs mean, and how their meaning when they occur transitively is related to their meaning when they occur intransitively. For example, to move is to change one's posture, position, or location; to move something is to change *its* posture, position, or location; and to change something is to cause it to change: as the OED puts it, it is to make something—i.e. cause it to become—other than it was. Every dictionary says this, or something very like it, and it is hard to think of a plausible definition of 'move' or 'change' as transitive verbs that is substantially different from these ones.*

We should therefore insist that to move something simply *is* to cause it to move, regardless of what is moved or how it is moved, while acknowledging that we tend to reserve the phrase 'cause . . . to move (open, close, etc.)' for the case where something is moved (opened, closed, etc.) more indirectly than usual; and equally that we tend to reserve the causative verb for cases where causation is relatively direct. (Compare 'to make a tree fall' and 'to fell a tree'.) But the proximity of the connection suggested by the causative expression is relative to what is normal in the kind of case concerned. For example, one might contrast 'opening a door' with a handle or a jemmy with 'causing a door to open' with a magic phrase.

What about the contract killing? If to kill something simply *is* to cause it to die, and if the man who hires an assassin causes his victim to die, then the man kills his victim. But surely (it is said) we would normally say that the assassin is the one who kills him. Gardner defends this claim, with the legal distinction between principal and accessory in mind:

> When I pay a hitman to kill an enemy, it is a straightforward consequence of what I do that the hitman kills my enemy, and hence that my enemy dies. Barring the special case of *novus actus interveniens*, I procure the killing and I also cause, through the hitman, the death. [But] he was the killer—and only one of us can be the killer. [. . .] My part in the causal story was not as principal but as accomplice.[13]

As a matter of fact, a principal in a murder need not pull the trigger or plant the bomb, and may be someone who has got another to do so. For example, if I cause my enemy's death by getting someone to plant a bomb without being aware that that is what he is doing, then I am a principal in the crime. So the distinction between principal and accessory (or accomplice) in a

---

* Hacker's defence of the position I reject underlines this point. He writes: 'Human beings [. . .] have the power to move, to act, at will. "To act" in this context does not signify causing a movement, but making one' (*Human Nature: The Categorial Framework*, p. 158). But this is a distinction without a difference. Making a movement *is* causing a movement, whether or not it is made voluntarily or 'at will'. (See OED, **make**, esp. 9.) For the view that it is impossible to explain the meaning of causative verbs, see Fodor, *The Language of Thought*, p. 130, n. 23.

murder cannot be explained purely in terms of causal proximity to the victim's death.

Setting that aside, my reply to this objection is that we do need to distinguish between the case where A kills B personally, and the case where A employs or induces C to kill B on his behalf, but we are not obliged to do this by confining the use of the verb 'kill' to the first case, and as a matter of fact our use of causative verbs, whether in daily life or in courts of law, does not conform to this rule. It is true that we sometimes use the word 'killer' to mean hitman. In Gardner's example, the man who was paid was obviously a killer in that sense, whereas presumably the man who paid him was not. But we are comfortable saying that Louis XIV built Versailles, that Hitler bombed London, and that Stalin killed millions, while acknowledging that they did not do these things with their own bare hands. If we wish, we can insist that the man who hires a hitman does not *strictly speaking* kill his victim, and perhaps this will be agreed. But if it is agreed, this will be because it is understood that by '*strictly speaking* kill' what is meant is kill personally, or kill with his own bare hands.[14]

For these reasons, I believe we can accept the account I have proposed of causative/mutative alternation and the meaning of causative verbs. Of course we could reserve the verb 'cause' for a particular kind of action—just as we could reserve the term 'agent' for a human being, an adult, etc.—and assign the role of expressing the broader causal concept to another word or phrase, such as 'produce' or 'bring about'. But this would merely be a terminological stipulation and it is hard to see what would be gained intellectually by making it.

2.3.4 Causation by agents and causation by acts

It might be objected that even if my account of causative/mutative alternation is convincing, we cannot *define* an act as an instance of an agent's causing some kind of change, because when we speak about an *agent*'s causing something, this is an elliptical way of speaking about an *act*'s causing something, and so the proposed definition is circular. For example, Davidson writes: 'Although we say the agent caused the death of the victim, that is, that he killed him, this is an elliptical way of saying that some act of the agent [. . .] caused the death of the victim.'[15]

It is not hard to see why philosophers diagnose ellipsis. A hidden piece of meaning can save a semantic theory in much the same way as a hidden heavenly body can save an astronomical one. But in this case the diagnosis is mistaken. Ellipsis is the omission of a word or phrase from a sentence, which is needed either to complete its grammatical structure or to fully express its meaning.[16] But

(1) Brutus killed Caesar

is a grammatically complete sentence as it stands, unlike, for example, '[be] Careful!' or '[it is] Nice to see you.' So the idea must be that the meaning of (1) is not completely expressed unless we amend it to read

(2) *Some act of* Brutus ~~killed~~ *caused the death of* Caesar.

But this cannot be right. (1) and (2) cannot have the same meaning, because if they did then so would

(3) Brutus moved his hand

and

(4) *Some act of* Brutus ~~moved~~ *caused the movement of* his hand.

But (3) does not imply (4). Arguably, (1) does imply (2), since Brutus cannot kill Caesar without doing so by doing another act that causes Caesar's death, such as stabbing him. By contrast, moving one's hand is the kind of act one can do directly, in other words, *without* doing it by doing another act. Hence, if Brutus moves his hand, there need not be an earlier act that causes the movement of his hand, so (3) does not imply (4). ((4) is not to be confused with 'Brutus caused the movement of his hand', which *is* implied by (3), as we have seen.)

It has been claimed in reply that (3) is ambiguous, since it can refer either to direct or indirect action, and that it is elliptical in one meaning and not in the other.[17] But this cannot be right. It is true that (3) does not say whether Brutus moved his hand by doing something else. Nor does it say whether he moved his right hand or his left hand, whether he moved it quickly or slowly, and so on. But these are not ambiguities: they are simply details not filled in. One might as well claim that 'Brutus killed Caesar' is ambiguous because it does not say whether he did it with a gun or a knife, on the Nones of February or the Ides of March.[18]

A more widely disputed question, which stands behind the one about ellipsis but does not bear on the definition of action proposed here, is whether causation by agents can be reduced to causation by events. In fact, philosophers have made reductionist claims about causation in both directions,[19] and arguments have been offered on both sides, purporting to show that the disfavoured kind of causation is paradoxical unless it can be reduced. In favour of reducing agent- to event-causation, it is claimed that causes must occur at specific times;* in favour of the opposite reduction, that causation must be an exercise of causal power. But both claims are question-begging—neither can be adequately supported except by assuming what it is supposed to prove—and no convincing reductive scheme has been proposed.

However, more persuasive arguments have been advanced, which do not impugn the reality of either kind of causation, or support reduction in either direction, but suggest that neither can exist without the other. Thus, partisans of agent-causation argue that event-causation alone cannot amount to any more than regularity or counterfactual dependence (isn't this the main lesson of the analysis of causation in Hume's *Treatise*?), and that the idea of an origin or source, which is essential to the idea of causation, cannot be captured in this way (isn't *this* the main lesson of the long history of inadequate Humean theories of causation?). For their part, partisans of event-causation argue that there cannot be causation by agents without causation by events, because a causal power must have a trigger, and the trigger is the event-cause of the exercise of the power. (I shall return to the question of triggers in Chapter 5.)

The truth is probably that the two kinds of causation are *interdependent*, and partisans on both sides are seeing one side of a symmetric relation. Roughly speaking, events can only acquire the status of causes by participating in action by agents, and agents can only exercise causal powers by dint of events. This is the solution suggested by our explanations of the behaviour of complex agents with functionally differentiated parts. For example, we can explain how a man moves his hand by describing the events inside his body that cause the motion of his hand: the release of neurotransmitters, the contraction of muscles, and so on. But these events are caused by nerve cells and muscle fibres, which are agents themselves, with their own distinctive causal powers. These powers in turn are activated

---

* This argument is sometimes attributed to Broad, but his claim is in fact the more cautious one that 'an essential factor' in 'the total cause' of an event must be other events, which is consistent with the interdependence of causation by agents and by events, on a reasonable interpretation of the phrase 'total cause' (*Ethics and the History of Philosophy*, p. 215).

by events caused by more minute agents. And so on, until, below the nanoscale, substance, power, action all dissolve, and causation is 'swallowed up in mathematics', in other words pure regularities, or patterns of functional dependence between events.[20]

2.3.5 A definition of action

In sum, the definition of action proposed in 2.3.1 is not invalidated by Davidson's specious claim about ellipsis, and the account of causative/ mutative alternation proposed in 2.3.2 is not disproved by our tendency to reserve the use of verb phrases with 'cause to' for cases where causation is relatively indirect. To act is to cause some kind of change, the agent being the one that causes the change and the patient being the one that undergoes it, the kind of act depending on the kind of change. Agents and patients are individual substances, such as a particular cat or man or stone, or else particular quantities of a kind of material, such as a particular vial of poison or a particular ounce of gold. But 'agent' and 'patient' do not refer to different kinds of entities, but to complementary roles. Nothing is active but immutable, i.e. able to cause change but unable to undergo it, except, according to some religious traditions, God.

This is not a reductive definition. I do not mean to suggest that the concepts of substance, causation, and change are simpler or more basic than the concept of action itself, or that the idea of action is composed of these other ideas in the way that molecules are composed of the elements in the periodic table. On the contrary, the definition reveals part of the pattern of relationships between a number of equally abstract ideas. It is, to use Strawson's term, connective rather than reductive.[21]

It is also conservative, for although it allows for a much greater range of agents than the chauvinist conception of action criticized in 2.1–2.2, it restricts the range of performances that count as acts. For instance, when I hold my breath, I prevent a certain kind of motion in my body, and when I drop to my knees I allow myself to fall to my knees. Both performances can be voluntary, intentional, or planned. And in the right context both might be described as acts. But to prevent motion is to cause it *not* to occur; and to allow motion is to fail to prevent it, or refrain from preventing it.*

---

* Notice that it is possible to prevent or allow *x* by causing *y*—for example, one can prevent a bath from overflowing by closing the tap or allow a prisoner to escape by opening a gate; and it

Neither of these things is equivalent to causing or bringing about the motion prevented or allowed. So I do not count them as acts.

Defining an act as an instance of an agent's causing some kind of change therefore presents a simple, indeed a simplifying, model of our thought—one that distinguishes between causing, preventing, and allowing with unnatural sharpness. It is, in effect, the result we obtain by using the concepts of substance, power, cause, and change to define in abstract terms the conceptual thread that runs through the thought of something raising, lowering, carrying, dragging, throwing, or in general moving something; or making, breaking, heating, cooling, wetting, drying, twisting, tearing, or in general creating, destroying, or changing something.

Returning to an example mentioned earlier, Paul is able to melt butter, and butter is liable to melt. A change in the patient is caused by the agent and the act is the causing of this change. The model is simple, and its value lies partly in its simplicity. It is not an exact record of our fluid and undisciplined thought and talk; it regiments it to some degree. But it makes our thought and talk more tractable, and fallacies easier to expose.

2.4 Action and integration

In 2.1–2.3, we saw that in the early modern period, the idea that all real action originates in the will arose out of a double misconception: the doctrine that matter is inert coupled with a not yet fully naturalized conception of human beings. We also saw that if we set these two ideas aside there is no reason to confine the idea of agency to human beings. Action in general is simply the exercise of an active causal power—i.e. the power or ability to cause some kind of change—the agent being the one that causes the change and the patient being the one that undergoes it. Far from applying exclusively to human beings, the concept of action applies to every substance able to cause change.

If the concept of action is the highly abstract causal concept these claims imply it is, will or intention may still play an essential role in *human* agency, for we may still need to refer to an act of will or an intention in order to

---

is possible to cause *x* by preventing or allowing *y*—for example, one can kill a man by suffocating him, or please a child by letting it stay up late. For a detailed treatment of allowing, see Bach, 'Refraining, Omitting and Negative Acts'.

distinguish between the changes in a person's body she causes personally herself, such as the movements of her legs when she walks, or her lips when she speaks, and the movements she does not cause personally, such as the contraction of her heart. But I shall reject this theory of human agency and propose an alternative that is not limited in its application to animals capable of having intentions, but applies to all agents with functionally differentiated parts. I shall confine attention to *physical* activity and passivity; the distinction between *mental* activity and passivity involves special problems of its own, and I shall ignore it here.

Davidson gave a new lease of life to the idea that intention is the mark of human agency: 'a person does, as agent,' he claimed, 'whatever he does intentionally under some description.'[22] But the idea had been around for a long time by then. In *The Passions of the Soul*, Descartes argues that our *volontés* cause all our active movements and active thoughts, for example, when we walk as opposed to when we fall, or when we apply our minds to a problem as opposed to feeling pain. The English words used in place of *volonté* were 'volition' or 'will', but Reid and Bentham substituted 'intention' (see the Appendix). Thus Reid says that if an act was done without the agent's 'will and intention', then 'it ought not to be imputed to him as the agent'; and Bentham insists that 'if the act be not intentional in the first stage, it is no act of yours.'[23]

If we take the main principles of Descartes's philosophy for granted, volition provides a plausible way of distinguishing between activity and passivity in human life. For, one might argue, any event that is attributable to a *res cogitans* as the agent must either be or be caused by one of its own thoughts. In other words, the acts of a *res cogitans* must all 'terminate', as Descartes puts it, in its own thoughts or their effects. Descartes assumes that these must be *active* thoughts, perhaps on the grounds that active thoughts will cause active movements, whereas passive thoughts will cause passive movements. And our active thoughts, he says, are our volitions: 'The ones I call [the soul's] actions are all of our volitions, because we find by experience that they come directly from our soul and seem to depend only on it.' (§17)

The strength of this theory lies in the first step: if a person is purely a thinking substance, then anything attributable to his agency must either be, or be caused by, one of his own thoughts. This must be right. For comparison: if Parliament were a purely legislative body—if the only thing Parliament could do was to legislate—then anything attributable to its agency would have to consist in its legislation or an effect thereof; if Tiger Woods were a purely golfing substance—if the only thing he could do was play golf—anything attributable to his agency would have to consist in his golfing or an effect thereof; and so on. But the two other ideas on which the plausibility of the theory depends are both questionable.

First, why should only active thoughts cause active movements? I defended Ryle's analogous assumption that only voluntary thoughts can cause voluntary movements in 1.5. But we are holding the ideas of voluntariness and agency firmly apart, and considered purely as an idea about agency this does not seem to be true. For if one billiard ball strikes another one and sets it in motion, the motion in the first ball need not be, and presumably *will* not be, caused by the ball itself. In other words, it will not be attributable to its own agency. But this does not count against the idea that setting the second ball in motion *is* attributable to the first ball's agency, in other words, that it is an exercise of active power by the first ball.

Second, why should every active thought, that is, every thought directly attributable to the thinker's own agency, be a volition? Descartes says that volitions 'come directly from our soul and seem to depend only on it'. But if he means that they are spontaneous, or that they do not seem to have an exogenous cause, many other kinds of thoughts can be described in these terms as plausibly as volitions: for example, spontaneously remembering a name one struggled in vain to remember the day before, suddenly finding the solution to a problem, and so on. Thoughts such as these may not be as spontaneous as they seem to be; but the same can be said of volitions.

We can see why Descartes held that causation by volitions is the mark of activity in human life, although his arguments are not entirely convincing, even if we assume that the main principles of his philosophy are true. But it does not matter for now whether the idea that will or intention is the mark of human agency is backed by a theory that postulates volitions, or for that matter by any theory about how active movements are caused. At present we are only concerned with the idea that being intentional 'in the first stage' or 'under some description' is what distinguishes active movements from passive ones.

If we set the history of philosophy aside, it is still understandable that the orthodox view is widely accepted. Surely, intending or willing is so central to human nature that human agency must involve it somehow or other? Besides, what is the alternative? Frankfurt, who rejected the orthodoxy for a while, writes as follows:

Consider the difference between what goes on when a spider moves its legs in making its way along the ground, and what goes on when its legs move in similar patterns and with similar effects because they are manipulated by a boy who has managed to tie strings to them. In the first case the movements are not simply purposive, as the spider's digestive processes doubtless are. They are also attributable to the spider who makes them. In the second case the same movements occur but they are not made by the spider, to whom they merely happen.[24]

Frankfurt insists that the contrast between these kinds of movement is the same whether we are concerned with a spider or a human being, and hence that it cannot 'be explicated in terms of any of the distinctive higher faculties which characteristically come into play when a person acts'. But unfortunately he stops there: 'the general conditions of [human] agency', he comments, 'are unclear.' And in a later article, he reverts to explaining the contrast between activity and passivity in terms of 'higher faculties'.[25]

So even discounting for Descartes's influence, the prevalence of the idea that intention is the mark of human agency is understandable. But I shall argue that it is wrong. I shall assume, contrary to Descartes, both that we are not purely thinking substances and that we are not simple substances, and approach the problem of defining human agency by considering the agency of complex substances—i.e. substances with parts—in general.

Complex agents can be animate (a spider) or inanimate (a turbine), and complex animate agents can be divided into three kinds: organisms; parts of organisms, such as cells and bodily organs; and super-organisms, that is, groups of organisms, such as colonies of ants or bees, which act as functionally integrated wholes. Institutions are complex inanimate agents of an unusual kind, being inanimate wholes with inanimate parts analogous to organs, and animate members analogous to cells. They include universities, incorporated businesses, government departments, and political parties.

All complex agents possess active and passive powers, that is, powers to cause and undergo particular kinds of change. Some of these powers are purely aggregative, others are not. For example, the weight of a body is aggregative: it is simply the combined weight of its parts. Consider an engine driving a flywheel. It exerts a downward force on whatever is supporting it, because of the gravitational force the earth exerts on it, but this has nothing to do with the structure that makes it an engine. By contrast, its ability to drive the flywheel is non-aggregative, because it depends on the interaction between functionally differentiated parts. We want to define the kind of motion that is attributable to the non-aggregative agency of a human being as a whole, such as the motion of your hand when you write or of your lips when you speak, but human agency is not the best place to start. In fact, the easiest cases to understand are institutions, because we design them ourselves. We don't need to reverse engineer them, because we engineer them.

For example, consider a university. Only a university as a whole can award degrees, but its administrative offices, exam boards, individual professors and lecturers, etc. all have to follow the procedures laid down in the university's statutes and regulations for it to do so. The university as a whole has the power to award degrees, and it is not a purely aggregative power, but its exercise depends on the integrated exercise of the powers of its functionally differentiated parts. So the agency of the whole supervenes on the agency of its parts, in the sense that if the acts of the university's departments, offices, and staff are fixed, the acts of the university as a whole are fixed as well. The whole cannot act independently of its parts.[26]

Super-organisms also provide examples where distinguishing between the agency of wholes and parts is straightforward. For example, when bees swarm they gather in a convenient place, such as the branches of a tree, while scouts set out to find a place for a new hive. When a scout encounters a candidate place, it returns to the swarm and communicates what it has discovered by performing the famous 'waggle dance', running through a figure-of-eight pattern, vibrating its body laterally as it moves through the central axis. Different features of the dance communicate the distance and direction of the place and how attractive it was. Other scouts respond to dances by investigating the places they advertise. More attractive candidate places elicit dances that are longer and more vigorous, which in turn are more likely to elicit a response from other scouts. So, gradually, and without any individual comparing one candidate place with another, the support for the more attractive places grows. When a sufficient number of scouts are indicating the same place with their dances, the swarm goes there and builds a hive. In this example, it is not difficult to distinguish between the agency of the swarm and the agency of individual bees, even though there are no statutes or regulations to refer to, where their powers are defined. As with the university, the swarm has a power that none of its members has alone— the ability to select the place for a new hive—but the exercise of this power depends on the interaction between its members.

The same model must apply to the agency of a spider or a human being, because all animal agency is really collective agency. There is a growing literature on the relationship between individual agency and collective agency, in which the idea of individual agency is taken for granted, and usually assumed to involve intention, and collective agency is explained in terms of individual agency. It is assumed that the right way of understanding agency is to proceed from the individual to the collective, the association, or the group. But I believe we need to turn this order of explanation on its head, because individual human agency is always really collective agency, since a human being, like every other multicellular organism with special-ized tissues, is in reality a highly integrated colony of functionally differen-tiated but genetically similar cells.

The similarity between an animal and a colony is especially clear if the individuals that make up the colony are compared with organs as opposed to cells. The colonial medusa *Nanomia Cara* illustrates this point (see Figure 2.1). As Maynard Smith and Szathmáry explain:

> [I]t looks like a single organism, with a bladder to keep afloat, pumps to propel it through the water, tentacles for killing prey, digestive organs, and organs for producing gametes. Yet all these different structures turn out to be modified individuals, or zooids. *Nanomia* is a colony of highly differentiated individuals.[27]

It differs from a colony of bees in that it develops from a single fertilized egg, so the parts of its body are as genetically similar as those of a single insect or vertebrate. But unlike the organs of higher animals, its body parts evolved from individual organisms, similar to the present-day *Hydra*.

The lesson of these examples is that the non-aggregative agency of complex substances with functionally differentiated parts depends on the integrated operation of these parts, rather than on the operation of a specific part. A spider spins a web, kills and eats its prey, selects and copulates with a mate. Some of these activities involve parts specifically adapted for them, such as poison- and silk-glands. But since they all involve complex inter-actions with the spider's environment—and mostly with moving targets—they all involve the integrated operation of its sensory and motor systems, as well as the metabolic systems on which its life and activity continuously depend. One plausible option is therefore to regard the integrated operation of metabolic, sensory, and motor systems as the mark that distinguishes the agency of the spider as a whole from the agency of its parts.

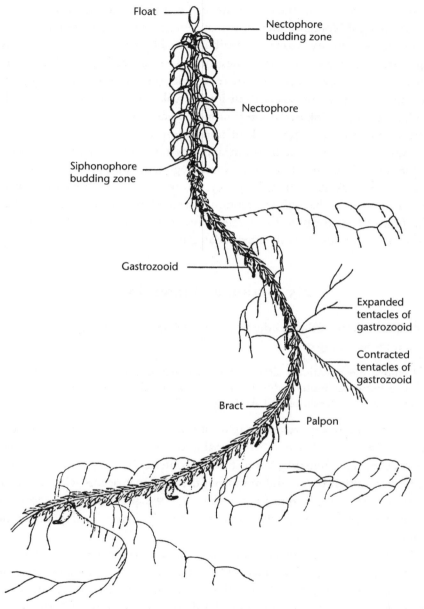

Figure 2.1. The colonial medusa, *Nanomia Cara* (from Maynard Smith and Szathmáry, *The Origins of Life*, reproduced by permission of Oxford University Press)

If this is plausible in the case of spiders, is it also plausible in the case of human beings? Not quite. Activities that depend on the integrated operation of motor and sensory systems *are* attributed to a human being as a whole, as opposed to particular organs, tissues, or cells—e.g. feeding, mating, locomotion, communication—but these activities involve the physiological systems that are responsible for our intellectual and emotional lives as well. So it is better to think of the integration of metabolic, motor, and cognitive systems in general as the mark of non-aggregative human agency, using 'cognitive' with the same broad meaning that it has in 'cognitive science'. Adopting this proposal involves some regimentation of our quotidian thought and talk about human agency, but it matches it more closely than the orthodox idea that will or intention is the mark of human agency, and has the merit of conforming to a general conception of agency by complex substances with functionally differentiated parts.

2.5 Action and intention

I shall turn to the orthodox doctrine now. Mele and Moser illustrate it with a picturesque comparison:

> Remove the intentional altogether from intentional action, and you have mere behavior: brute bodily motion not unlike the movement of wind-swept sand on the shores of Lake Michigan.[28]

This is obviously a grotesque simplification. Spiders have a complex repertoire of patterns of behaviour that enable them to survive to maturity and reproduce, and while they can be blown around by a strong wind, this kind of bodily motion is very different from the kind that occurs when a spider spins a web. Still, it remains possible that the presence or absence of intention coincides with the division between activity and passivity in human life.

But in fact there are several kinds of exceptions to the generalization that all human action is intentional under some description or stems from an intentional movement, including the following: automatic reactions, such as ducking or drawing back one's head to avoid a blow, or making an involuntary adjustment to one's posture to maintain balance; some kinds of habitual action, including verbal tics such as echolalia (the automatic repetition of words and phrases spoken by a person one is conversing with) or interspersing speech with words or phrases like 'you know'; some kinds of uncontrolled action done in abnormal or pathological states of mind, such as panic or psychosis; unconscious action such as murmuring in one's sleep; and the spontaneous expression of emotion in facial expressions, vocalizations, and gestures, such as smiling, scowling, pouting, shrugging, and laughing, or crying out with pleasure or pain.[29]

It is true that a great deal of behaviour expressing emotion *is* intentional, often despite being spontaneous and not fully controlled, for example kissing a lover or throwing crockery at a spouse.[30] It is also true that there are many changes in the body that express emotion, which we do not typically attribute to the person as agent, such as blushing and shedding tears. And others are borderline cases or perhaps treated inconsistently. For example, we do not regard goosebumps as the result of personal agency, but we describe a dog as raising its hackles, and think of this as an act, on a par with growling or baring its teeth. But that leaves a large range of cases that are undeniably *un*intentional expressive acts, such as the ones Norfolk mentions in a speech about Cardinal Wolsey in Shakespeare's *Henry VIII*, which Darwin quotes in *The Expression of the Emotions in Man and Animals*:

> Some strange commotion
> Is in his brain: he bites his lips and starts;
> Stops on a sudden, looks upon the ground,
> Then, lays his finger on his temple; straight,
> Springs out into a fast gait; then, stops again,
> Strikes his breast hard; and anon, he casts
> His eye against the moon: in most strange postures
> We have seen him set himself.[31]

The truth seems to be that *most* human acts that matter sufficiently to be reported or recorded stem from an intentional movement—in Bentham's phrase, they are intentional 'in the first stage'—with the important exception of spontaneous expressions of emotion. The reason is simple. Roughly speaking, an act is intentional if, and only if, the agent does it either because she wants to do it or values doing it for its own sake, or because it is, or seems to be, a means to a further end that she wants or values. When acts are considered unintentional, it is usually because the agent did them by accident or by mistake, or because she was unaware of doing them, or because they were anticipated but unwanted concomitants of intentional action, such as giving oneself a hangover when one drinks. But the movements our acts stem from are not concomitants of these acts, and it is unusual for us to move parts of our bodies without being aware of doing so, or by accident or mistake, at least when the movements are liable to have significant consequences. It is even more unusual for us to move parts of our bodies unintentionally in ways in which we cannot also move them intentionally, although even this may happen on occasion. For example, Darwin claims that few people can control the muscles involved in in the facial expression of grief.[32]

Furthermore, even if every human act *did* stem from an intentional movement, it would not follow that the distinction between activity and passivity is explained by intention. For comparison, if every human act were selfish, or stemmed from a movement of the agent's body that has a selfish purpose, it would not follow that this explains why it qualifies as an act. In fact, the proportion of human acts that stem from an intentional movement is neither here nor there, as far as defining the distinction between activity and passivity is concerned. For the agency of complex substances with functionally differentiated parts *always* depends on the integrated operation of these parts, rather than on the operation of a specific part or faculty—e.g. the amygdala or the will. This applies to human beings in the same way as it applies to other animals and colonies of animals, and all other complex agents, including institutions and machines. Hence if some basic human activity that involves the integrated operation of cognitive and motor systems, such as feeding or copulating, were only conscious and controllable to the extent that breathing is, a smaller proportion of human acts would stem from an intentional movement than is actually the case, but activity and passivity in human life would be distinguished in exactly the same way.

Of course, this does not prevent us from asking which part of the body initiates motion in a limb. We can still ask Locke's question, 'my right hand writes, whilst my left hand is still: what causes rest in one, and motion in the other?', and choose between Aristotle's answer, which is the heart, and Chrysippus's, which is the brain. We can even distinguish the part of the brain that causes motion in a hand from the part that makes the heart contract. But this will not tell us why we assign one kind of motion and not the other to the agency of a human being as a whole. The key to answering *this* question is integration, and not the activity of a specific organ or mental faculty—the imaginary locus of the active self. It was impossible for Descartes to appreciate this, because he conceived of a person as a simple substance, without parts. But it should be obvious once we abandon this idea, because the activity of any part of a complex agent is exactly that: the activity of a part as opposed to the activity of the whole.

Descartes also says that man is 'in a special way the author of his actions and deserving of praise for what he does'.[33] (See the Appendix.) Philosophers have tried to pin down this special kind of agency in various ways, sometimes describing it in terms of free will, voluntariness, autonomy, reason, or intention—Descartes himself refers in this connection to 'the control we have over our volitions'[34]—but I have not tried to define it here. No doubt most normal human acts, or most that would be included in a biography, differ from acts by other animals in several respects, and it is important that we understand them. This is generally what philosophers who use phrases like 'full-blooded agency' and 'agency in the strict sense' are trying to do. But it is also worth understanding the idea of human agency as such, even if it turns out to be less special than we thought.

3
Acts and Events

3.1 Action and motion

The orthodox view in modern philosophy is that a physical act is a bodily movement or a muscular contraction.[*] This is asserted repeatedly by philosophers and jurists (see 1.3.3), but is it true? As we shall see in a moment, Prichard briskly rejects the idea in an article published posthumously in 1949, and some of the philosophers who reformed the philosophy of action in the first few decades after 1945 also challenge it, or at least call it into question—e.g., J.L. Austin, Kenny, and von Wright—but most do not.[1]

Ryle comes close to doing so in *The Concept of Mind*:

> According to the theory, the workings of the body are motions of matter in space. The causes of these motions must then be either other motions of matter in space or, in the privileged case of human beings, thrusts of another kind. In some way which must forever remain a mystery, mental thrusts, which are not movements of matter in space, can cause muscles to contract. To describe a man as intentionally pulling the trigger is to state that such a mental thrust did cause the contraction of the muscles of his finger.[2]

But instead of rejecting both parts of this conception of human action, both the mental thrusts and the contractions of the muscles, Ryle directs his fire exclusively against the first.[3]

Wittgenstein also seems to accept the equation between action and motion. In a passage in *The Brown Book*, he describes how one can press

---

[*] Hornsby (*Actions*, ch. 1) distinguishes between two senses of 'movement', corresponding to transitive and intransitive uses of the verb 'move': 'movement' meaning the act of moving something; and 'movement' meaning motion of something. I shall use 'movement' in the latter sense throughout.

the back of one's hand against the wall, then step away from the wall and let one's arm rise 'of its own accord', commenting:

> There is a difference between the voluntary act of getting out of bed and the involuntary rising of my arm. But there is not one common difference between so-called voluntary acts and involuntary ones.[4]

Wittgenstein is right in saying that there is not one common difference between voluntary and involuntary acts, as we shall see in Chapter 4; but the difference between his getting out of bed and the rising of his arm is the difference between action and motion, and not, I shall argue, the difference between two kinds of act.

In the next generation, Anscombe follows Wittgenstein closely, describing voluntary acts as 'bodily movements' and contrasting these with 'involuntary movements', such as 'the lift of the arm from one's side after one has leaned heavily with it up against a wall'.[5] Davidson claims that 'if I raise my arm, then my raising my arm and my arm rising are one and the same event'.[6] And Armstrong claims that 'the rising of my arm is the *raising* of my arm provided that it is part or the whole of a pattern of behaviour that has an objective'.[7]

All these philosophers either claim explicitly, or else assume, that if someone raises her arm, her act of raising her arm and the motion of her arm are one and the same process or event. But this cannot be right. For to raise one's arm is to cause one's arm to rise. The act is the agent's *causing* of the motion; and the causing of the motion cannot be identical with the motion caused. It makes no difference what is raised. If Mary raises her arm and the pencil she is holding in a single gesture, her raising of her arm is just as certainly distinct from the motion of her arm as her raising of the pencil is from the motion of the pencil, despite the fact that her arm is part of her body whereas the pencil is not.[*]

Prichard, whose theory of action seems to me confused on practically every other point, understood this. He writes (this is the passage I referred to earlier):

---

* Coope rejects this argument on the grounds that an agent does not cause motion or change, but the state in which motion or change terminates ('Aristotle on Action' pp. 109–38). But it is hard to see how an agent can cause an end-state without doing so by causing the motion or change that terminates in it; for example, how Brutus can cause Caesar to be dead without doing so by causing his death.

When I move my hand, the movement of my hand, though an effect of my action, is not itself an action, and no one who considers the matter carefully would say it was, any more than he would say that the death of Caesar, as distinct from his murder, was an action or even part of an action.[8]

Prichard's own view, that the movement of my hand is an effect of my act, cannot be right, for reasons I shall explain shortly. But he surely is right to insist that it is not itself an act, and of course it follows that it cannot be identified with my act of raising my hand, which self-evidently *is* an act.

Compare causing motion with taking a bath or meeting one's death. The phrases 'take a bath' and 'meet one's death' are examples of a fairly common construction in English, which uses a verb with a so-called eventive object. One can take a bath and have a chat; one can make a choice or a promise; and so on. The verb is often 'have', 'give', 'make', or 'take', but it can also be cognate with the noun-phrase. For instance, instead of saying that Socrates lived well and died peacefully, we can say that he lived a good life and died a peaceful death. The construction allows us to qualify a noun with an adjective instead of qualifying a verb with an adverb, but it is merely a syntactic expedient, and the verb does not express a genuine relation. On the contrary, it refers to one of the very things that it appears, syntactically, to relate. For example, when Socrates took a bath, the taking of it *was* the bath he took; and when he met his death, their meeting *was* his death. But causing motion is different, because an instance of causation cannot be identical with the event caused, any more than an instance of a spatial or social relation can be identical with one of its relata, for instance, a marriage with a spouse.

So whereas Socrates's taking a bath and meeting his death *can* be identified with the bath he took and the death he met, Mary's raising of her arm *cannot* be identified with the motion of her arm. Perhaps one reason why philosophers confuse them is a tendency to focus on acts that consist in moving parts of one's own body. The distinction between action and motion is less salient in this kind of case. It is much easier to confuse the act of raising an arm and the motion of the arm than the act of raising a flag and the motion of the flag, because we can imagine the motion of the flag without the act. We can cut the agent out of the picture, so to speak. But if the motion caused by the agent is in her own body, we cannot do this; and if we imagine ourselves pointing to the act and pointing to the motion, we shall imagine ourselves pointing in the same direction.

If Mary's raising of her arm is not the same event as the rising of her arm, is it an event that causes her arm to rise? Pritchard claims that it is: 'When I move my hand, the movement of my hand [is] an effect of my action.' But this cannot be right either, for three reasons.

(A) The first reason is that a *causing* is not a cause. This is related to the point I made earlier about verbs with eventive objects. The verb 'raising' in the phrase 'Mary's raising of her arm'—like the nouns 'life' and 'death'—is a nominalization, i.e. a noun or noun-phrase derived from another part of speech. The nouns 'kiss' in the phrase 'the kiss Judas gave Jesus' and 'love' in the phrase 'Tom's love for Lucy' are other examples. Now we can use the phrase 'the kiss Judas gave Jesus' to refer to the act reported in the sentence 'Judas gave Jesus a kiss' (or 'Judas kissed Jesus'), since to give someone a kiss is to kiss them ('give a kiss' is like 'take a bath'). Clearly, the phrase 'the kiss Judas gave Jesus' does not refer to something that kissed Jesus. The kiss is not the one that kisses, it is the act of kissing itself.

The same applies in the case of 'raising', 'killing', 'turning', and so on. 'Mary's raising of her arm' refers to the act reported in the sentence 'Mary raised her arm', just as 'Brutus's killing of Caesar' refers to the act reported in the sentence 'Brutus killed Caesar' and 'Paul's turning of his head' refers to the act reported in the sentence 'Paul turned his head'. But again, these phrases do not refer to objects or events that raised Mary's arm, killed Caesar or turned Paul's head, and no one who considers the matter carefully would say they do. In fact, we can state it as a general principle that where 'a' and 'b' are names of particulars (of whatever categories or kinds) and 'ϕ' is a causative verb or verb phrase, 'a's ϕing of b' does not refer (except by accident) to an object or event that ϕs b. In every case, it refers to the ϕing not the ϕer: the killing not the one that kills, the raising not the one that raises, and in general the causing and not the one that causes. This principle is not merely about words. The phrase 'a's causing of b' refers to a's causing of b. Hence if 'a's causing of b' does not *refer* to an object or event that causes b, then a's causing of b is not an object or event that causes b. In short, a *causing* is not a cause.

Thus, we only need to consider the grammar of nominalizations to see that Prichard was mistaken in thinking that when I move my hand, the motion of my hand is an effect of my act. Some philosophers are inclined to dismiss arguments that appeal to grammar with a vague mention of differences between 'superficial' grammatical form and 'deep' logical form. But this is quite unconvincing. The distinction between grammatical form and logical form is real, but it cannot be used in this way. For if a philosophical doctrine implies something false, then it must itself be false, and if it is implied by something true, then it must itself be true, regardless of the subject-matter of the truth or falsehood concerned. For example, if someone proves the existence of God from the premise that ginger is hot, we cannot object that this is merely a fact about root vegetables. Equally, if a philosophical doctrine implies that nominalizations of verbs such as 'love', 'kiss', 'kill', or 'cause' refer to things that love, kiss, kill, or cause, it cannot be defended on the grounds that the behaviour of parts of speech is mere grammar.

(B) Many of the verbs we use to refer to causation by agents can also be used, without any change of meaning, to refer to causation by events. For example, 'broke' has exactly the same meaning in the sentences 'Mary broke the vase' and 'Katrina broke the levee': in both cases it means cause to break, in conformity with the pattern described in 2.3.2, although Mary is a person and Katrina, the hurricane, is an event. So if Mary's breaking of the vase were an event that causes the vase to break, the hurricane's breaking of the levee would be an event that causes the levee to break—that is, a third event, distinct both from the hurricane and the levee's breaking; and this third event's causing the levee to break would be a fourth event; and so on ad infinitum. An infinity of such events may not be a logical or physical impossibility. But the idea that a mundane statement like 'Katrina broke the levee' implies that there are infinitely many such intermediate events is absurd. Hence, the hurricane's breaking of the levee cannot be an event that causes the levee to break, and Mary's breaking of the vase cannot be an event that causes the vase to break either.*

(C) The third reason why Mary's raising of her arm cannot be an event that causes her arm to rise is that, if it were, it would have to be an event that

---

* Hornsby seems to be aware of the regress when she defends Prichard's view. Distinguishing between transitive and intransitive uses of causative verbs by means of the subscripts '$_T$' and '$_I$', she writes: 'Where 'a' designates something in the category of a continuant (rather than event), it is a necessary condition of the truth of 'a ϕ_T-s b' that a cause b to ϕ_I. In that case movements$_T$ of the body are events that cause bodily movements$_I$' (*Actions*, p.13). The argument is a non-sequitur, but the principle that if a ϕ_T-s b then a causes b to ϕ_I is true. However, there is no logical justification for excluding events from its scope. So why does Hornsby circumscribe it in the way she does? Presumably the reason is that if she included events in the scope of the principle, she would have had to include them in the scope of the conclusion stated in the second sentence too, and this would generate the regress.

occurs inside her body: a contraction of a muscle or a release of a neuro-transmitter, or some other event in Mary's nervous system. For these are the events that cause the motion of a person's arm, when she raises it. But if Mary's action were such an event, we would not be able to see it. The act, as opposed to its effect, would be hidden from view. One might think that this would not present a serious practical difficulty, since we would still be able to see Mary's arm go up. But that is not the point. The point is that we *do* see acts of this kind, and not merely their effects. If I say that I saw Mary raise her arm, wave her hand, or turn her head, my statement may be true, without being an elliptical or inaccurate way of saying that I saw an event that was caused by one of these acts, as opposed to the act itself. Witnessing an act is not like witnessing a heart attack. We do not merely see the symptoms.

Despite this formidable difficulty, the view that acts occur inside the agent's body has been seriously advanced. As we have seen, Hornsby follows Prichard in holding that an act is an event that causes motion in the body, and she accepts this implication of the view. She replies to the objection as follows:

> The objector thinks that we see actions themselves, and I am inclined to agree. But he says 'If actions are inside the body, then we cannot see them.' Some doubt is cast on his conditional when we remember that to say that actions take place inside the body is not to deny that they take place in larger portions of space [...] Perhaps then we see actions in virtue of seeing some place where they occur when they occur; perhaps we see actions in virtue simply of seeing the people whose actions they are at the time of their happening. Or again, perhaps we see actions in seeing their effects.[9]

Hornsby does not say which of these alternatives she prefers, but none of them can be right. For we do not see events in a person's nervous system in virtue of seeing some place where they occur when they occur, any more than we see a man walking in Hyde Park in virtue of seeing Hyde Park while he is walking there. Nor do we see an event in someone's nervous system in virtue simply of seeing him when the event occurs, any more than we see a door open inside a house in virtue simply of seeing the house when the door opens. And we do not see events in a person's nervous system in seeing their effects, any more than we see the pistons of an engine move in seeing the car accelerate along a highway. So no doubt is cast on the objector's conditional by the alternatives canvassed here, and the objection stands.[10]

For these reasons, it is not only a mistake to identify the causing of a change with that change itself; it is also a mistake to identify it with another event that causes it. The act of raising one's arm is not an event that causes the motion of one's arm, the act of killing Caesar is not an event that causes Caesar's death, and so on. Suppose therefore—to take another well-known example—that a queen kills a king by pouring poison into his ear. We can imagine tracing our way back from the king's death along a sequence of causally related events that led up to it—events that occurred inside the king's body as the poison took effect, earlier events that occurred in the space between his body and the queen's body, such as the motion of the phial beside his ear, and yet earlier events that occurred inside the queen's body, such as the contraction of a muscle and the release of a neurotransmitter. But it follows from these arguments that we shall not find either the queen's killing of the king or her pouring of the poison into his ear anywhere along this sequence of events.

Figure 3.1. Acts and events

The situation is schematically represented in Figure 3.1. 'A' stands for an agent, each '*e*' stands for an event, the dotted line represents the causal connectedness of the events that are ranged along it, and the curved arrows represent A's causings of events, in other words, A's acts. (I shall comment on the relationship between these acts below.) This is sharply at odds both with the view that an act is a bodily movement and with the view that it is an event that causes a bodily movement, both of which would include A's acts somewhere among the events on the dotted line.

3.2 Acts and events

Should we therefore exclude acts entirely from the category of events? Von Wright says that we should:

> It would not be right, I think, to call acts a kind or species of events. An act *is* not a change in the world. But many acts may quite appropriately be described as the bringing about or effecting (at will) of a change.[11]

We can set aside the parenthetical phrase 'at will'. The immediate import-ance of this passage is that von Wright saw—as Prichard had seen before him—that the student's raising of her arm and the motion of her arm cannot be the same event, any more than the murder of Caesar can be identical with his death. But whereas Prichard rejected the idea that an act can be the causing of the motion of her arm, precisely on the grounds that this would exclude it from being an event, von Wright accepted this implication.[12]

According to von Wright, then, the motion of the student's arm *is* a change in the world, it is a change in the position her arm, but her raising of her arm, her act, is *not* a change in the world, it is the 'bringing about' or 'effecting', in other words the causing, of a change. If we think of events vaguely as occurrences, we shall certainly think of acts as events. But von Wright has a more restricted conception of an event as 'a change in the world'. Perhaps this is a stipulation, but if so, it is a useful one, and I shall follow it.

An act, then, is the causing of an event or change. Now if changes necessarily occur in an underlying substance, then not only does the identity of an act depend on the event of which it is the causing, but the identity of an event depends on the substance that undergoes the change.[13] So events are dependent particulars and acts are doubly dependent particulars, since they are dependent on events. This does not mean that acts are less real than events, or that events are less real than substances, or that substances could exist in a world without events, or that events could occur in a world without acts. And of course it does not prevent us from including acts, events, and substances in Quine's super-category of 'objects', an object being 'the material content of any portion of space–time'.[14] But even if some events depend on others, as well as on an underlying substance, because events themselves can change, these systematic relations of dependence between substances, events, and acts justify placing them in a hierarchy of categories, which the grosser distinction between occurrents and continuants ignores.

The implications of doing so come out clearly when we consider the identity and location of acts. I shall say something more about these things in a moment, but first I shall introduce a distinction between two kinds of event, or rather two kinds of relations between acts and events.

We commonly talk indifferently about a 'result' or a 'consequence' of an act, but I shall distinguish between them in a way introduced by von Wright.[15] An act is a causing of an event by one or more agents. (Agents perform an act jointly if they cause an event jointly.) The *result* of an act is that very event, and its *consequences* are effects of its result. For example, to kill something is to cause it to die; the *result* of a killing is the death caused; and its *consequences* are effects of that death. Again, to break a window is to cause it to break; the *result* of breaking a window is the window's breaking, and the *consequences* of breaking a window are the effects of the window's breaking, such as rainwater getting in. It is useful to distinguish between results and consequences in this way because the identity and location of an act depend on the identity and location of its *result*, and an act belongs to a certain kind of event if and only if its *result* belongs to the corresponding kind: for instance, an act is a killing if and only if its result is a death, a raising of an arm if and only if its result is a rising of an arm, and so on.

Figure 3.2.   Opening a trap by pulling a lever

Figure 3.3.   Giving a signal by flashing a torch

We can approach the question of how acts are identified and distinguished by comparing two cases. First, Tom opens a trap by pulling a lever (Figure 3.2). In this case, the trap's opening (e_m) is caused by the lever's motion (e_n), and so the trap's opening is the *result* of Tom's opening the trap and a *consequence* of his pulling the lever. The *result* of one act is a *consequence* of another. Second, Lucy gives a signal by flashing a torch (Figure 3.3). In this case, the signal *is* the flash (e_n), so Lucy's flashing the torch and her giving the signal are one and the same act, and the signal is the *result*, not the *consequence* of Lucy's flashing the torch. The distinction between these kinds of cases is sometimes marked in our common idiom with the prepositions 'in' and 'by'. But there are also cases, some of which involve legal, social, or ad hoc conventions, in which idiom alone does not record whether two events, and therefore two acts, are involved, or only one. The example of Lucy's giving the signal *by* flashing the torch is one of these.

Now if we describe these two kinds of cases in this way—i.e. as cases which involve two descriptions of a single act, and as cases which involve descriptions of two acts, the *result* of one of which is a *consequence* of the other—we are implicitly applying a criterion of identity for acts, which can be formulated explicitly as follows. Let 'a_1' and 'a_2' be two expressions, each of which refers to an act:

(I) Necessarily, $a_1 = a_2$ if, and only if, the result of a_1 = the result of a_2.

But (I) contradicts the popular claim that *whenever* an agent ϕs by ψing, her ϕing and her ψing are one and the same act. This claim is an obvious corollary of the doctrine that an act is a movement of the body, or alternatively an event that causes such a movement to occur. For example, suppose in the case just mentioned that Tom's opening of the trap and his pulling of the lever were both identical with a thrust of Tom's arm. They would have to be identical with the same thrust, since only one is presumed to have occurred. Then, by the transitivity of identity, his pulling of the lever would have to be the same act as his opening of the trap.

(I) implies, on the contrary, that when an agent ϕs by ψing, her ϕing *may* be the same act as her ψing, as it is in the case where Lucy gives a signal by flashing a torch; but when the result of her ψing is the effect of the result of her ϕing, as it is in Tom's case, her ϕing and her ψing are distinct acts because they have distinct results. Davidson and others, who have denied this, were right to reject the view that Tom's opening the trap and his pulling the lever are related either as cause and effect or as whole and part.[16] But they were wrong to infer that the acts must therefore be one and the same.

Davidson defends his view about the identity of acts with the following example. Suppose the queen moves her hand in such a way as to pour poison in the king's ear:

> The moving of her hand by the queen on that occasion was identical with her doing something that caused the death of the king. Doing something that causes a death is identical with causing a death. But there is no distinction to be made [in this sort of case] between causing the death of a person and killing him.

It follows, Davidson argues, that 'the killing [...] did not differ from the movement of the hand'.[17] He also asks, rhetorically:

> Is it not absurd to suppose that, after the queen has moved her hand in such a way as to cause the king's death, any deed remains for her to do or complete?[18]

But neither the argument nor the question proves its point. The argument is a *petitio*, because the question whether doing something that causes a death is identical with causing a death is precisely what is at issue. Necessarily, if the queen does something that causes a death, then she causes a death, and vice versa; but it does not follow that her doing whatever she does—in this case, her moving her hand—is *identical* with her causing a death. I maintain, on the contrary, that causing one event and causing another event are no less distinct than the events themselves.

But, one might protest, there is surely a difference between the case where the result of one act (a death) is the consequence of another (a movement of a hand), and the case where two acts (a killing and a movement of a hand) have nothing to do with each other. Surely, the second case is the one in which there really are distinct acts, the case, as we might say, in which the agent was *busier*. The answer to this objection is that we do indeed want to mark the difference between the two cases, but the difference is simply this: only in the first case was the result of one act the consequence of the other. As Davidson suggests, we leave it to nature to unfold the consequences of our acts, and can busy ourselves with other things while it does so. But it does not follow that the queen's moving of her hand and her killing of the king are one and the same act if nature ensures that the result of the second ensues from the result of the first.

As for Davidson's question, 'Is it not absurd . . . ', it simply fails to prove that the killing 'did not differ from the movement of the hand'. There was nothing more for the queen to do, because she killed the king by moving her hand, and not by moving her hand and then doing something else, say, flaring her nostrils. But this is not a reason to accept that her moving her hand and her killing the king were one and the same act. Compare events. If one event, such as the white ball's striking the red ball with a certain force, is all that needs to happen for another event to happen, such as the red ball's beginning to move, it does not follow that only one event occurred.

Now the doctrine that acts are movements of the agent's body, or muscular contractions, or causes of muscular contractions in the agent's nervous system, creates a puzzle about the location of acts—in fact two puzzles: one concerning acts that consist in an agent moving part of her own body, and the other concerning acts with remoter results.

The first puzzle is stated concisely by Davidson himself: 'If a man's arm goes up, the event takes place in the space–time zone occupied by the arm; but if a man raises his arm, doesn't the event fill the zone occupied by the whole man?'[19] Davidson takes the example to show that we do not have adequate criteria for the location of an event. I take it to show that the motion of the man's arm cannot be identified with his act of raising it. 'Fill the zone' may not be exactly the right phrase, but if the motion of a limb occurs in a certain place, and the act of moving it does not occur in that place, then they cannot be identical.

The second puzzle is that if acts are movements of the agent's body, then a murder may already have taken place a month before the victim dies, in a place where he has never set foot. (The doctrine that acts are muscular contractions or events in the agent's nervous system carries the same implication.) Strawson argued that we should not be troubled by the implication, pointing out that a man shot in a duel may say to his opponent, 'You have killed me.'[20] But it is doubtful whether the remark should be taken literally, any more than the despairing statement by someone expecting to be killed, 'I'm a dead man.'

Abandoning the doctrine that acts are events permits a more plausible view about their location.

Many acts are done at times and in places which we can readily identify as precisely as we normally identify the place where a object is to be found, or the time at which an event occurred. For example, Sylvia may pour a glass of water at three-fifteen, in the kitchen, by the sink. But if an agent did one act by doing another—for example, if the queen killed the king by pouring poison in his ear—and the results of these two acts occur in different places or at different times, then the only direct answer to the question of where she did the act, which is dictated by the nature of the case, will be sufficiently imprecise to embrace the results of both acts, in this case, the poison entering the king's ear, and the king's death. (The qualification 'which is dictated by the nature of the case' is needed because legal arrangements may sometimes require a more precise answer, for example to decide on the jurisdiction in which an alleged crime occurred, in which case we gerrymander.)

For example, if the queen killed the king by poisoning him, she poisoned him last Tuesday in Elsinore, and he died last Thursday in Horsholm, then the queen killed the king last week in Denmark. This is a *direct* answer to the question, 'Where and when did the queen kill the king?' But we can always answer the question indirectly: that is, by locating one or more events and one or more other acts by the same agent. For example, 'Where and when did the queen kill the king?' 'She poisoned him last Tuesday in Elsinore; and he died last Thursday in Horsholm.' This answer provides more precise information than the direct one; but although it implies that the queen killed the king last week in Denmark, it does not say explicitly where or when the killing took place.

That concludes my comments on the identity and location of acts. The principal lesson is that acts are not events. It is an old lesson. As we saw in 2.1, philosophers in the early modern period found it hard to accommodate the activity of matter within the emerging scientific picture of the world. The picture is fully realized in Hume's *Treatise*, where causation is treated solely as a relation between events, and 'power or efficacy' is accorded no more reality than sound or smell. It is only the mind's 'propensity to spread itself on external objects' that persuades us that they 'lie in the objects we consider, not in our mind'. Hume saw that there is no place for active causal power or its exercise in a mere flux of events.* Indeed Leibniz had already pointed out that the elimination of action is implicit in Descartes's metaphysics:

> There is in matter something else than the purely Geometrical, that is, than just extension and bare change. And in considering the matter closely we perceive that we must add to them some higher or metaphysical notion, namely that of substance, action, and force.[21]

Leibniz and Hume both saw that there is nothing dynamic in extension and bare change, but the insight was discarded. Twentieth-century philosophers mostly fail to distinguish between my raising of my arm, which is an act—a dynamic episode, so to speak—and the motion of my arm, which is a mere kinetic episode, or as Leibniz puts it, bare change. When action and motion are not simply identified, as they are by Wittgenstein, Ryle, Anscombe, Davidson, and Armstrong, the act is either identified with the cause of the motion, as it is by Pritchard and Hornsby, or with a combination of the motion and its cause, as it had been by Mill. Staring myopically at a sequence of events, like Edwin Abbot's Flatlanders, they do not see any alternative to locating the act somewhere along its length.

---

* In *The View From Nowhere*, Nagel describes the result well: 'When we view action from an objective or external standpoint, [acts] no longer seem assignable to individual agents as sources, but become instead components of the flux of events in the world of which the agent is a part' (p.110; cf. Velleman, 'What Happens When Someone Acts?'). Nagel sees this as a problem about assigning acts to individual agents, but acts that cannot be assigned to agents and dissolve into a flux of events are not acts at all.

3.3 Acts and relations

In *Action, Emotion and Will*, Kenny points out that names, definite descriptions, predicates, and relational expressions had been studied intensively by logicians, whereas verbs of action had received scant attention:

> If a verb of action is intransitive, like 'doodles', it is treated as a one-place predicate, like '... is blue'; if transitive, like '... killed ...', it is classed with dyadic relation expressions, such as '... is larger than ...'; if it 'takes a dative', like '... gives ... to ...' it is put on a par with triadic relation expressions, such as '... is between ... and ...'.[22]

As a corollary of this way of looking at things, Kenny adds, the grammatical distinction between the subject and the object of a transitive verb is assumed to be philosophically useless. For example, Prior writes: No doubt grammarians would have no hesitation in identifying the subject of ['Brutus killed Caesar'] as 'Brutus', dismissing 'Caesar' as merely the 'object'; and it is certainly true that the proposition is about Brutus, and that what it says of him is that he killed Caesar. But it is equally true that the proposition is about Caesar, saying of him that Brutus killed him. 'Brutus' and 'Caesar' are *both* of them 'subjects' in the logical sense, and the predicate is the 'dyadic' predicate '... killed ...'.[23]

According to Prior, 'killed' in 'Brutus killed Caesar' expresses a relation between the two Romans, just as 'is west of' in 'Tunis is west of Pisa' expresses a relation between the two cities, and 'is the father of' in 'Abraham is the father of Isaac' expresses a relation between the father and his son.

However, Kenny points out that if we analyse 'Brutus killed Caesar' in this way, it is hard to see how we can deduce 'Caesar was killed' from it:

> 'Caesar was killed' is a complete sentence [...] and it is not a relational sentence. But the logic books give us no rules by which we can pass from a dyadic relational proposition to a proposition made up of a single-place predicate and a name.[24]

Kenny dismisses the idea that 'Caesar was killed' is elliptical, and that what it really means is 'Caesar was killed by someone or something'. We can lengthen the sentence by adding information about whom Caesar was killed by, when, where, by what means, and so on. But the fact that the sentence can be filled out in this way is not evidence of ellipsis. If it were, it would apply to 'Brutus killed Caesar' in the same way, since although this sentence already says whom Caesar was killed by, we can lengthen it the other ways just mentioned as well. Furthermore, the problem with the inference from 'Brutus killed Caesar' to 'Caesar died' also arises with the inference *to* 'Brutus killed Caesar' *from* 'Brutus killed Caesar in Pompey's Theatre', which combines three names—'Brutus', 'Caesar', and 'Pompey's Theatre'—with the three-place predicate 'x killed y in z'. For the logic books do not give us any rules to pass from three-term relational propositions to two-term ones either.

For these reasons, among others, Kenny concludes that we should agree with Aristotle, who distinguishes between *pros ti* and *poiesis*, and assigns acts to a category of their own.*

Kenny's argument initiated an extensive debate about the logical analysis of sentences reporting acts, to which the best-known contribution was made by Davidson, who proposed that we treat the verbs in these sentences as predicates with one more place than they appear to have. For instance, 'killed' in 'Brutus killed Caesar' is to be treated as a *three*-place predicate, with one place for Brutus, one for Caesar, and a third for a variable ranging over events. (Davidson holds that acts are events, as we have seen; but we could stipulate instead that the variable ranges over acts.) Accordingly, 'Brutus killed Caesar' is rewritten in the notation of standard formal logic as

(1) $\exists e$ (Killed (Brutus, Caesar, e)),

roughly, some event is a killing by Brutus of Caesar. This allows us to represent adverbial phrases—such as 'in Pompey's Theatre', 'on the Ides of March', or 'with a knife'—by means of predicates, which can be added by conjunction and subtracted by conjunction elimination. For example, 'Brutus killed Caesar in Pompey's Theatre on the Ides of March' is rewritten as

(2) $\exists e$ (Killed (Brutus, Caesar, e) & in (Pompey's Theatre, e)) & on (the Ides of March, e),

from which we can validly infer (1). Similarly, Davidson proposes that we treat intransitive verbs as two-place predicates. For example, 'Caesar died' and 'Spirit of St Louis flew' are rewritten as

(3) $\exists e$ (Died (Caesar, e))

and

---

* Aristotle was mainly interested in distinguishing the kind of thing that is in its nature related in a certain way to something else—e.g. a father or a child—from a part of something, such as a head or a hand. See *Categories* 7b15–8a24.

(4) $\exists e$ (Flew (Spirit of St Louis, e)),

roughly, some event is a dying of Caesar, and some event is a flying of Spirit of St Louis. (Notice that 'flew', unlike 'died', can be transitive or intransitive; here it is intransitive.) And of course the inferences we make by dropping adverbs can be represented in these cases in the same way, for instance from 'Spirit of St Louis flew from New York to Paris' to 'Spirit of St Louis flew'.

The success of these formal paraphrases in handling adverb-dropping inferences persuaded Davidson that 'flying is basically a relation between an event of flying and a thing that flies',[25] despite the grammatical structure of English sentences like 'Spirit of St Louis flew.' Similarly, killing is a *three*-termed relation, despite the grammatical structure of sentences like 'Brutus killed Caesar.'

Davidson's formal proposal is ingenious, but it is not entirely successful. It does not license the inference from 'Brutus killed Caesar' to 'Caesar died', since the inference from

(1) $\exists e$ (Killed (Brutus, Caesar, e))

to

(3) $\exists e$ (Died (Caesar, e))

is formally invalid, or indeed any inference that moves from the transitive to the intransitive form of the verb, according to the scheme

A {broke, twisted, turned, moved, burned, melted, . . . } B
therefore,
B {broke, twisted, turned, moved, burned, melted, . . . }.

Hence it requires us to hold that each of these inferences is attributable to the meaning of a particular verb, which formal logic can properly ignore.

This is the obvious objection to Davidson's proposal, judged on his own terms, and some years later he acknowledged its force.* But there is an

---

* Davidson concedes that the validity of inferences that move from the transitive to the intransitive form of the verb should be attributed to the logical form of the sentences involved in *Essays on Actions and Events*, p. 126, n. 15. The concession must extend to the inference from 'Brutus killed Caesar' to 'Caesar died', since it is an accident of English that 'die' is not cognate with 'kill'. Hebrew, for example, differs from English in this respect (Alvarez, 'Actions and Events: Some Semantical Considerations', p. 220). There are other ways of representing action sentences in standard formal logic, which also depend on the idea that they quantify over events, and which validate a broader range of inferences than Davidson's own method. Alvarez proposes one in the same article.

equally obvious objection to the claim that flying is a relation between an event of flying and a thing that flies, or that killing is a three-termed relation between a killer, a victim, and an event, which is quite independent of the question about how best to represent the logical structure of sentences reporting acts and events in standard logic. For, as we have seen, Davidson's formalizations use two-place predicates to represent intransitive verbs. For example, 'Spirit of St Louis flew' is rewritten as

(4) ∃e (Flew (Spirit of St Louis, e)),

roughly, some event is a flying of Spirit of St Louis. But although the syntax of the formula suggests that flying is a relation, this cannot possibly be right. For if flying *were* a relation, then a particular 'event of flying', such as the Spirit of St Louis's flying from New York to Paris, would be *both* an instance of this relation *and* one of its own relata, which is absurd. It is as if something were both the wisdom of Socrates and Socrates himself.

Recall the sentences discussed in 3.1, which combine an adjective with a noun instead of an adverb with a verb—e.g., 'Caesar died a painful death' instead of 'Caesar died painfully'. As we saw there, 'died' in 'Caesar died a { . . . } death' cannot express a genuine relation, any more than 'took' in the sentence 'Caesar took a { . . . } stroll', because if one takes a stroll, the taking of it is not a relation to a stroll, it *is* a stroll, and if one dies a painful death, one's dying this death is not a relation to an event, it *is* the event—that is, the painful death—itself. We cannot take the syntax of these English sentences at face value, because doing so has the paradoxical implication that an instance of a relation can be identical with one of its relata. Exactly the same applies to (3) and (4), which are formal equivalents of these sentences.

This is not an objection to Davidson's proposal considered simply as an exercise in formal logic. But if we are interested in whether acts are relations, the objection shows that rewriting sentences that report acts in the notation of standard formal logic cannot be the right way to decide. For even if Davidson's method were entirely successful on its own terms, this would not show that 'died' in 'Caesar died' expresses a relation between Caesar and his death, or that 'killed' in 'Brutus killed Caesar' expresses a three-termed relation between Brutus, Caesar, and a killing, at least if we continued to regard the principle that an instance of a relation cannot be one of its own relata as non-negotiable, as I believe we should. But notice that this argument cuts both ways. For if we cannot prove that killing *is* a relation by matching sentences in natural languages with formulae in standard logic, we cannot prove it is *not* a relation by failing in the attempt. In other words, if predication, truth-functional composition, and quantification are too limited a repertoire of structures to represent adverb-dropping inferences in a formal logical notation, it does not follow that 'Brutus killed Caesar' is *not* a relational sentence.

Perhaps a better argument against the proposition that acts are relations is that the relation between the active and passive forms of a verb is not the same as the relation between a term expressing a binary relation and a term expressing its converse. For example,

(5) Brutus killed Caesar

and

(6) Caesar was killed by Brutus

evidently refer to one and the same act, with a single 'direction' or dynamic orientation, whereas

(7) Brutus is older than Caesar

and

(8) Caesar is younger than Brutus

do not refer to the same relation, but to converse relations. If this is right, then acts should not be assimilated to relations. But it has also been argued that while they may appear to come in pairs, converse relations are in reality identical, so that (7) and (8) *do* refer to the same relation, approaching it from opposite directions, as it were, just like (5) and (6).

Fine, who defends the claim that converse relations are identical, compares a relation to a road, a favourite medieval trope:

> There is a road from Princeton to Trenton and a road (with the same tarmac) from Trenton to Princeton. Are they the same or different? There is perhaps a directional sense of 'road' in which they are different. But even if we concede that there is such a sense, we should surely acknowledge that there is a more basic adirectional sense of 'road' in which they are the same. Roads in the directional sense are merely roads in the adirectional sense upon which a direction has been imposed. And similarly for the relational 'routes' between objects.[26]

But this comparison is unconvincing, because a stretch of tarmac between two towns is a substance, not a relation, and the fact that substances do not have an inherent direction has no tendency to show that relations do not either. Why not compare converse relations to the equal and opposite forces that two objects exert on each other instead? For example, if block a sits on block b, a is above b and exerts a downward force on b, and b is beneath a and exerts an upward force of the same magnitude on a. Two equal and opposite forces, two equal and opposite relations. The comparison with forces, which was not available to the medievals, may not be better than the comparison with substances, but it is no worse.

Fine introduces the idea of a *completion*, where the completion of a relation R by the objects $a_1, a_2, \ldots$ is 'the state of the objects $a_1, a_2, \ldots$ standing in the relation R'.[27] He also calls this state a 'complex' and an 'arrangement'. For example, if block a sits on top of block b, this arrangement of the blocks is a completion of the relation *sitting on top of*. Fine points out that the doctrine that converse relations are identical can be deduced from two assumptions: first, any completion of a relation is a completion of its converse, and, second, no state is the completion of two distinct relations. But why should we accept the second assumption? Why should we not assume instead that a relation and its converse are distinct, and deduce that *every* state that is the completion of a relation with a converse is the completion of two distinct relations? Fine says 'we are [. . .] inclined to think' of the state of two blocks a and b where a is above and b is beneath as 'some sort of relational complex, consisting of a [single] relation in appropriate combination with its relata'.[28] But this is what the argument is meant to prove, and even if we are inclined to think it, or can be persuaded to think it, we are also inclined to think that converse relations come in pairs, and he does not explain why we should give the second thought less weight than the first.

Williamson defends the view that converse relations are identical with a different argument. Suppose a language E^* is exactly like English in every other respect, but differs from it in two ways. First, the word or phrase it uses to refer to a relation is the one English uses to refer to its converse; second, it places the names of relata in the reverse order in which they occur in English. So for example the E^* statement 'a is to the left of b' means that b is to the right of a; and the E^* statement 'a is to the right of b' means that b is to the left of a. In these circumstances, Williamson claims, the use of an E^* phrase expressing a relation would be indistinguishable from the use of the same phrase in English. But semantic facts supervene on facts about use ('there are no brute semantic facts', he says),[29] so if their uses were indistinguishable, we ought to conclude that they would express the same relation, in other words, that converse relations such as *being to the left of* and *being to the right of* are identical, and not distinct.

Williamson's argument is more complex than this précis indicates, but it is not convincing, partly because he assumes that acts are relations and the sentence he discusses in most detail is 'Brutus stabbed Caesar', which reports an act. But he does also mention some comparative and spatial relations, and the weakness of the argument becomes apparent as soon as we consider these. For example, the E* statements '*a* is wetter than *b*' and '*a* is drier than *b*' mean respectively that *b* is drier than *a* and that *b* is wetter than *a*. But how would an E* speaker say that *a* dried the dishes, or that *b* is bone dry? Presumably, '*a* wetted the dishes' and '*b* is bone wet'. But in that case the use of 'wet' and its cognates in E* *would* be distinguishable from their use in English, and the fact that E* places the names of relata in the reverse order in which they occur in English would soon emerge. Similarly, the E* statements '*a* is to the left of *b*' and '*a* is to the right of *b*' mean that *b* is to the right of *a*, and that *b* is to the left of *a*, as we have seen. But how would an E* speaker say that *a* turned right at the junction, or that *b* is left-handed? Presumably, '*a* turned left at the junction' and '*b* is right-handed'. So again, the use of 'left' and 'right' in E* would be distinguishable from their use in English, and again, the order in which E* places the names of relata would emerge.

For these reasons, Fine's and Williamson's arguments do not prove that converse relations are identical, or that the grammatical contrast between 'killed'/'was killed by' and 'was older than'/'was younger than' is superficial or misleading.[30] But while this contrast supports the view that acts should not be assimilated to relations, it does not explain why. Perhaps the best we can do to explain this is simply to appeal to the traditional conception of a binary relation as a way in which one thing can stand to another thing, which predates the development of modern formal logic.* Spatial, temporal, comparative, and familial relations all belong in the category of relations on

---

* Here is Locke's definition: 'The Nature of Relation consists in the referring or comparing two things one to another' (*An Essay Concerning Human Understanding*, 2.25.5). Notice that this definition confines relations to two terms and precludes something from standing in a relation to itself. The general notion of a many-termed relation was formed only in the second half of the nineteenth century.

this conception, but acts are excluded from it because they are dynamic rather than static. Statements such as 'Brutus killed Caesar' and 'David begat Absalom' *entail* that the agent stands to the patient in a certain relation, and hence that the patient stands to the agent in its converse. Thus, if David begat Absalom then David was the father of Absalom, and hence Absalom was the son of David. But begetting Absalom is one thing and being his father is another. For example, begetting Absalom may have been pleasant, while being his father was painful, and we can ask when and where David begat Absalom, and how long it took, but not when and where David was the father of Absalom, or how long *that* took.[31]

3.4 Conclusion

In the first three chapters, I have argued that a convincing philosophy of human action needs to disaggregate its physical, psychological, intellectual, and ethical dimensions, and I have tried to show how we can think about action in general—its metaphysics and its logic—and individual human action in particular, without confusing agency with either voluntariness or intention (Chapters 1 and 2), and without confusing action and motion (Chapter 3). In Chapter 1, I criticized Wittgenstein and Ryle for failing to escape completely from these confusions, and therefore from the influence of the modern theory of the will, but I hope it is clear that I see the argument in these chapters as continuing their radical attack on the modern theory, and taking it a stage further. In the next three chapters I shall explore the ethical, psychological and intellectual dimensions of human action in turn.

4

Voluntariness and Choice

4.1 Voluntariness and guilt

Philosophers have shown little interest in voluntariness during the past fifty years. Related concepts, such as coercion, obligation, and free will, have been the subject of intense scrutiny and lively debate, but voluntariness has been neglected. The reason seems to be that just a few years after Ryle and Wittgenstein attacked the theory of volitions with such spectacular success, Anscombe's book *Intention* persuaded philosophers that voluntariness plays a relatively minor role in our thought about human action, compared to the concept of acting intentionally or acting for a reason, and does not raise any interesting problems of its own, once the nature of intentional action has been explained. The theory of volitions had been demolished, and the delicate task of lifting voluntariness out of the ruins did not seem worth the trouble.

Anscombe says at the beginning of *Intention* that 'the object of the whole enquiry is really to delineate such concepts as the voluntary and the intentional', but she gives voluntariness short shrift.[1] In fact, she devotes exactly two pages to it. She claims, (i) that every intentional act is also voluntary; (ii) that there are two kinds of unintentional voluntary action: 'mere physical movements', such as drumming one's fingers, and causing an 'antecedently known concomitant of one's intentional action', such as so-called collateral damage in a military attack; and (iii) that acts can also be called involuntary because one regretted doing them, although (she adds) '"reluctant" would be the more commonly used word'.[*] She also adds, in a rare acknowledgement of voluntary passivity:

---

[*] As noted in 1.3.1, some philosophers reserve the term 'involuntary' for thoughts or changes in the body that the agent is unable to control, and distinguish between 'involuntary' and 'not

> Things may be voluntary which are not one's own doing at all, but which
> happen to one's delight so that one consents and does not protest or take steps
> against them: as when someone on the bank pushes a punt out into the river.[2]

In an article published a couple of decades later, Anscombe effectively
equates voluntary action and intentional action. Davidson makes the same
equation, Kenny follows Anscombe in maintaining that every intentional
action is also voluntary, and Bernard Williams claims that 'a certain thing is
done voluntarily if (very roughly) it is an intentional aspect of an action
done in a normal state of mind'.[3] Since Anscombe, many philosophers have
assumed that voluntariness can be defined in terms of knowledge, intention,
and self-control.

But these views are questionable in detail and misguided in approach. They
are questionable in detail because (i) it is commonly assumed that an act is not
done voluntarily if the agent is compelled to do it by a sufficiently grave threat,
despite the fact that an act of this kind is done knowingly and intentionally,
and the agent has not normally lost self-control; (ii) if this assumption is right,
some known concomitants of intentional action are caused voluntarily, while
others are not, viz. those which are known concomitants of intentional action
that is not voluntary itself; and (iii) it is doubtful whether regret cancels the
voluntariness of an act.

The approach is misguided because voluntariness is at root an ethical
concept, unlike knowledge, intention, and self-control. Of course, morally
neutral acts can be voluntary. But the basic function of the concept is to
inform the appraisal of individual conduct and in particular the assessment of
innocence and guilt, and we cannot understand its structure if we do not
understand its function, any more than we can understand the structure of
the liver if we believe its function is to make blood. Ryle was wrong to claim
that the question whether a person acted voluntarily can only arise when
the act appears to have been wrong.[4] It can arise because the act was, or
might have been, harmful or detrimental to another person, or to himself.
For example, we may want to know whether someone placed himself in
danger voluntarily. Or it may matter for another reason that involves the
agent's responsibilities and commitments, such as when the validity of a

voluntary'. But although English usage matches this convention to some extent, it is not cut and
dried, and Anscombe uses 'involuntary' simply as the negation of 'voluntary', which is how it is
generally defined in dictionaries, and also how Locke and Blackstone use it in the remarks
quoted in this chapter.

contract is in doubt. But Ryle was right in thinking that voluntariness is basically concerned with innocence and guilt.

What is voluntariness? Roughly, a certain thing is done voluntarily if, and only if, it is *not* done out of ignorance or compulsion. This is not the same as saying that it *is* done knowingly and freely. Regarding knowledge, if a man drives the wrong way down a one-way street, and it transpires that although he believed the street was one-way, he did not *know* that it was—e.g. because the information he relied on came from an untrustworthy source—he cannot be excused on the grounds that he did not do it voluntarily. Knowledge and ignorance are contraries, not contradictories, and voluntariness is defined in terms of ignorance, not knowledge. As for freedom, it can be opposed either to necessity or to compulsion. As we shall see, these are not the same, and if voluntariness were defined in terms of freedom it would have to be made clear that 'freely' here means without compulsion.

But what does ignorance have to do with compulsion? Why do we have a concept that yokes together these disparate ideas? The answer, I suggest, is that both are normally exculpations. The qualification 'normally' needs to be borne in mind, and I shall return to it. Ignorance is not always an exculpation because negligence can be culpable; and compulsion is not always an exculpation because it may be a consequence of voluntary or negligent conduct by the individual concerned. But I suggest that the concept of voluntariness is formed by negation, in fact by double negation, by excluding factors that exculpate, in other words, factors that exclude guilt. So it has not just *turned out* to be useful for assessing a person's culpability, in the way that probability theory, which was originally developed to analyse games of chance, turned out to be useful in thermodynamics. On the contrary, it was designed for this purpose. That is what I mean by saying that voluntariness is at root an ethical concept.

The factors that negate voluntariness are ignorance and compulsion, regardless of whether the thing whose voluntariness is in question is an act, omission, event, relation, condition, and so on. Aristotle states this explicitly with respect to action and emotion.[5] But the idea that ignorance and compulsion are exculpations was already ancient in the classical age, and it does not seem to have originated in any single ethical tradition. Indeed, it is hard to see how the ideas of guilt and innocence, as opposed to the simple idea of causing harm, could exist without it. If there is 'a massive central core of human thinking which has no history—or none recorded in the histories of thought', it includes the concepts of freedom, compulsion, knowledge and ignorance, as well as physical concepts such as causation, space, and time.[6]

Ignorance is identified as an exculpation in the *Iliad*, in a passage where Agamemnon excuses his seizure of Briseis; in a passage in *Genesis* that describes how Abimelech has Abraham's wife Sarah brought to him, mistakenly believing her to be unmarried; in a provision in the *Code of Hammurabi* concerned with branding slaves for sale; in the most important ancient Indian legal treatise, the *Manava-Dharmasastra*, in passages concerned with penances for sexual offences and fines for perjury; and in a Chinese legal text from the Qin dynasty, in a provision concerned with receiving stolen goods. Compulsion is identified as an exculpation in the *Odyssey*, when Phemius excuses himself for having performed for the suitors at their banquets and Telemachus confirms his innocence; in provisions in *Deuteronomy* and the *Code of Hammurabi* concerned with adultery and rape (a married woman who is raped is not guilty of adultery); in the passage about fines for perjury in the *Manava-Dharmasastra* mentioned above, and another passage concerned with the loss of animals in a herdsman's care; and in a Qin dynasty provision about pledges extorted or made voluntarily while in debt.[7]

The ancient connection between voluntariness and exculpation is a cornerstone of ethics, but it can easily be misunderstood, either by falsifying the relationship between voluntariness and intention or by misunderstanding guilt. Regarding guilt, Bernard Williams's study of agency and responsibility in Greek thought, *Shame and Necessity*, is a case in point.

The principal claim defended in *Shame and Necessity* is that the idea that we moderns, heirs of the enlightenment, possess a 'developed moral consciousness', by comparison with the 'primitive' ethical conceptions of the Greeks, is a self-aggrandizing myth. The differences are exaggerated, Williams argues, and the ones that do exist are not signs of moral superiority or intellectual progress, because our 'supposedly more developed conceptions do not offer much to rely on'.[8] In particular, the modern idea that voluntariness and guilt are closely associated is an illusion. Guilt, Williams explains, is a 'moral emotion' that can 'direct one towards those who have been wronged or damaged':

> [But] insofar as it concerns itself with victims, [it] is not necessarily or obviously restricted to voluntary actions. I may rightly feel that victims have a claim on me, and that their anger and suffering look towards me, even

though I have acted involuntarily. The conceptions of modern morality, however, insist at once on the primacy of guilt, its significance in turning us towards victims, and its rational restriction to the voluntary.[9]

The passage is compressed, but Williams seems to believe (i) that guilt cannot be 'restricted to voluntary actions', because 'I may rightly feel that victims have a claim on me [. . .] even though I have acted involuntarily'; and (ii) that modern morality does restrict guilt, or at least rational feelings of guilt, to the voluntary. The argument in (i) is enthymematic, the unstated premise being (iii), that if I rightly feel that victims have a claim on me, then I rightly feel guilty.

I shall not contest Williams's anti-progressive views about ethical thought, although I do not share them. What concerns us here is the argument about voluntariness and guilt. I suggest that it depends on three mistakes.

Williams's first mistake is confusing the feeling of guilt with guilt itself. Unlike shame, guilt is not an emotion, as he claims, although the feeling of guilt—the 'reproach of conscience', as the OED calls it—is.[*] So although it is true that we may rightly—or, better, understandably—*feel* guilty when we have involuntarily caused harm or failed to prevent it, say, because although we exercised a reasonable or even an exceptional degree of care, we could have done more, this does not support the claim that we *are* guilty in these circumstances, and hence that guilt itself, as opposed to the feeling of guilt, is not restricted to voluntary conduct.

Second, regarding (ii), Williams claims that according to modern morality, guilt *is* restricted to voluntary conduct—or perhaps that according to modern morality, feelings of guilt are irrational unless they are so restricted. But this is not true. The reason has nothing to do with the emotions felt by those who inadvertently cause harm. As noted earlier, it is because of negligence: our negligent acts and omissions can be culpable whether they are voluntary or not, and modern morality does not imply otherwise.

Third, regarding (iii), Williams seems to assume that if someone acknowledges or 'rightly feels' that a victim has a claim on him—i.e. that he has an obligation to compensate him, or at least apologize, for some loss or harm—then he must 'rightly feel' guilty. But in fact this is not true. For example, if my dog savages my neighbour's prize marrow, I may accept that I have a

---

[*] The once-popular contrast between 'shame-cultures' and 'guilt-cultures' invites the confusion, 'guilt' here meaning 'feeling of guilt'. The phrase 'reproach of conscience' is quoted from OED, **guilt**, 5a.

moral and legal obligation to compensate him despite the fact that I took care to ensure that nothing like this would occur. I may rightly feel that he has a claim on me, even that his anger and suffering look towards me, without either being guilty of wrongdoing or feeling guilty.

Williams's conclusion, that the close connection between guilt and voluntariness is a modern myth, is therefore doubly wrong: it is neither modern nor a myth. Perhaps the idea that one may be right to feel guilty about harm one has caused inadvertently is plausible, although it can seem more telling than it is if we imagine that the only alternative to feeling guilty is indifference. (One can feel awful or despairing without feeling guilty.) But it cannot touch the ancient and indispensable idea that the factors that negate voluntariness are exculpations.

What role does voluntariness play in assessing innocence and guilt? The eighteenth-century jurist William Blackstone said that 'an involuntary act, as it has no claim to merit, so neither can it induce any guilt'.[10] But this cannot be quite right, since (as already noted) negligent acts can be culpable, whether they are voluntary or not. The truth is that moral censure and criminal liability, the latter with a few exceptions and a certain roughness at the edges, are confined to voluntary or negligent conduct *and its foreseeable consequences* (foreseeable by the agent, that is). When the law departs from this principle it either does so for policy reasons—crimes of strict liability are commonly justified on the grounds that they supply an especially strong incentive to take care—or because the courts cannot enquire into the mind of a defendant with either the subtlety or the access of Proust or Henry James. So they follow the rule that an adult who does not suffer from a gross form of mental impairment is capable of exercising a reasonable amount of foresight and imagination. The qualification '*and its foreseeable consequences*' is important for both moral and legal purposes. For example, a person who gives way to duress will not be excused if he exposed himself to the risk of coercion by associating with known criminals. Guilt is not ruled out by the fact (assuming for the moment that it is a fact) that he did not do the act demanded of him voluntarily, because the question remains whether the duress was a foreseeable consequence of something that *was* voluntary on his part. As Lord Bingham put it in a review of the law relating to duress (the point is also made by Aristotle in the *Eudemian Ethics*): 'The defendant may not rely on duress to which he has voluntarily laid himself open.'[11]

4.2 An antinomy about duress

Traditionally, voluntariness is associated with choice. The two concepts must surely be closely related, because it is natural to think that a person does something voluntarily if, and only if, he chooses to do it, or at least could choose not to do it. But the connection between voluntariness and choice is not straightforward. It is deeply entrenched in our conception of voluntariness that acts that are obligatory, compulsory, or mandatory are not voluntary—e.g. paying a fine as opposed to making a donation, or joining the army as a conscript rather than a volunteer—and that an act is not voluntary if it is done because of a sufficiently grave threat. Yet in most cases a person who gives way to duress *could* choose to resist, even if doing so would be dangerous; and a person who pays a fine or joins the army as a conscript could refuse to do so, even if this would be unwise, futile, or wrong.

Consider duress first. (I shall comment on obligations in 4.5.) For present purposes, we are not interested as such in whether the courts should recognize a defence of duress, or in the range of offences to which it should apply, or the kinds of threats it should include. The only questions that concern us are whether a person who acts under duress acts voluntarily, and whether he has a choice. (I shall say that someone has a choice whether to ϕ when he can choose to ϕ and can choose not to ϕ.)

Duress is generally regarded as a species of necessity, its distinguishing feature being that the circumstance that compelled the defendant to commit the act consisted in a threat by another person. But duress also differs from other cases of necessity in two other significant respects. First, the harm to be averted in cases of necessity may be of many different kinds—a ship's sinking, a fire's spreading, and so on; whereas the courts have on the whole restricted the plea of duress to threats of death or serious personal injury to the defendant or someone closely associated with him. Second, in cases of duress the act demanded is specified together with the threat, whereas it is often a matter of judgement what course of action is made necessary by the elements (e.g. trespassing to take shelter from a storm), by illness (e.g. crossing a red light while driving someone to a hospital), or by some other pressing circumstance.

Lord Widgery, then Lord Chief Justice, summarized the English legal position regarding duress as follows, in the perjury case *Hudson and Taylor*:

It is clearly established that duress provides a defence in all offences including perjury (except possibly treason or murder as a principal) if the will of the accused has been overborne by threats of death or serious personal injury so that the commission of the alleged offence was no longer the voluntary act of the accused.[12]

'The will of the accused has been overborne' is figurative language. It appears to mean that duress affords a defence if the person threatened was unable to resist the pressure exerted on him, but this cannot be what Lord Widgery intended. A person who gives way to a threat may do so coolly and without any loss of self-control, after assessing the risks he would run if he refused, and the courts have not rejected a plea of duress because the act was done calmly or preceded by deliberation in this way. Frankfurt claims that when a person acts under duress, giving way to the threat is 'made inescapable by forces within himself which he is unable to overcome'.[13] But this is a much narrower idea of duress than that adopted by the courts or sanctioned by common sense. So for present purposes the important point is not about whether the will of the accused was overborne, it is that if a plea of duress is accepted, it is thereby accepted that the commission of the alleged offence was not a voluntary act.

Now the majority of judgements in criminal and civil cases involving duress have endorsed Lord Widgery's position, but some judges and a considerable number of jurists have opposed it, on the grounds that the person subjected to duress has a choice. No one disputes that if one course of action is absolutely necessary no other is possible, and the agent does not have a choice. But giving way to duress is not absolutely necessary. It *is* necessary *if the threatened harm or risk of harm is to be avoided*—since, we assume, it is the only means by which this can be done—but hypothetical necessity does not necessarily abolish choice. For example, it may be necessary for Henry to divorce Catherine *if he is to marry Anne*; but it does not follow that he has no choice, unless marrying Anne is something he *must* do. However desirable it may be to avert a threat, it is not obvious that this is something a person subjected to duress *must* do. As Hart and Honoré point out: 'The person threatened is literally able to choose whether to act as instructed or suffer the threatened harm, so that a choice exists.'[14] So it is plausible that threats, however terrible, change the incentives associated with a course of action, just as offers and bribes do, so that they *influence* but do not *abolish* choice, and therefore do not negate voluntariness. This is the revisionist position, as I shall call it. As Lord Simon summarizes it in *Lynch*:

[In cases of duress] there is power of choice between two alternatives, but one of the alternatives is so disagreeable that even serious infraction of the criminal law seems preferable. [. . .] duress is not inconsistent with act and will, the will being deflected, not destroyed.[15]

The revisionist position has serious implications. At the limit, it might seem to undermine the justification for a defence of duress entirely. For if Lord Simon's dictum is accepted, it is hard to resist Sir James Stephen's argument, quoted in the Privy Council case of *Abbot*:

Criminal law is itself a system of compulsion on the widest scale. It is a collection of threats of injury to life, liberty and property if people do commit crimes. Are such threats to be withdrawn as soon as they are encountered by opposing threats? The law says to a man intending to commit murder, If you do it I will hang you. Is the law to withdraw its threat if someone else says, If you do not do it I will shoot you? Surely it is at the moment when temptation to crime is strongest that the law should speak most clearly and emphatically to the contrary.[16]

As Kenny points out, the conclusion to which this seems to point is that criminal acts done under duress should be punished *more* severely than other crimes, 'since a more severe threat of punishment will be necessary to counterbalance the threats constituting the duress'.[17] But even if it is allowed that deterrence must be tempered with humanity—that is, humanity for the defendant rather than the victim—the revisionist position still makes it much harder to defend the principle that duress is an absolute defence, which completely exonerates the defendant, rather than merely mitigating the criminality of the act.[18]

It cannot be denied that the argument for the revisionist position is persuasive, but it remains difficult to accept, because the idea of voluntariness or choice is normally taken to involve not only the contrast between acts we are physically able to prevent ourselves from doing, such as waving to a friend, and ones we are not, such as putting out our arms to break a fall, but also the contrast between making an autonomous decision and submitting to another person's will. As Nozick puts it, when a person gives way to coercion, we want to say that 'it is not his own choice but someone else's, or not fully his own choice, or someone else has made his choice for him'.[19]

So there appear to be good reasons to agree with Lord Widgery's view that if duress is established, 'the commission of the alleged offence was no longer the voluntary act of the accused', and good reasons to think the opposite.

4.3 Is 'voluntary' ambiguous?

One way of responding to this antinomy is to claim that the word 'voluntary' is ambiguous, so that giving way to duress is voluntary in one sense and not in another. Hart and Honoré claim that 'voluntary' is ambiguous in this way.[20] They identify a 'narrow sense of "voluntary"' that excludes duress: '[W]hen we take a step reluctantly, as the lesser of two evils, this is one way in which, for common sense and the law, our act is something less than fully voluntary.'[21] But alongside this 'narrow sense', they detect 'a wider sense', which they do not define, but which they say *does* apply to acts done under duress, and in evidence of which they cite the Latin maxim *coactus volui* (which I shall explain and comment on shortly).[22] Kenny draws a similar distinction. In one sense, he claims, voluntary action is contrasted with action taken reluctantly, while, in the other, it is contrasted with action the agent is unable to control, such as reflex action, sleepwalking, or the 'gasping admissions of an exhausted man broken by torture'.[23] Clearly, most cases of duress would be voluntary in the second sense but not the first.

But this response to the antinomy is unconvincing. First, it is doubtful whether the 'narrow' sense of 'voluntary', the sense in which acts are not voluntary if they are done reluctantly, as the lesser of two evils—such as travelling easyJet instead of Ryanair—is really a sense of 'voluntary' at all. Being reluctant is contrasted with being willing, and 'voluntary' does not mean the same as 'willing'. One can join the army as a conscript or as a volunteer, and either willingly or reluctantly, but a willing conscript is not a volunteer and a reluctant volunteer is not a conscript. An act is done willingly if it is done with a certain attitude or in a certain frame of mind, if the person welcomes doing it or at least does it without reluctance, whereas an act is done voluntarily if the agent does not do it out of ignorance or compulsion, or, as we also say, if he has a choice. 'Voluntary' does not describe a person's attitude or state of mind, whereas 'reluctant' and 'willing' do exactly that. That is why an individual can be willing or reluctant but not voluntary or compulsory, whereas an option, such as second-year logic, can be voluntary or compulsory but not willing or reluctant; and it is why willingness is a matter of degree whereas voluntariness is not, so that A can do something, such as join the army or study formal logic, more willingly, but not more voluntarily, than B.[24]

Second, suppose 'voluntary' *is* sometimes used to mean willing as opposed to reluctant. The voluntariness of an act done under duress in *this* sense cannot have a bearing on the agent's culpability, because reluctance does not excuse, or even mitigate, wrongdoing. For example, squeamishness does not make a murderer less guilty. So presumably the learned judges who deny that acts done under duress are voluntary do not have *this* sense of the word in mind. It is true that Hart and Honoré speak of taking a step reluctantly, *as the lesser of two evils*. But giving way to duress may *not* be the lesser evil, judged from an impartial point of view. If it *always* were, then someone subjected to duress who attached more weight to the prohibition they were instructed to violate than to their own safety would *always* be irrational or wrong. So the point stands: the sense of 'voluntary' in Lord Widgery's statement of the English legal position regarding duress cannot be the 'narrow' sense.

Third, in the 'wider' sense, an act is supposed to be voluntary unless the agent is unaware of doing it or unable to control himself. But again, it is doubtful whether this *is* a sense of 'voluntary'. The evidence Hart and Honoré cite, the maxim *coactus volui*, derives from a well-known dictum by the Roman jurist Paulus, recorded in Justinian's *Digest*: 'Si metu coactus adii hereditatem, puto me heredem effici, quia quamvis si liberum esset noluissem, tamen coactus volui.'[25] (If I am compelled by fear to accept an inheritance, I believe that I become heir, because although I would have refused if I had been free to do so, I do consent, albeit under compulsion.) But their interpretation of the maxim is unconvincing. It is surely not evidence of ambiguity, let alone ambiguity in an English word: it is evidence of a controversy about whether or not agreements of a certain kind should be considered valid despite having been elicited by coercion. Paulus held that they should—on the grounds, as we might put it, that whether they were made voluntarily or not, they *were made*—whereas Ulpian, who was the other principal contributor to the *Digest*, held the opposite opinion: 'Nihil consensui tam contrarium est [...] quam vis atque metus.'[26] (Nothing is so opposed to consent as force and fear.) It is a mistake to imagine that this was a terminological disagreement, which could be settled by disambiguating a word, and Paulus's maxim is not evidence that 'voluntary' sometimes has the 'wider' sense postulated by Hart and Honoré.

Fourth, suppose again that my comments are unconvincing, and there *is* a sense in which an act is voluntary unless the agent is unaware of doing it or unable to control it. Giving way to duress is obviously voluntary in most cases, in this sense. So presumably the judges do not have this sense of 'voluntary' in mind either.

Finally, it is possible to insist that the judges are confused. One could argue: 'There are two senses of "voluntary". In one, voluntariness is contrasted with reluctance and negated by duress, while in the other it is contrasted with lack of control and is necessary for guilt. Unfortunately, the courts have failed to notice the ambiguity, so they have equivocated and mistakenly held that duress excuses crime.' But confusing reluctance and lack of control would be a monumental error, and besides, if these two senses of 'voluntary' *do* exist, how can we be sure that there is not a third, which is negated by duress (like the first) and is necessary for guilt (like the second)?

For these reasons, I do not believe we can solve the antinomy by postulating multiple senses of 'voluntary'. Instead, I shall set aside the idea that voluntariness can be contrasted with reluctance or regret, and return to the simple fact that it is negated by compulsion—in other words, that one cannot be compelled to do something voluntarily.[27]

4.4 Voluntariness, compulsion, and consent

There are two basic oppositions involved in thinking about voluntariness: one is between knowledge and ignorance, the other is between freedom and compulsion. I commented briefly on the former in 4.1, but I shall not examine it in detail, because the latter is the one that bears on the antinomy about duress.[28] The difficult question about the opposition between freedom and compulsion is whether the scope of compulsion includes pressures that fall short of main force and do not leave a person so psychologically debilitated that he is literally unable to resist the demands of the one who exerts the pressure.

Aristotle seems to have changed his mind about this question. In the *Nicomachean Ethics*, he argues that an act is voluntary if the agent is aware of doing it and if he is able not to do it, which implies that a person who gives way to duress acts voluntarily in every case except perhaps for torture. If this view is correct the answer to the question about the scope of compulsion is no. In the *Eudemian Ethics*, by contrast, he concludes that duress *does* negate voluntariness, unless the agent could have avoided or escaped from the situation in which he was coerced, which implies that the answer is yes.[29] I shall argue that there is convincing evidence in favour of the *Eudemian* doctrine, which becomes apparent as soon as we consider the voluntariness of an act from the patient's perspective, and acknowledge the relationship between voluntariness and consent.

To begin with, some brief comments about consent.

Consenting to something is not the same as welcoming it or liking it: reluctance and aversion are compatible with consent. But submission alone does not imply consent. Consent itself is agreement or acquiescence. 'Agreement' can mean either concurrence or consent: agreeing *that* is concurring, whereas agreeing *to* is consenting. For example, if A agrees that B should kill or marry C, or agrees that he should kill or marry C himself, he concurs; whereas if he agrees to B's killing or marrying C, or agrees to kill or marry C himself, he consents.

Some philosophers maintain that consent is a state of mind, while others hold that it is an act.[30] In fact, like agreement and disagreement, but unlike assertion and denial, consent can consist either in a communicative act or in the state of mind it normally expresses, so both views are right. But, as Raz points out, it is express consent that changes, or purports to change, a person's rights or duties.[31] Thus, if I expressly consent to do something, then, as long as it is something I am permitted to do, I impose a duty on myself to do it; and if I expressly consent to someone else's doing something, I give them my permission to do it, and generally purport to give them the right to do it, although it does not follow that they do in fact have the right to do it.[32]

Consent must be *to* something, which can be specified with a certain form of words; and what is consented to may be in the present or in the future, but it cannot be in the past. One can condone or ratify an act after it has been done, but one can no longer consent to it. One cannot consent to something unless one is conscious of doing so and understands what one is consenting to, although even so-called informed consent is consistent with an incomplete or vague understanding, for example, because the patient does not want to know more. But it is possible, indeed quite normal, to consent in advance to something that will occur when one is unconscious (e.g. surgery) or dead (e.g. organ donation).

The scope of consent has been over- and understated. On the one hand, Kenny claims that 'all voluntary action [. . .] must be accompanied with at least consent',[33] but this is an idiosyncratic use of the word 'consent'. As it is normally understood, one can only consent, just as one can only agree, to do what one has been (explicitly or implicitly) invited, asked, or told to do. For example, a child sucking on a sweet does not normally consent to suck. On the other hand, Simmons claims that 'consent in the strict sense is always given to the actions of other persons',[34] but this is mistaken in two ways. First, one can consent to be or become something, or to another's being or becoming something, such as the leader of the party; second, one can consent to do something oneself. In the criminal law, the consent of the person against whom an act is directed is generally at issue, but heteronomous action—action proposed or commanded by another—can also be done with or without consent.

Returning now to the *Eudemian* doctrine, I said that there is convincing evidence in favour of it, which becomes apparent when we consider the voluntariness of an act on the part of the patient. In the modern period, most philosophers have ignored voluntary passivity. Empiricists did so because they explained voluntariness by postulating a special kind of conscious thought which causes motion in our limbs. So they only considered the voluntariness of an act from the agent's point of view—the act considered as something done by the agent and not as something received by the patient—and made it hard to see that activity and passivity are equally capable of being voluntary. But Ryle and Wittgenstein also ignored voluntary passivity, and so did most of their followers, except for those who denied that it exists.[35] (See 1.3.2.)

The truth is that voluntariness can be attributed to several things apart from action: conditions such as exile and unemployment; attitudes, such as forgiveness; being acted on by another agent—for example, being tickled, kissed or killed; inaction or quiescence; failures to act, such as neglect; relations, such as occupancy and possession; and events that can occur by choice, such as when one falls asleep or dies. Whether we describe someone as joining a trade union voluntarily, being kissed or carried voluntarily, or dying voluntarily, we use the same word to express the same idea. Indeed, it should be obvious that it can be just as important to know whether someone *underwent* or *received* an act voluntarily, for example a medical procedure or a sex act, as to know whether someone *performed* an act voluntarily. And it is clear that coercion and voluntariness are opposed, where the patient of an act is concerned, because whether an act is voluntary on the part of the patient depends on whether it is done with her consent, and a sufficiently grave threat vitiates consent. In some cases it is a matter of judgement how grave the threat must be. But if a rapist threatens a woman with violence and she makes a conscious decision to submit—as she may, if the circumstances allow her to weigh the risks involved—the idea that she must therefore have consented to the act and submitted to it voluntarily is repugnant and absurd, regardless of whether she was 'literally able to choose' whether to submit or risk being killed.

Now as soon as we think about voluntary passivity, the advantage of the *Eudemian* doctrine is obvious. For the *Nicomachean* doctrine requires us to say that if terror and panic made the victim unable to resist—in other words, if her submission was 'made inescapable by forces within herself which she was unable to overcome'[36]—then she did not consent to the act or submit voluntarily, whereas if she made a conscious decision to submit because she judged resistance to be too dangerous, then she did consent to the act, and did submit voluntarily. But this cannot be right, because, by definition, rape is sexual penetration that is 'not truly voluntary or consensual on the part of the victim'. (This is identified in a comparative study by a UN Criminal Tribunal as 'the basic underlying principle' in the law of rape, in the various legal systems surveyed.[37]) So, if the *Nicomachean* theory were right, it would be a defence against a charge of rape that the victim was 'literally able to choose whether to act as instructed or suffer the threatened harm'.

Admittedly, statements to the effect that 'the more extreme the pressure, the more real is the consent of the victim' appear from time to time in articles about economic duress, and we have already encountered Paulus's maxim *coactus volui*.[38] But this is not a reason to rewrite the law of rape. The difference between these branches of the law exists because cases of economic duress are customarily decided on the basis of what sorts of threat are permissible, without involving the concepts of voluntariness or choice, since the legitimacy of commercial pressure does not depend on how painful it would be to resist; whereas rape is a violation of a person's autonomy and dignity, whether it involves threats or not, so it is generally accepted that the question of consent cannot be bypassed.[39] There may be good policy reasons to follow the maxim *coactus volui* in the law of contracts—which is what Paulus was actually commenting on—but it does not express a philosophical insight into the relationship between coercion and consent, any more than it is evidence of a 'wide' sense of 'voluntary' that encompasses deliberate submission to a threat. Indeed, it cannot be sensibly applied to every kind of contract or agreement, marriage being an obvious case where it does not apply.

But if the victim in a case of rape does not consent, and does not submit voluntarily, despite being 'literally able to choose', it cannot follow from the fact that a defendant who pleads duress was 'literally able to choose' that he *did* act voluntarily. In fact, the defendant could be in a situation closely resembling that of the victim in a case of rape. For example, in *R* v. *Bourne*, a man who had compelled his wife to have intercourse with a dog was convicted of aiding and abetting an illegal sex act, but Lord Goddard stated that if the woman herself had been charged with the offence, she could have successfully pleaded duress.[40] And if it is conceded that the wife in *Bourne* did not have intercourse with the dog voluntarily, presumably the same can be true in other cases of duress as well, for example, cases of perjury, criminal damage, theft, or receiving stolen goods. The fact that the defendant in these cases would be active whereas the victim of a rape is passive is immaterial, and besides, receiving stolen goods may amount to no more than allowing someone to put them in one's garage and not telling the police. If the threat is less credible or if the person subjected to duress can seek protection, this is not immaterial. But for the purposes of argument, we can assume that the cases do not differ in these respects. So the *Eudemian* doctrine must be right. A sufficiently grave threat *can* negate the voluntariness of an act without the person threatened being literally unable to resist, although it does not follow that it is unjust to blame or punish him for the act, since he might have been able to avoid getting into the situation in which he was coerced.

The case of rape, and other cases where the voluntariness of an act on the part of the person who receives it is the issue, confirm that Hart and Honoré's disambiguation of 'voluntary' provides the wrong solution to the antinomy about duress. For on the one hand, if a person who receives an act acquiesces in it reluctantly, as the lesser of two evils, it does not follow that the act is not voluntary on her part, since reluctance is compatible with consent. On the other hand, if a woman who is threatened by a rapist is 'literally able to choose' whether to submit or resist, and chooses to submit, it does not follow that the act *is* voluntary on her part, because deliberate submission is not sufficient for consent. So the disambiguation is nothing of the sort: both definitions miss their target, as already argued in 4.3. The right solution to the antinomy is to acknowledge that the scope of compulsion is *not* limited to pressures that a person is literally unable to resist. As Locke points out, '*voluntary* is opposed to *involuntary*, not *necessary*'.[41] (I shall return to this remark later.)

Defending the *Eudemian* doctrine means fighting on two fronts. On the one hand, the theories of the will defended by empiricists from Hobbes and Locke to James and Russell—the theories Ryle and Wittgenstein attacked—support the *Nicomachean* doctrine, because if we picture voluntary action as bodily motion triggered by kinaesthetic sensations or *sui generis* acts of will, the contrast between submitting to another person's will and making one's own choice—even if the choice is to comply with another person's wishes—will tend to disappear from view. For example, if someone commits perjury, the kinaesthetic sensations or volitions that cause the motion of his lips will be the same whether he is acting under duress or not. On the other hand, many of the philosophers who were persuaded by Wittgenstein's and Ryle's arguments to reject these theories embraced an alternative to them that is still broadly *Nicomachean* in inspiration, which implies that an act is voluntary if the agent knows he is doing it and if he is 'literally able' not to do it. So this theory *also* implies that a person who gives way to duress acts voluntarily.

Beginning with the perspective of the patient makes it is easier to escape the influence of both theories, and supports the orthodox view, as stated by Lord Widgery, that if a plea of duress is accepted, it is thereby accepted that the alleged offence was not the voluntary act of the accused. It does not follow that the proposal canvassed in England in the 1980s, that duress should become a plea in mitigation rather than an absolute defence, must be wrong; or that duress ought to be available as a defence to a principal in a case of murder; or that the established rule that economic duress makes a contract voidable rather than void is unjust. These are all matters of policy as much as of philosophy. It does not follow either that it is always possible to decide whether an act done under duress was done voluntarily purely on the basis of the severity of the threat, without regard to the value of the interest sacrificed by giving way. (I shall return to this point later.) But it *does* follow that voluntariness cannot be defined in terms of deliberation, intention, or physical control. All of these may be present when a person submits to a sexual assault or a rape, and generally *are* present when a person does a criminal act under duress.

4.5 Voluntariness, choice, and obligation

This leaves us with a puzzle about the relationship between voluntariness and choice. If an act elicited by a threat may not be voluntary despite the agent's being 'literally able to choose whether to act as instructed or suffer the threatened harm', does it follow that the equation we find it natural to make, between doing something voluntarily and having a choice whether to do it or not, must be rejected?

No doubt part of the answer is that the word 'choice' can express more than one idea. For example, suppose a defendant charged with perjury pleads duress. If he was capable of answering the questions put to him truthfully, then he was capable of choosing whether to perjure himself or not. And yet he may claim that he had no choice—not in the playful way in which one may say that one 'had no choice' but to do something one found especially tempting, but seriously and with conviction. And the members of the jury may agree. If they do, we are not bound to conclude that they are unable to think intelligently about choice, because two ideas of choice are evidently in play: the theoretical idea of an alternative the agent was 'literally able to choose', and the practical idea of an *acceptable* alternative—what Hart and Honoré call a 'real choice' and Lord Scarman calls a 'practical choice'— in other words, an alternative that meets an appropriate standard of eligibility, because it does not conflict with a binding obligation or because it is not too high a price to pay.[42] So we can acknowledge that the defendant was literally able to choose whether to act as instructed or face down the threat, so that in theory a choice existed, while insisting that in practice he had no choice.

It remains true that in any particular case in which someone claims that he had no choice, a more courageous or more reckless person may disagree. But this is not a way of insisting on intellectual rigour; it is a way of insisting that there *was* an acceptable alternative to giving way—and perhaps that he should have taken it—and we are not bound to agree. Moreover, if we do not agree, this need not be because we have less exacting moral standards. Think of the case in which the threat is to harm the defendant's wife or child. But whatever the right ethical stance may be in a particular case, no legal or logical principle requires us to reject the plea of someone who gave way to duress that he had no choice, on the grounds that he was 'literally able to choose'. It is undeniable that our ordinary thought and talk about choice can be confused, even mendacious. For example, an angry parent may say to a child 'You leave me with no choice', when this is obviously untrue. But the idea of a 'real choice'—i.e. an acceptable or eligible alternative—is not confused or contradictory, and so the claim that a person who gives way to duress does not have a choice cannot be dismissed a priori as hyperbole or mere 'popular speech'.[43]

It is not confused or contradictory, but it is a clue rather than a solution to the puzzle about voluntariness and choice. To solve the puzzle, we need a clearer picture of the relationship between ability, possibility, and choice.

As the word 'choice' is normally used, the choices we have—the alternatives that are open to us—can depend on several different factors, including our abilities and skills, our resources, our circumstances, and our obligations.[44] And while some of the factors that exclude choices do so by making things impossible, others do not. For instance, it is impossible to run if one is lame, and it is impossible to drink gin if gin is unavailable. But obligations and prohibitions do not make it *impossible* for us not to do the things they require us to do, or to do the things they prohibit, since they can be overridden, forgotten, renounced, or ignored.

For example, Jewish dietary laws do not make observant Jews incapable of eating pork. Laws can only remove abilities that laws confer, as English law currently makes convicted prisoners ineligible to vote. Nor do the dietary laws remove the opportunity to eat pork, except indirectly in some places, by making it impossible to obtain. A Jew who disregards the prohibition because he is tempted by a dish of pork eats pork voluntarily, and one who accepts it remains capable of rejecting it. Yet the prohibition is not meant to offer Jews a choice between abstaining from eating pork and incurring the consequences of disobedience, whatever these are, or are thought to be. To imagine that it is is to ignore the difference between a sanction and a charge. Hart explains this as follows in *The Concept of Law*:

> A punishment for a crime, such as a fine, is not the same as a tax on a course of conduct, though both involve directions to officials to inflict the same money loss. What differentiates these ideas is that the first involves, as the second does not, an offence or breach of duty in the form of a violation of a rule set up to guide the conduct of ordinary citizens.[45]

Thus, on the one hand, if a person is 'literally able to choose' whether to act in a certain way or not, a prohibition will not remove his ability to do so. If it did, there would be no need to back it with a sanction. On the other hand, a prohibition does not offer the choice between obedience and a sanction. English law offers a choice between ways of disposing of a body: burial in a cemetery and cremation. But a prohibition does not offer a choice, it excludes one. A sanction attached to a prohibition is designed to discourage the prohibited act, rather as a tax may be designed to disincentivize a certain kind of transaction rather than to raise revenue, but taxing and prohibiting are not the same.

It therefore seems best not to say without qualification either that the prohibition does or that it does not eliminate a choice. On the one hand, a prohibition limits what is *permitted*, not what is *possible*. So there is a sense in which a choice—an 'alternate possibility'—exists. For assuming that pork is available, someone who accepts the prohibition remains 'literally able to choose' whether to eat pork or not. But although a prohibition cannot remove the *ability* or the *opportunity*, it can remove the *freedom* to eat pork. What we are *able* to do depends on our physical and mental constitution, our skills, and our resources; what we have the *opportunity* to do depends on our circumstances; but what we are *free* to do depends on our obligations. Hence, on the other hand, someone who *accepts* the prohibition accepts that pork is excluded from the range of alternatives between which he is free to choose—he accepts, so to speak, that pork is off the menu—so we can also say that he does not abstain from pork voluntarily, out of choice.

The same applies in the case of a positive obligation, whether it is assumed voluntarily or not. A person who does an act in order to fulfil an obligation, such as submitting a tax return or repairing a fence, is normally able either to do the thing in question or not do it. But the fact that one is *able* to do or not do a certain act does not imply that one is *free* to do it or not do it. If I place myself under an obligation to repair a fence—e.g. by making a contract or a promise—I am no longer free to choose whether to repair it or not. In signing the contract or making the promise, I bind myself—in other words, I relinquish the freedom to make that choice. But of course I do not render myself physically incapable of leaving it in a state of disrepair.

In sum:

- Both threats and obligations can be obliging factors, in other words, *factors that compel someone to adopt a course of conduct without making it impossible for him not to do so.*[*]

- We contrast the things we do because we are obliged to do them with the things we do because we are physically compelled to do them, but we also contrast them with the things we do voluntarily, because we prefer doing them to an alternative.

- If we accept that an agent did an act because he was obliged to do it, we thereby accept that he did not choose to do it in preference to an alternative, because *the alternative was excluded by the obliging factor.*[46]

But threats and obligations oblige in different ways. First, a person subjected to duress is permitted to disregard it, unless the threats are made against someone he has an obligation to protect, whereas a person who is subject to an obligation is not permitted to ignore it. Second, a threat constrains a person's freedom of choice by making an option—in other words, a possible course of conduct—too costly to pursue, whereas an obligation does so by excluding it from the range of options that are permitted. Third, a binding obligation justifies doing what it obliges one to do, and makes it wrong not to do it; whereas a sufficiently dire threat can *either* justify doing an act, if giving way is a lesser evil than resisting, or excuse doing it *without it ceasing to be wrongdoing.* By this I do not mean without its ceasing to be a prohibited *kind* of act, such as committing perjury, which one generally ought not to do, but without its ceasing to be a *particular* act one ought not to have done. For, as we noted earlier, submitting to coercion may *not* be the lesser evil, judged from an impartial point of view.

None of these differences casts doubt on the claim that both threats and obligations can be obliging factors. But some people are more inclined to accept that a threat can negate the voluntariness of an act than that an obligation can. For obligations are not always backed by sanctions, and one can discharge an obligation willingly, without being compelled to do so by a threat. Does one not act voluntarily in this kind of case?

---

[*] 'Oblige' here is to be understood as meaning *compel, force, or constrain* (the OED's sense 12) and not *impose a duty or an obligation* (sense 1). So the statement that someone was obliged to do something, in this sense, implies that she did it, whereas the statement that she had an obligation to do something does not.

Not necessarily. It is true that we often discharge an obligation willingly, whereas acts done under duress are only done willingly in exceptional cases, if at all. For example, Jews who abstain from eating pork do not normally do so with reluctance. But whether someone does an act willingly and whether she does it voluntarily are different questions. One can choose to do something, and do it voluntarily, despite feeling intensely reluctant to do it, as when someone with a phobia treats it with exposure therapy; and one can do something willingly despite being unable to resist doing it, as when an exhausted man falls asleep. Some people die voluntarily, because they could save themselves, but choose not to. But those who do not have a choice, and do not die voluntarily, may still die willingly in the end.

But it is also true that we *do* often discharge obligations voluntarily, because an obligation only compels a person who does an act because of it, just as a threat only compels a person who gives way. So if one does something one has an obligation to do, it does not follow that one does not do it voluntarily, since one's motive need not be the obligation. For example, parents are typically motivated by the desire to care for their children, rather than the desire to fulfil their obligation to care for them, and often continue to want to care for them after they have grown up. Whereas it is very unusual for someone to want to do an act he does under duress for independent reasons, so that he would continue to want to do it if the threat were lifted. Equally, if one chooses to conform to a rule or custom, without regarding oneself as being under an obligation to do so, one conforms voluntarily, such as when a secular Jew abstains from eating pork while in the company of religious Jews, to avoid causing offence.

So acts that are done in order to discharge obligations, unlike acts that are done under duress, are commonly done willingly, and acts that do in fact discharge obligations, but are not done for that reason, are commonly done both willingly and voluntarily. This, I believe, accounts for the intuition that threats are more plausibly regarded as impediments to voluntariness than obligations. Nevertheless, if one does in fact have an obligation to do something, and this is one's whole reason for doing it, then one does not do it voluntarily. For to acknowledge that one has an obligation to do something is precisely to think of it as compulsory, non-optional, so that whether one does it is *not* a matter of choice.

4.6 Voluntariness, ability, and choice

I suggested at the beginning of this chapter that one of the principal mistakes in Anscombe's influential treatment of voluntariness is the idea that intentional conduct must also be voluntary. *Intention* includes a rare reference to voluntary passivity, which identifies the role of consent in deciding whether an act is voluntary from the perspective of the patient:

> Things may be voluntary which are not one's own doing at all, but which happen to one's delight so that one consents and does not protest or take steps against them: as when someone on the bank pushes a punt out into the river.

But apparently Anscombe failed to notice that intentional submission to an act may not be voluntary because it may not be accompanied by consent. It is possible that she missed this because she had in mind an antiquated conception of consent, according to which withholding consent must involve resistance or audible protest.* Perhaps that is why she wrote, 'so that one consents and does not protest or take steps against them'.[47] Be that as it may, I hope it is clear that intentional conduct need not be voluntary, because the scope of compulsion encompasses cases in which a person is compelled to do, not do, or undergo something by an obligation or a threat. But reflecting on compulsion by threats and obligations yields several other conclusions, which show how profoundly the idea of voluntariness differs from the (narrowly) modal ideas of ability and possibility, and which remind us that voluntariness, unlike intention, is at root an ethical concept.

Subjectivity: First, as was just pointed out, a choice is only excluded by an obligation if one accepts it, and one is only compelled to do an act by a threat if one does the act to avoid the threatened harm. If someone does what he has an obligation to do, or what is demanded of him, for his own reasons, *without* accepting that he is obliged to do it, he does it voluntarily, out of choice.[48] So there is an inescapable subjective element in the concept of voluntariness, which is not present in the concepts of ability or possibility, as these are normally understood. Whether someone acted voluntarily may turn on whether he believed he had a choice, so that it is impossible to

---

* The provision in *Deuteronomy* 22.23–27 cited in 4.1 makes a woman punishable if an illegal sex act occurs in a town but not if it occurs in the countryside, where she could protest without being heard. See also Brundage, *Law, Sex, and Christian Society in Medieval Europe*, p. 396.

decide whether he acted voluntarily without knowing what he thought. But whether someone is able to do something does not depend in this way on whether he believes he is able to do it, although it may depend on it in a different way, as, for example, when an ability, such as the ability to speak effectively in public, depends on self-confidence.

Evaluation: Second, whether we accept a person's claim that he was obliged to give way to a threat depends both on the severity of the threat and on the value of the interest sacrificed by giving way. (But remember: it does *not* depend simply on whether giving way was the lesser evil, judged from an impartial point of view.) For example, Hart and Honoré point out that if a man hands over his wallet because he is threatened with violence, we would normally accept that he was forced to do so, whereas if he hands over strategic plans to the enemy for the same reason, we might not.[49] (Why not? Because we might think it reasonable to demand the degree of heroism of him that resisting would require.) Similarly, one kind of situation will release someone from an obligation, while another will not. For example, if a man cuts short a friendly conversation because he has a dinner engagement, he is entitled to say that he is obliged to do so, and is not cutting it short voluntarily, out of choice, whereas if he leaves the bedside of a dying friend for the same reason, he is not entitled to say this. Hence, deciding whether a person's conduct was voluntary can involve making a value-judgement.

Modality: Third, a person who is compelled to do something by a threat is generally *able* not to do it, although he does not do it voluntarily. So if it is *possible* for someone to avoid doing something, it does not follow that he does it voluntarily. Equally, if someone does something voluntarily, it does not follow that it is possible for him to avoid doing it. Locke describes the case of a man who chooses to remain in a locked room in the company of a friend, in the mistaken belief that he is able to leave: 'I ask, is not this stay voluntary? I think nobody will doubt it: and yet, being locked fast in, it is evident he is not at liberty not to stay, he has not freedom to be gone.' (See the Appendix.)

Locke is surely right in saying that the man stays in the room voluntarily, but we need to be clear about the reason. The reason is not that he stays willingly, or that he does not regret staying; for if he stays reluctantly, out of politeness, and *does* regret staying, it remains true that he stays voluntarily. (We saw in 4.3, when we considered the idea that 'voluntary' is ambiguous,

that contrasting voluntariness with reluctance is a mistake.) The true reason
is that he is not *actually* prevented from leaving the room by the locked door,
although he would be prevented if he tried. So we need to interpret Locke's
statement that 'he has not the freedom to be gone' as expressing a contrast
between freedom and necessity rather than freedom and compulsion, since
the man is not *actually* compelled to stay. If we replace the lock in the story
with a guard stationed outside the door, this becomes more obvious. The
guard is there to prevent the man from leaving, in other words, to compel
him to stay, *should that be necessary*, but only the guard's *actual* intervention,
or the lock's *actual* resistance to the pressure the man applies to it, prevents
him from leaving, and of course this only happens if he attempts to leave.
Similarly, if an adult of sound mind freely consents to sex without being
aware that her partner would have raped her if she had refused, she has sex
voluntarily, since she is not *actually* compelled to do so by force or threats.
Again, this remains true whether she consents willingly or reluctantly, and
whether she regrets doing so or not.

So, these cases and cases where acts *are* done because of obliging factors
confirm Locke's important claim that '*voluntary* is opposed to *involuntary*, not
necessary' in different ways. Acts done because of obliging factors show that
involuntary (i.e. *not voluntary*) does not imply *necessary*, while Locke's own case
and the sex case show that *necessary* does not imply *involuntary* (ditto).[50] Both
kinds of case also show that the relationship between doing something voluntarily and having a choice whether to do it is not straightforward. On the one
hand, someone who does an act under duress is able to choose whether to do
it or not, and yet he does not do it voluntarily. On the other hand, the man
in Locke's example chooses to stay in the room, and he does so without
being coerced; but in fact, although it is a fact he is not aware of, he does not
have a choice whether to stay or go. The choice he does have is whether to
try to go, and whether he stays voluntarily depends on which choice he makes,
since he will be compelled to stay if, and only if, he tries to leave.

4.7 Desire and causation

As we saw in 1.1, Ryle claims that the question, 'What makes a bodily
movement voluntary?' is not a causal question. But if the conception of
voluntariness defended here is correct, this is not quite right. True, what

makes an act voluntary is not the fact that it has a specific kind of cause, such as a volition or an intention. Ryle has to be right about this for three main reasons:

(A) If the voluntariness of an act consisted in its having a specific kind of mental cause, we would be able to ask whether this cause is voluntary itself, and as Ryle showed, 'either answer leads to absurdities':

> If I cannot help willing to pull the trigger, it would be absurd to describe my pulling it as 'voluntary'. But if my volition to pull the trigger is voluntary, in the sense assumed by the theory, then it must issue from a prior volition and that from another ad infinitum.[51]

(As we saw in 1.5, no such regress would afflict an attempt to define human agency in causal terms, because there is no reason why a specific kind of cause of bodily motion that makes it attributable to the agency of the individual whose body moves should be attributable to his agency as well.)

(B) Passivity is just as capable of being voluntary as activity, and it is obvious that voluntary passivity need not be caused by a volition-like thought in the mind of the individual concerned. For example, if a soldier falls asleep on duty or if a man dies on a cross, the cause will probably be tiredness in one case and asphyxiation in the other, whether they fall asleep and die voluntarily or not.

(C) The questions involved in deciding whether an act was voluntary can include ones that are neither about its causes nor about the agent's state of mind. For as we have seen, they can be about the value of the interest sacrificed by giving way to a threat, or about whether the circumstances in which the agent found herself nullified or overrode the obligation she acted to fulfil.

So Ryle is right in saying that what makes an act voluntary is not the fact that it has a specific kind of cause. But it *is* the fact that the act does *not* have specific kinds of causes, such as physical force or threats. And this means that it *is* a causal question whether an act is voluntary or not.

Now Kenny takes the idea that the voluntariness of an act excludes certain kinds of cause a step further. For it is natural to think that voluntary action is caused by the agent's wants. For instance, when a child eats ice-cream voluntarily, and not under duress, its desire for ice-cream causes it to eat. But Kenny denies that voluntary acts are caused by wants, on the grounds that causes make their effects inevitable—in other words, given the cause, the effect *must* follow—whereas if someone does something voluntarily, it is *not* inevitable that he will do it:

> If there were a causal link between the want and the action, the action would cease to be voluntary. It may be that there is a causal generalization to the effect that those who have been without food for *n* days cannot help grabbing the first food they see, irrespective of all consideration for others. If so, there is a good case for saying that their movements are causally determined by their hunger. *Eo ipso*, they cease to be voluntary actions. In the normal case of motivated action this is not so. A man who gives a present out of generosity is not compelled to give by anything, not even by his generosity.[52]

If this were right, a voluntary act could not have *any* kind of cause. For if causes made their effects inevitable, a voluntary act would be made inevitable by its cause, whether or not this was a want. This does not show that the argument is fallacious. The idea that an act may be uncaused is not manifestly absurd, and it is not self-evident that if an act did not have a cause, the physical changes in the body that need to occur for the act to take place would not have causes either. But in fact Kenny's argument *is* fallacious, because causes do not invariably make their effects inevitable, so that given the cause, the effect must follow. Causes do not always compel.

Clearly, the distinction between what does happen and what does not happen is not the same as the distinction between what must happen and what need not happen, so explaining why something *did* happen is logically different from explaining why it *was bound to* happen. A reason that explains why something was bound to happen need not also explain why it did happen. For example, if Brett was bound to fail because she had not revised her coursework, she may in fact have failed because she did not turn up for the exam. Equally, a reason that explains why something did happen need not also explain why it was bound to happen. For example, if Lucy called a taxi because she wanted to get home before dark, it does not follow that wanting to get home before dark made it inevitable that she would call a taxi. She might have chosen to take the tube instead.

But we can acknowledge this and still insist that voluntary acts are caused by wants. Kenny assumes that if a want causes someone to do something, then it must 'determine' its effect, so that, given the want, it is inevitable that the act will occur, and the agent cannot help doing it. But in fact *some* causes make their effects inevitable, whereas others do not. For example, a fatal injury is one that causes death. But the fact that someone received a fatal injury only implies that he *did* die, and not that he *was bound to* die. Some fatal injuries are so severe that the victim could not have survived under any circumstances, but in other cases the victim *could* have survived, for example, if he had been treated. In a case of this kind, the fact that the victim received the injury does not by itself imply that he was bound to die, it only implies it in conjunction with the fact that he was not treated, and the injury did not make his death inevitable, unless it was inevitable that he would not be treated.

Similarly, if Lucy calls a taxi because she wants to get home before dark, her desire to get home will not normally be irresistible, as the hunger of a starving man might be. But it does not follow that wanting to get home does not cause her to call a taxi, because there is no more reason to think that only irresistible wants can cause acts than to think that only injuries that make death inevitable can be fatal. So if we maintain that wanting to get home before dark *did* cause her to call a taxi, we can still also maintain that wanting this did not make it inevitable that she would call the taxi, since she could have chosen to take the tube. Of course, there is a difference between the cases, as described, because if someone dies because an injury is not treated, he is not likely to have chosen not to get it treated. But this does happen occasionally, for example, when the victim is a Christian Scientist.

It is therefore a mistake to argue on these grounds that voluntary acts cannot be caused by wants. Hume was right to argue that coercion is inimical to responsibility, whereas causation is not. But of course it does not follow that voluntary acts *are* caused by wants. I shall consider whether they are or not in the next chapter.

5

Desire and Intention

5.1 A turning of the tide

According to the positivist view that dominated philosophy in the first half of the twentieth century, the human sciences are comparable to the exact natural sciences in their infancy. Mill's *System of Logic* contains the classic nineteenth-century statement of this view:

> The Science of Human Nature may be said to exist, in proportion as the approximate truths, which compose a practical knowledge of mankind, can be exhibited as corollaries from the universal laws of human nature on which they rest.[1]

The logical positivists shared Mill's belief in the unity of science and agreed that scientific explanations of events subsume them under laws of nature. Hempel's paper 'The Function of General Laws in History', published in 1942, contains the most influential defence of Mill's view of the human sciences in the twentieth century.[2] But the balance of opinion had shifted by the early 1960s, in particular because of three books published in 1957–8. In *Laws and Explanation in History*, Dray argued that if we try to state the laws on which historical explanations are supposed to rely, they will either be so vague as to be useless or so precise and detailed as to be indistinguishable from a narrative of the events they are meant to explain. In *Intention*, Anscombe contrasted the teleological explanation of intentional action with the explanation of behaviour in terms of causes. And in *The Idea of a Social Science*, Winch defended the claim that the behaviour of social agents, unlike the behaviour of the objects studied in the natural sciences, can only be understood in terms of their own concepts and social rules.

Their opposition to positivism was not new, but it had new elements, which were mainly due to Collingwood and Wittgenstein, and it gave anti-positivism such a powerful impetus that von Wright called 1957–8 'a turning of the tide', while Davidson described Hempel as 'swimming [in 1961] against a very strong neo-Wittgensteinian current of small red books'.[3]*

Collingwood's influence was mainly due to his rejection of the positivist doctrine of the unity of science. He claimed that the eighteenth-century ambition to construct a science of human nature had failed 'because its method was distorted by the analogy of the natural sciences'. Historians investigate the causes of events, just as natural scientists do, but in historical studies the term 'cause' is used in 'a special sense'. In natural science, discovering the cause of an event means 'bring[ing] it under a general formula or law of nature', whereas in history, it means discovering 'the thought in the mind of the person by whose agency the event came about', the thought expressed in the action.' It is, Collingwood says, a positivist misconception that history is 'the study of successive events lying in the dead past, events to be understood as the scientist understands natural events, by classifying them and establishing relations between the classes thus defined'. Unlike the natural scientist, the historian is not interested in events as such, 'he is only concerned with those events which are the outward expression of thoughts, and is only concerned with these in so far as they express thoughts'. Hence, 'all history is the history of thought'.[4]

Wittgenstein's influence was mainly due to two ideas, one of which was about the nature of philosophy itself.

(A) In the early 1930s, Wittgenstein abandoned the doctrines, which he had defended in the *Tractatus*, that a sentence is a logical picture composed of names, that the meaning of a name is the object it stands for, and that the intelligible use of language always serves the same purpose, to describe the facts. He came to believe, on the contrary, that sentences do not have a uniform logical structure, that the meaning of a word is its use in the language, and that language serves an indefinitely broad and heterogeneous range of human purposes. And this new conception of language changed his conception of philosophy. He continued to think of philosophy as a critique of language, and as a critical activity rather than a doctrine. But he now argued that the right method in philosophy is not analytic but hermeneutic. Philosophy, he now claimed, should not consist in logical analysis, in

---

* Books published in the Routledge & Kegan Paul series *Studies in Philosophical Psychology* were indeed small and red. They included Winch's *The Idea of a Social Science*, Melden's *Free Action*, and Kenny's *Action, Emotion and Will*.

seeking to discover the logical form of a sentence disguised by its grammatical form, or in policing the language of science, but in describing various 'language-games'—in particular, language-games involving mathematical, logical, linguistic, and psychological concepts—which the author of the *Tractatus* and Russell and earlier philosophers had misunderstood.

A language-game is simply a human activity involving speech or writing in which a distinctive range of concepts is employed. The word 'game' is there to remind us that the use of language is constrained by rules, and occurs both in the context of a specific human culture and in the larger context of human life in general. But some philosophers and social scientists came to regard language-games as paradigms of the complex patterns of social behaviour—the rituals, customs, institutions, and social structures—that exist on every scale in human societies, and argued that the correct method of enquiry in sociology and anthropology is the hermeneutic method Wittgenstein had described in the 1930s, rather than the scientific method Mill had described a century earlier, in which data obtained from experiments and observations confirm or disconfirm predictions deduced from hypotheses or laws. The human sciences, they held, should renounce theoretical explanation and seek instead to formulate synoptic pictures of symbolic activities informed by rules, as Wittgenstein had thought philosophy should do.

(B) The other influential idea Wittgenstein defended in the 1930s is not about methodology. It is simply that *an intentional act is normally explained by identifying the agent's own reason or motive for his act, and this is not a kind of causal explanation*:

The double use of the word 'why' asking for the cause and asking for the motive, together with the idea that we can know, and not only conjecture, our motives, gives rise to the confusion that a motive is a cause of which we are immediately aware, a cause 'seen from the inside', or a cause experienced.— Giving a reason is like giving a calculation by which you have arrived at a certain result.[5]

The philosophy of action today is deeply divided between those who accept Wittgenstein's view that explanations of intentional action are not normally causal explanations, and those, mostly followers of Davidson, who reject it. The dispute is not about *every* explanation of intentional action. For example, we might explain why Sally bit a policeman by saying that she was drunk. The act was almost certainly intentional. As a London magistrate pointed out in 1961, you don't bite policemen without intending it.[6] But the explanation doesn't indicate a motive. For all we have said, it might have been an affectionate nibble or a violent assault.

But while there are exceptions, *most* explanations of intentional action *do* indicate a motive, either explicitly or implicitly. This includes ones that mention desires or intentions ('Sally bit a policeman because she wanted to impress Tom', '...in order to impress Tom', '...with the intention of impressing Tom') and ones that mention reasons or beliefs ('...because it would impress Tom', '...because she knew it would impress Tom', '...because she believed it would impress Tom'). These are the explanations whose character is controversial.

In this chapter, I shall concentrate for the most part on intentions or desires. I shall examine the concept of a reason in general, and the concept of an agent's reason for an act in particular, in the next chapter. The purpose of this chapter is not to defend a full-dress analysis of the concept of intentional action or the concept of desire, but purely to shed light on the long-running dispute about the explanation of intentional action. I shall argue that both sides are partly right and partly wrong, and that the dispute has seemed intractable because of a failure of percipience about dispositions and a commitment to Humean orthodoxies about causation on both sides.

I do not propose to discuss the controversy about methods of enquiry in the human sciences. It animated the study of intentional action in the 1960s, but the connection between the two topics was simplified to an implausible degree, and the idea that philosophy can define the methods suited to different areas of scientific enquiry never made much sense.[*]

5.2 Desires and dispositions

Aristotle's statement in the *Nicomachean Ethics* is a convenient point of departure:

> The origin of action—its efficient, not its final cause—is choice, and that of choice is desire and reasoning with a view to an end.[7]

---

[*] Von Wright argued that the logical analysis of practical reasoning could provide an explanation schema that stands to the human sciences as the covering-law model was thought to stand to the natural sciences. But by this time the prestige of the covering-law model was already in decline and methodological monism and dualism now seem equally unrealistic. See von Wright, *Explanation and Understanding*, chs. 3 & 4; and 'A Reply to My Critics', p. 839. An astute assessment of the covering-law model can be found in Woodward, *Making Things Happen*, ch. 4.

Not all intentional action, let alone all action, issues from instrumental reasoning or involves conscious choice. I take my keys out of my pocket when I get home with the intention of opening my front door, but I do not make a conscious choice to do so or rehearse the reason in my mind. But intentional action always (or almost always) involves desire, as long as 'desire' is understood in the broad sense (it is often given by philosophers,) so that it refers to the whole gamut of wanting and valuing, from the most egoistic to the most altruistic, from the most idealistic to the most mundane, and from the desire to live to a hundred, which depends on having abstract concepts, so that only language-users can have it, and whose satisfaction, if it occurs, may be very remote in time, to the appetites we share with non-human animals, such as hunger and thirst.*

All (or almost all) intentional acts involve desire in this broad sense, because an intentional act is always (or almost always) done either because the agent wants to do it or values doing it for its own sake, or in order to achieve something else she wants or values. If urges and cravings are not counted as desires, there will be some exceptions to this rule. For example, arguably, the compulsive hand-washer has no desire to wash her hands the twentieth time she does so on the same day, but finds it difficult to control the urge. But perhaps urges and cravings should not be distinguished from desires, in which case the hand-washer has an intense desire to wash her hands, which she may also want to resist.

I shall assume that a simple and conventional conception of desire is approximately right.[8] A desire is a disposition, in the broad sense of the term that corresponds to Aristotle's *hexis*. But desires differ in important ways from the simple physical dispositions that philosophers tend to focus on, such as fragility and solubility. The basic difference is that a simple physical disposition is manifested by causing or undergoing change, whereas a desire is manifested in two main ways: first, by purposive or goal-directed behaviour, specifically, behaviour aimed at satisfying the desire—in other words, at getting what it is a desire to have, or doing what it is a desire to do; and second, by feeling glad, pleased, or relieved if the desire is satisfied, and sorry, displeased, or disappointed if it is frustrated.†

---

* It is controversial whether one can do something, say, take one's keys out of one's pocket, *intentionally* or *with the intention of opening the door* without also intending to take one's keys out of one's pocket. The argument in this chapter is consistent with both views.

† Pleasure at a desire's satisfaction and displeasure at its frustration can in turn be manifested in behaviour that is not purposive, as when a child claps her hands with delight or stamps her foot

There can be other signs or symptoms of desire, but signs and symptoms are not manifestations. As Wittgenstein put it, they are not *criteria*.[9] *Only the manifestation of a desire is constitutive of its identity, and how it is defined.* This is true of dispositions in general. The green colour of a leaf is a reliable sign that it is photosynthetic, but only photosynthesizing is a manifestation of the disposition. Similarly, salivating can be a *sign* or *indication* of the desire to eat a steak, but eating a steak, and action aimed at getting and eating a steak, are not merely signs of the desire, they are manifestations.

The fact that desires are manifested in goal-directed action has two direct consequences, both of which distinguish desires from simple physical dispositions, and even from primitive adaptive behavioural dispositions like the phototropic disposition of a plant. First, the object of a desire—i.e. what it is a desire for or a desire to do—and its expression in action can be related teleologically, as end and means. For example, Lucy's desire to dance can be expressed in dancing, but it can also be manifested in, say, buying a tutu, as long as buying a tutu seems to Lucy conducive to dancing. Second, the way in which a desire is manifested in purposive behaviour depends on cognition: it depends on what the agent senses, knows, and believes—for example, James's desire to please his mother will not be expressed by his going to church unless he knows or believes that doing so might please her. And it can be manifested in behaviour that will actually displease her, if he is under a misapprehension about what she would like.

There is a good deal to be said for this simple conception of desire. First, it is clear that if one is disposed to do X, it does not follow that one wants to do X. One may be disposed to catch colds or to stammer when one is nervous without wanting to in the least. But it is equally clear that if one wants to do X one is disposed to do X, or something conducive to doing X. Someone who wants to do something, say dance, may be prevented or dissuaded from doing it, may want to do something else more, may feel lazy, or may change her mind. But as long as she wants to dance, she is disposed to dance. The same applies to someone who wants to do something idiotic,

---

with annoyance, so these kinds of behaviour are also indirect manifestations of the desire that is satisfied or frustrated. Empiricists from Locke to Mill insist on the intrinsic relation between desire, pleasure, and pain. For example, Mill claims that 'desiring a thing and finding it pleasant, aversion to it and thinking of it as painful, are phenomena entirely inseparable or, rather, two parts of the phenomenon' (Mill, *Utilitarianism*, p. 49).

such as punch a slot machine, and controls the desire so well that he never gets close to doing it. This is part of what distinguishes a desire from an idle wish. It also distinguishes a desire from a felt need. For although some desires, especially the appetites we share with other animals, are for things we need, it is conceivable, as Kenny points out, 'that a felt need might be like a felt ache: it might just cause one to hug oneself and lie immobile'.[10]

Second, it explains why one cannot want to get something one knows one already has—although of course one can want to keep it—and why wanting shades into hoping or wishing when one knows that one cannot do anything to satisfy one's desire, either because of the limitation of one's powers, such as hoping the weather will be fine next week, or because the thing is settled or in the past, such as wishing the weather had been fine last week.[11] (But the boundaries between wanting, hoping, and wishing are not sharp. Our mental concepts draw distinctions in sfumato, so that one feature blends into another.)

Third, it explains the behaviourist idea, which Russell learned from the psychologist John Watson, that 'desire must be capable of being exhibited in action'.[12] But what exactly does this mean? In fact, it is similar to Wittgenstein's remark that 'an "inner process" stands in need of outward criteria'.[13] It does not mean that one cannot desire something if one is unable to express the desire in action, so that an animal cannot be hungry if it is unable to seek food, say, because it is too weak. It means that if there is such a thing as the desire for X, then there is such a thing as exhibiting the desire for X in action. For example, there is such a thing as wanting to die, but there is no such thing as wanting, as opposed to wishing, one had not been born. And it means that one can have conflicting desires, such as the desire to eat trifle and the desire to be slim, and even contradictory desires, such as the desire to eat trifle and the desire not to eat trifle, but not a desire with a contradictory content, such as the desire to eat trifle and not to eat it. Wanting to have one's cake and eat it is not one desire but two.

Fourth, it also explains Wittgenstein's criticism of Russell's theory of desire. Russell argued that the object of a desire, what it is a desire for, or to do, is the result that brings action manifesting the desire to an end, it is 'the state that brings quiescence':

A hungry animal is restless until it finds food; then it becomes quiescent. The thing which will bring a restless condition to an end is said to be what is desired.[14]

Wittgenstein's well-known comment on the theory is this:

> I believe Russell's theory comes to the following: if I give someone an order and what he thereupon does pleases me, then he has carried out the order. (If I should like to eat an apple and someone gives me a punch in the stomach, so that the desire to eat goes away, then it was this punch that I originally wanted.)[15]

The objection is decisive. Russell's theory cannot be right because something that eliminates a desire is not necessarily what the desire is for. The more a desire is like a craving or an urge, the more plausible the theory seems. For example, an alcoholic in a play by Tennessee Williams—Brick, in *Cat on a Hot Tin Roof*—says that he drinks for the click, 'the click I get in my head when I've had enough of this stuff to make me peaceful'. In this case, Russell's remark that 'the thing which will bring a restless condition to an end is said to be what is desired' is a close fit. But most desires are not merely for quiescence, and Wittgenstein's example shows that unless that *is* what a desire is for, eliminating it and satisfying it will not necessarily be the same thing. Like any disposition, the *object* of a desire—what it is a desire *for* or *to do*—is constitutive of its identity and how it is defined, whereas what eliminates it is not.

Finally, the simple conception of desire proposed here explains why the object of a desire, like the object of any disposition, is standardly identified in English with an infinitival clause, and not, as philosophers who believe desires are propositional attitudes would prefer, a sentential clause.[16] It is true that the object of a desire is also commonly identified with a nominal clause, but if one desires a thing, such as an apple or a house, one desires to eat it, occupy it, or inhabit it, or minimally have it under one's control.

This simple conception of desire may not provide an accurate characterization of every desire or a complete characterization of any desire. Perhaps some desires are too fleeting to be dispositions, although perhaps dispositions can be fleeting too. And desires can be manifested in ways I have not discussed, for example, in obsessions, preoccupations, and subtler patterns of thought. But it is sufficient for our present purposes if it provides a partial characterization of many desires, and it certainly does that. As I have said, I shall assume that it is approximately right.

Now if desires are dispositions, then presumably they explain action in the way dispositions in general explain action. But it is sometimes said that explanations that refer to dispositions are vacuous or uninformative, and explain nothing at all. The complaint has some merit when the disposition mentioned is to produce the effect whose cause we want to know. Molière's joke about a student who is congratulated for explaining that taking opium makes one fall asleep because of its *virtus dormitiva*—i.e. its soporific power—is a case in point.[17] The explanation is not quite vacuous, since it excludes the hypothesis that opium activates the *virtus dormitiva* of some other popular part of the French diet, such as asparagus or red wine, but its value is limited. It is like explaining that Henry kicked a lamp post because he wanted to, which excludes the hypothesis that he did it under duress, but is likely to leave us wanting to know more.

But explanations that refer to dispositions are not all alike. For example, 'Lead is poisonous because it is a neurotoxin' is a better explanation than the one Molière lampooned, because it excludes a larger range of alternatives. Most explanations referring to desires are better than 'Because he wanted to', for the same reason. All explanations without exception are informative to the extent that they rule out alternatives, and since one act can be expected to have many different consequences, it can express many different desires. For example, one can open a window because one wants to let the cool air in, because one wants to let the smell of frying bacon out, because one wants to hear what the neighbours are saying, and so on. The right explanation will say which desire or desires the act actually manifested, and rule out the rest.

5.3 The explanation of intentional action

The idea that our desires cause the acts we do in order to satisfy them was never disputed before the twentieth century, except by philosophers, such as Malebranche, who denied the existence of psycho-physical and physical causation entirely. The controversy was initiated by Wittgenstein's writings in the 1930s, and the arguments he and his followers advanced rely on different elements of what I shall call, with deliberate vagueness, the Humean (as opposed to Hume's) theory of causation. I use the term to refer indiscriminately to various combinations of doctrines or assumptions about causation which were defended by or have been imputed to or derive from Hume, and not to refer to Hume's own theory of causation in particular.

These are the principal arguments:

- *Causes are events, which are distinct from and precede their effects*; whereas desires are not events, and, in most cases, if one says what desire an act was meant to satisfy, one does not identify a feeling, image, or idea that precedes the act the desire explains: one does not answer the question 'What did you see or hear or feel, or what ideas or images cropped up in your mind and led up to it?'[18]

- *Our knowledge of causes is uncertain, and relies on inductive inference from a plurality of cases, because causation cannot be observed in any particular case*; whereas our knowledge of our own motives is normally certain and non-inferential.[19]

- *A singular causal statement is implicitly general: it implies that events resembling the cause are invariably followed by events resembling the effect.* But the statement that a particular act was done with a particular motive does not imply that the same motive invariably leads to the same act. For instance, a defendant's assertion that he did a certain act because of threats does not imply that he would act in the same way if he was threatened again, or that he or others always respond to threats in that way.[20]

- *It is conceivable that any kind of cause should have had a different kind of effect from the one it actually has*, whereas what a desire is for, or to do, is constitutive of its identity and how it is defined. For example, it is not a contingent fact that a desire for an apple is satisfied by an apple rather than a punch in the stomach, or a pear.[21]

Of course, none of these arguments has to be taken to show that desires are not causes, even if it is accepted that it shows that desires are not causes *as the Humean theory conceives of them*. They can be taken to reveal a defect in the Humean theory instead. And if they *are* taken this way, different diagnoses regarding the defect in the theory are possible.

Davidson's ingenious and influential response to these arguments is minimalist: a refinement of the Humean theory—perhaps no more than a clarification—is sufficient to meet them:

- True, desires are not events; but the 'onslaught' of a desire is, such as when the smell of food makes one feel hungry; and so is a perception that triggers the manifestation of a desire, such as when catching sight of its mother makes a child run towards her.

(So desires are better described as causal factors than as causes; but explanations that refer to desires *are* causal explanations.)

- True, our knowledge of our own motives is normally certain and non-inferential; but Hume himself points out that we can 'attain knowledge of a particular cause merely by one experiment.'

  (In fact Hume adds the qualification, 'provided it be made with judgment and after a careful removal of all foreign and superfluous circumstances'.[22] But we normally know what desire motivated us in the ordinary circumstances of our daily lives, and not just in an experimental situation that is carefully contrived to exclude confusion about motives.)

- True, the statement that an act was done because of a certain motive does not imply that the same motive would always lead to the same act; but it can imply that a law covering the events concerned exists without implying that the law can be stated in the language of motives and desires. If desires are physical states, it can be stated in the language of physics.

- True, what a desire is for is constitutive of its identity qua desire; but it does not follow that it is constitutive of its identity qua physical state.

I agree with Davidson that desires are causal factors, but I think the arguments of Wittgenstein and his followers exposed a more serious flaw in the Humean theory of causation. The root of the problem, the reason why it seemed to them that desires could not be causal factors, is that the Humean theory cannot explain the exercise of dispositions. But neither side in the dispute saw this. (Of course Hume himself never intended to explain the exercise of powers, but only to explain how the *idea* of power can be produced by impressions of sequences of events.) In effect—although I do not mean to suggest that this is how it appeared—Wittgenstein and his followers faced a choice between challenging the Humean theory and excluding causation by desires, and they made the wrong choice. For his part, Davidson adhered just as closely to the Humean theory, and the principal difficulty faced by his solution—eliminating the 'deviant' causal chains from desires to acts—which Anscombe and others sympathetic to Wittgenstein's position seized on, is a residual sign of the same weakness in the Humean theory.

In sum, the opposing views about explanations of intentional action arrived at an impasse because of a failure of percipience on both sides regarding dispositions. But it can be broken if this is put right. Or so I shall argue.

If this account of the matter is correct, the four arguments above should be answered rather differently. Expressed with the same brevity, the answers should be roughly as follows:

- True, desires are not events; they are dispositions. But dispositions are causal factors, which belong to the causal history of the acts and events that they explain.

- True, our knowledge of our own motives is normally certain and non-inferential. But there is no inherent difficulty in the idea that knowledge of a singular causal fact can be certain and non-inferential, unless we accept the Humean doctrine that a singular causal statement is made true by a regularity in the general pattern of events, rather than by anything present locally in the particular case.

- True, the statement that an act was done because of a certain motive does not imply that the same motive would always lead to the same act; but it is normal for many dispositions to contribute to a particular act, and when this happens, the outcome depends on the exact mix.

- True, what a desire is *for*, or *to do*, is constitutive of its identity, and how it is defined; but this is true of every disposition.

I said that the opposing views about explanations of intentional action arrived at an impasse. Here it is. On the one hand,

(A) if James went to church and wanted to please his mother (and knew or believed that going to church would please her), it does not follow that he went to church *because* he wanted to please his mother.

On the other hand,

(B) if James went to church and wanted to please his mother (and knew or believed that going to church would please her), and his churchgoing was caused by his desire to please his mother, it *still* does not follow that he went to church *because* he wanted to please his mother (as this would normally be meant and understood), because the 'causal chain' running from the desire to the act could be 'deviant' or 'freakish'.

(A) suggests that explanations of intentional action are causal explanations. Davidson writes:

If, as Melden claims, causal explanations are 'wholly irrelevant to the understanding we seek' of human action then we are without an analysis of the 'because' in 'He did it because...', where we go on to name a reason. Hampshire remarks, of the relation between reasons and action, 'In philosophy one ought surely to find this...connection altogether mysterious'. Hampshire rejects Aristotle's attempt to solve the mystery by introducing the concept of wanting as a causal factor [...] But I would urge that, failing a satisfactory alternative, the best argument for a scheme like Aristotle's is that it alone promises to give an account of the 'mysterious connection' between reasons and actions.[23]

Arguably, Davidson's Humean conception of efficient causes is so different from Aristotle's that it was misleading of him to present himself as a champion of Aristotle's doctrine at all. Be that as it may, (B) shows that postulating a causal connection between the desire and the act does not provide 'an analysis of the "because"', or explain the '"mysterious connection" between reasons and actions'. Anscombe writes:

> [Davidson's solution] lacks acumen. True, not only must I have a reason, it must also 'operate as my reason': that is, what I do must be done *in pursuit* of that end and *on grounds* of the belief. But not just *any* act of mine caused by my having a certain desire is done in pursuit of the object of desire; not just *any* act caused by my having a belief is done on grounds of the belief. Davidson indeed realises that even identity of description of *act done* with *act specified in the belief*, together with causality by the belief and desire, isn't enough to guarantee the act's being done *in pursuit of the end* and *on grounds of the belief*. He speaks of the possibility of 'wrong' or 'freak' causal connexions. I say that any recognisable causal connexions would be 'wrong', and that he can do no more than postulate a 'right' causal connexion in the happy security that none such can be found. If a causal connexion were found we could always still ask 'But was the act done for the sake of the end and in view of the thing believed?'[24]

This is not perfectly clear: 'any recognisable causal connexions would be "wrong"' suggests that *no* act caused by a desire is done with the intention of satisfying it, whereas 'not just *any* act of mine caused by my having a certain desire...' suggests, on the contrary, that some intentional acts *are* caused by desires, but that a causal connection between a desire and an act does not guarantee that the act is done with the intention of satisfying it. Be that as it may, the principal point here is that Davidson 'can do no more than postulate a "right" causal connexion in the happy security that none such can be found'. And by the time Anscombe had published this remark, Davidson had decided that this was true. 'Several clever philosophers have tried to show how to eliminate the deviant causal chains,' he wrote, 'but

I remain convinced that the concepts of event, cause, and intention are inadequate to account for intentional action.'[25]

If this is true, it does not follow that when desires explain intentional acts they are *not* causal factors, or that 'any recognisable causal connexions would be "wrong"'. But it *does* follow that if the relation between intentional acts and desires is mysterious, the idea that desires are causal factors will not dispel the mystery. Hence the impasse.

In outline, the solution I propose is this.

First, the fact that there can be a 'deviant' causal connection between a desire and an act that is conducive to satisfying it has nothing particularly to do with reasons or desires. The reason is simply that desires are dispositions, and with certain exceptions, such as radioactive decay and rest mass, to which I shall return, every disposition can be connected to the kind of occurrence that normally manifests it by a 'deviant' or 'freakish' causal chain. Take Molière's example of a disposition, the *virtus dormitiva*. A man might take a soporific drug before driving, and the drowsiness induced by the drug might make him crash the car and knock himself unconscious. If this happened, he would lose consciousness because he took the drug, but the exercise of its *virtus dormitiva* would be pre-empted by the crash. (It is true that the drug's soporific power is manifested to some degree in this case, but if that is thought to be a defect in the example, we can instead imagine the man taking the drug while driving, choking on it, crashing, etc.)

Second, if Anscombe and Davidson are right in thinking that the 'deviant' causal chains from a desire to an act cannot be eliminated—in other words, if the 'right' causal chain cannot be defined, except as one where the act is done 'in pursuit of that end'—again, this has nothing particularly to do with intentional action as such. It has nothing particularly to do with 'the normative character of psychological concepts' (contra Davidson), and it is not because teleological explanations are not causal explanations (contra Anscombe). It is because *the exercise of a disposition cannot be defined as a specific kind of sequence or concatenation of events.*[26]

Third, if the 'deviant' causal chains between taking a soporific drug and losing consciousness cannot be eliminated, it does not follow that the fact that a man took the drug explains why he lost consciousness *causally* if the causal chain was 'deviant' and *non-causally* if it was not. It obviously explains it causally in both cases. But the causal chain can be described as 'deviant' in the case of the man who crashes his car, *because the disposition is not manifested.*

Exactly the same is true of desires. It is a mistake to imagine that a climber's wanting to rid himself of the weight and danger of holding another man on a rope explains why he loosened his hold on the rope *causally* if the connection was 'deviant' and *non-causally* if it was not. His desire is a causal factor either way, but the process can be described as 'deviant' if letting go is an effect or 'symptom' but not a manifestation or 'criterion' of the desire.

Finally, many explanations that refer to the agent's own reasons for doing an act, and every explanation that refers to his aim or intention in doing it, contains non-redundant information about the desires manifested by the action. For example, 'James's reason for going to church was that it would please his mother' and 'James went to church with the aim (or intention) of pleasing his mother' contain the information that James's going to church manifested his desire to please his mother. Hence, if desires are causal factors, both these explanations contain non-redundant information about causal factors, and this makes them causal explanations, in one perfectly good sense of the phrase.[27]

I shall explain this in more detail in 5.4 and 5.5.

5.4 Wittgenstein and Anscombe

Wittgenstein returned repeatedly to the topic of intentional action, but his influence on the controversy about explanations of intentional action is mainly due to his writings in the 1930s, especially the following passage in the *Blue Book*:

> The proposition that your action has such and such a cause, is a hypothesis. The hypothesis is well-founded if one has had a number of experiences which, roughly speaking, agree in showing that your action is the regular sequel of certain conditions which we then call causes of the action. In order to know the reason which you had for making a certain statement, for acting in a particular way, etc., no number of agreeing experiences is necessary, and the statement of your reason is not a hypothesis. The difference between the grammars of "reason" and "cause" is quite similar to that between the grammars of "motive" and "cause". Of the cause one can say that one can't *know* it but can only *conjecture* it. On the other hand one often says: "Surely *I* must know why I did it" talking of the *motive*. [...] The double use of the word "why", asking for the cause and asking for the motive, together with the idea that we can know, and not only conjecture, our motives, gives rise to

the confusion that a motive is a cause of which we are immediately aware, a cause 'seen from the inside', or a cause experienced.[28*]

Anscombe points out in *Intention* why this argument is unconvincing. She comments on a case where someone is startled by a face appearing at a window: 'the subject is able to give the cause of a feeling or bodily movement in the same kind of way as he is able to state the place of his pain or the position of his limbs.'[29] These kinds of statement—for example, 'The pain is in my ankle' or 'My legs are crossed'—do *not* seem to be conjectures or hypotheses, whose credibility depends on 'a number of agreeing experiences'. And Anscombe is surely right to suggest that saying what made one start is similar. We *are* immediately aware of causation in this case—'a cause experienced' is an apt description, just as it is when one is stung by a bee or knocked over by a blow—and there is no obvious reason why we should not also normally be able to state the desire that caused us to act, in a similar way. If singular causal statements were invariably conjectures, Wittgenstein would be right in saying that stating a motive is not stating a cause, because stating a motive is not normally a conjecture. Unconscious motives, such as the ones Freud postulated to explain verbal slips, are exceptions. But examples like the one Anscombe mentions disprove Wittgenstein's assumption.

Anscombe does not endorse the Humean doctrine that a particular instance of causation counts as such only by conforming to a general pattern, which Wittgenstein took for granted when he wrote the passage quoted above. On the contrary, she implies that our ability to give the cause of a feeling or bodily movement, such as when we are startled, is incompatible with it.[30] But she still insists, now in agreement with Wittgenstein, that explanations of intentional action are not generally causal explanations, because she assumes that causes are events.[31] The desire an act is intended to satisfy, she points out, is not generally a 'mental cause' in the sense in which catching sight of a face at the window is, because it is not generally 'an event that brings the effect about'.[32] There are exceptions, 'feelings of desire' such as pangs of hunger, but in most cases, if one says what desire an

* Wittgenstein refers here to motives rather than desires, but this is not an important difference, and in fact he made similar remarks about desires to Waismann, which are recorded both in Waismann's notes of their conversations and in *The Principles of Linguistic Philosophy*, which was based on dictations by Wittgenstein. See Baker, *The Voices of Wittgenstein: The Vienna Circle*, pp. 424ff; Waismann, *The Principles of Linguistic Philosophy*, p. 123.

act was meant to satisfy, one does not answer the question 'What did you see or hear or feel, or what ideas or images cropped up in your mind and led up to it?'

But if the desire is not 'an event that brings the effect about', how does it explain the act? Anscombe's answer is that it *interprets it*.

> Motives may explain actions to us; but that is not to say that they 'determine', in the sense of causing, actions. We do say: 'His love of truth caused him to . . .' and similar things, and no doubt such expressions help us to think that a motive must be what produces or brings about a choice. But this means rather 'He did this in that he loved the truth'; it interprets his action.[33]

What kind of interpretation does Anscombe have in mind? If a doctor interprets a tremor as a symptom of a disease, the interpretation is a causal explanation. The text is elusive, and the phrase 'in that' is unhelpful, since it occurs in different kinds of explanations, like 'since' and 'because'. For example, 'Let him die, in that he is a fox' is a justification, whereas 'For in that he himself hath suffered being tempted, he is able to succour them that are tempted' is a causal explanation.[34] But although it is hard to be certain, Anscombe seems to believe that motives (like the desire for gain) (another of her examples) and the love of truth) explain an act by identifying the good, or apparent good, the agent aimed to realize or achieve, in other words, what it was about the act that made it seem worth doing—say, that it was (so he thought) likely to enrich him, or that it served (so he thought) the interests of truth.

If this is an accurate summary, Anscombe denies that an explanation of an intentional act in terms of the agent's motive or desire is a causal explanation because of a combination of two reasons. First, with the exception of pangs of hunger, sudden impulses to kiss lovers, and the like, desires are not events, and a fortiori not events that trigger actions. Second, explanations of intentional acts that refer to non-trigger-like desires interpret them, in the way explained. As she also puts it, they 'say something like "See the action in this light"'.[35] If she is right, empiricists like Locke and Russell thought of all desires as if they were urges and cravings. They regarded the exceptional case as the normal one, and so they imagined that explanations of conscious purposive behaviour by human beings postulate efficient causes—uncomfortable feelings that initiate behaviour—when in fact they postulate final causes, aims, or goals towards which the behaviour is directed.

But neither reason Anscombe gives for doubting whether explanations referring to desires are causal explanations is convincing. Regarding the first, we have seen that causal explanations do not invariably refer to triggering events. Since the desire for gain and the love of truth are abiding properties, asking whether a man launched a Sunday paper out of one or the other is *not* like asking what kind of sensation made Brick pour himself a vodka, and cannot be made to look like one without changing its meaning. It is more like asking whether a ship displaced a certain quantity of water because of its size or its weight, or whether a flower attracted a bee because of its colour or its scent. But these are evidently causal questions about the events concerned, and the answers are evidently causal explanations. So we have as yet no reason to deny that explanations which refer to desires are causal explanations too.

Regarding Anscombe's second reason, it is true that 'His love of truth caused him to . . .' and 'He did it to make money' identify the good or apparent good the agent wanted to realize or achieve. But we do not have to choose between saying this and saying that these explanations are causal, and we have every reason to say both. For *what* the man desires, in other words, his aim or goal—*to make money* or *to serve the truth*—is an intensional object, an object of thought, and therefore *not* a causal factor. But the desire itself is a disposition to act in ways that seem conducive to satisfying it, and so presumably *is* a causal factor. So the explanations do interpret the act, in the way Anscombe suggests; but they also explain it causally. They attribute a justification to the agent, because they say what kind of good he saw in doing the act; but they wrap up the justification in a causal explanation, because they say that seeing this kind of good in the act is what caused him to do it (see 6.1). Russell's assimilation of desires to urges and cravings was a mistake because it led him to equate the object of a desire with whatever extinguishes it, and thereby to eliminate teleology from the definition of desire, not because explanations of intentional action are not causal explanations.

If this is right, a desire is part of the causal history of the act or event it explains, just as a person's other physical or mental dispositions are: 'Cecilia came out in a rash because she is allergic to peanuts', 'Abe blushed because he is shy', 'Sam laughed because he was nervous', 'James went to church because he wanted to please his mother', and so on. Of course there are important differences between desires and simple physical dispositions, as we have seen, and there are also important differences between the desires of adults and older children and the desires of animals and infants, inasmuch *as* the former normally know what they desire; many of their desires can be assessed as reasonable or unreasonable, wise or foolish; and their desires normally leave room for choice, by which I mean that they are normally able to resist exhibiting them in intentional action. But for all that, explanations that refer to dispositions are *echt* causal explanations, whatever kind of dispositions they refer to. *How* they explain, exactly *what part* of a causal story they tell, and whether a disposition is the cause, or part of the cause, of its manifestation—these are contentious questions.[36] But *that* explanations that refer to dispositions are causal explanations should be beyond doubt.

5.5 Dispositions and deviant causal chains

By common consent, the most difficult objection faced by the claim that desires are causal factors arises from the existence of deviant causal chains. The best-known example is Davidson's, which I mentioned earlier. Here it is again, in his own words:

> A climber might want to rid himself of the weight and danger of holding another man on a rope, and he might know that by loosening his hold on the rope he could rid himself of the weight and danger. This belief and want might so unnerve him as to cause him to loosen his hold, and yet it might be the case that he never *chose* to loosen his hold, nor did he do it intentionally.[37]

Davidson and Anscombe agree that we cannot distinguish the case where the climber loosens his hold because he wants to rid himself of the weight and danger of holding another man on the rope from the case where his desire causes him to loosen his hold 'deviantly' by defining the 'normal' causal route from the desire (or its 'onslaught', or an event that triggers it) to the act. But this is not a problem about desires in particular; it is about dispositions and powers in general.

Deviant causal chains have been around in philosophy for longer than we might think. In fact, occasionalism is the arch-theory of deviant causal chains.[38] According to Malebranche, the pre-eminent early-modern occasionalist, there is no psycho-physical or physical interaction, but God's will ensures that whenever a physical or mental event occurs, the events we are inclined to think of as their effects follow. For example, when a person walks or speaks, we tend to attribute the motion in her legs or her lips to *her* agency, but in fact the only power that is manifested is God's power, and so the only real agency is God's agency. She has a volition to move her body in a certain way, but God causes the motion. Exactly the same is true when she pricks her finger and feels pain, and also when one billiard ball strikes another one and the second ball begins to move. It seems to us as if the pin causes the pain and the first ball sets the second ball in motion, but in reality it is God. In Malebranche's system, God's monopoly on power is absolute, and *every* sequence of events that counts as cause and effect by Humean criteria is 'deviant', except for the ones where the cause is the will of God.

Hume has been described as Malebranche without God, because he reduces causation to the recurring sequences of events that remain when God's agency is removed from Malebranche's system. But if we start out with occasionalism and eliminate God's power to cause events, we eliminate the distinction between deviant and normal causal chains as well. For if causation consists simply in the regular or law-like concatenation of events, one causal chain may be more circuitous or more surprising than another, but the question 'Deviant or normal?' cannot arise, because there is no power in the world from which an act or event can either proceed, if the chain is normal, or fail to proceed, if it is not. This is why the Humean theory of causation cannot 'eliminate the deviant causal chains'—for example, why it cannot distinguish between the case where the climber loosens his hold *in order to* kill the other man, and the case where his desire to kill the other man causes him to loosen his hold without him doing so for this reason. This is just a particular instance of a more general failure to distinguish between 'true' causes and 'occasional' causes. We deem the causal chain to be normal if, and only if, the climber loosens his hold *in order to* kill the other man; and in general we deem the process running from a power's standard trigger to an act or event of the kind that manifests it to be normal if, and only if, this act or event is in fact a manifestation of the power. But this process cannot be reduced to a specific kind of sequence or concatenation of events.

The reduction of powers in modern philosophy was originally part of the campaign to liberate science from Aristotelianism, which was led by Galileo and Descartes. But since powers cannot be perceived with the senses, there is a perennial tendency for empiricists to clarify, or falsify, or reform our talk about them (which verb seems apt depends on one's point of view).

In the twentieth century, most reductionists about powers employed the method of contextual definition. Instead of identifying powers with geometrical structures, as Descartes had done, or defending Hume's notorious claim that the distinction between a power and its exercise is 'entirely frivolous',[39] reductionists argued that categorical statements referring to powers can be explicated as hypothetical statements relating the stimulus that triggers the power to the response that manifests it. Armstrong summarizes the approach when he claims that powers are 'congealed hypothetical facts or states of affairs'.[40] But in recent years the reductionist programme has come under sustained attack. I shall not try to prove that its opponents are right. It is enough, for my purposes, to show that the question whether the deviant causal chains between a desire and an act can be eliminated can be subsumed under the same general question about powers.

The simplest approach to contextual definition is to hold that the statement that an object or substance has a certain power is revealed by analysis to be the hypothetical statement that if the appropriate stimulus occurs the response follows. For example, Ryle writes as follows:

> Dispositional statements are neither reports of observed or observable states of affairs, nor yet reports of unobserved or unobservable states of affairs. [...] To say that this lump of sugar is soluble is to say that it would dissolve, if submerged anywhere, at any time and in any parcel of water.[41]

Generalized, and relativized to a specific time, Ryle's analysis can be expressed thus:

(C) A substance x is disposed at time t to give response r to stimulus s if, and only if, x would give response r if x were to receive stimulus s at time t.

This is known as the conditional analysis of dispositions, or sometimes the 'simple' or 'naive' conditional analysis. As these names suggest, more complex and sophisticated conditional analyses have been proposed, which are designed to avoid some of the counterexamples to (C), but I shall confine my remarks to (C), and direct readers to more comprehensive studies in the notes.[42]

(C) is vulnerable to several kinds of counterexample. To begin with, Molnar argues that some dispositions are exercised without a stimulus or trigger.

Evidently, most action is interaction, and so (i) _most dispositions are powers to interact._ This includes the examples that crop up in the literature most often, such as the solubility of sugar in water and the brittleness of glass. And in most cases, (ii) _the exercise of a complementary pair of active and passive dispositions is triggered by the agent and the patient coming into contact in a certain way._ Sugar is submerged in water; the brittle sheet of glass is struck. But there are exceptions to both generalizations. Regarding (i), an unstable atom's propensity to decay is not exercised in any kind of interaction; it simply disintegrates in a specific way. Similarly, some desires are to interact with apples, lovers, and so on, in various ways, while others, such as the desire to die or sleep or compose a sonnet, are not. Regarding (ii), radio-active decay occurs spontaneously, without any kind of trigger, and a body's rest mass—according to General Relativity, its disposition to deform space-time—does not have a trigger either, not in this case because it is exercised spontaneously at a specific time, but because it is exercised continuously, for as long as the body exists. As Molnar puts it, it does not have a toggle, it cannot be switched on or off.[43]

Does the expression of desire in action invariably have a trigger? It is not _obvious_ that it does, but it is plausible. I may often have no reason—i.e. no justification—for doing something at a particular moment, rather than a few moments earlier or later, but it does not seem plausible that it can be a matter of pure chance. In some cases, the trigger is contact, but in more cases, it is seeing, hearing, or smelling something—contact at a distance, as it were—as when a child catches sight of its mother and runs towards her. And in many cases the trigger is inside the agent's body and we do not know what it is. For example, I want to tell the children to be quiet, but say nothing, hoping they will settle by themselves. After a while, I say some-thing. Perhaps the volume of chatter rose above a certain threshold, perhaps my blood sugar dropped below a certain threshold. I may not know why I spoke exactly when I did. Whatever the trigger was on this occasion, it was not necessarily a thought or feeling or perception.

If radioactive decay and rest mass are dispositions without triggers, then (C) cannot provide a template for the contextual definition of every dis-position, and Armstrong's claim that powers are 'congealed hypothetical facts or states of affairs' cannot be true without exception. But I do not think the reductionist should be troubled by this conclusion, because a body's rest mass and an unstable atom's propensity to decay are reducible to strict—that is, indefeasible—laws, deterministic in the first case and stochastic in the second. Perhaps it is a mistake to regard them as dispositions at all. As Strawson says, 'in the most sophisticated reaches of physical theory [. . .] causation is swallowed up in mathematics'.[44] What *should* trouble the reductionist is that there are various kinds of counterexamples to (C) involving dispositions that *do* have triggers, which suggests that *only* dispositions without triggers are reducible to strict laws.

Some of these counterexamples rely on the fact that the process running from a disposition's trigger to its manifestation takes some time, so an intervention can prevent the manifestation from occurring. So if a device is set up to intervene in this way if the stimulus occurs, it will not be true that the stimulus would cause the manifestation, or that if the stimulus occurred the manifestation would follow. One well-known example of this kind is due to Martin.[45] A wire is live if, and only if, it has the disposition to transmit a current when it is touched by an earthed conductor; it is dead if, and only if, it is not live. But suppose a live wire is attached to a safety device which detects when the wire is touched, and makes it dead before the current flows. If the wire is touched at t it will be live but it will not transmit a current, and so the right-hand side of (C) is false. The device could also have a 'reverse cycle', so that it detects when a dead wire is touched and makes it live. In this case, the right-hand side of (C) will be true although the wire is dead.

Johnston describes a different kind of example:

> A gold chalice is not fragile but an angel has taken a dislike to it because its garishness borders on sacrilege and has decided to shatter it when it is dropped. Even though the gold chalice would shatter when dropped, this does not make it fragile because [. . .] something extrinsic to the chalice is the cause of the breaking.[46]

Or, leaving the realm of fantasy, something that is not fragile, such as a sheet of toughened glass, could have an explosive device with a sensitive detonator attached to it, so that it would be shattered by the explosion if it were dropped.[47] In this case, the hypothetical statements are true, but the glass is not fragile. This example does not rely on the possibility of switching the disposition on or off after the trigger has occurred. Instead, like the example of the driver who takes a soporific drug and crashes his car, it relies on the fact that a response will only count as a manifestation of a disposition if it is the result of the right kind of process. As Molnar puts it, the relation between a disposition and its manifestation is *process-specific*, at least to some degree, whereas the relation between a cause-event and an effect-event is process-unspecific.[48]

In both the example about conductivity and the one about fragility, the situation is abnormal, and the abnormal element is an extrinsic factor: it is not part of the wire or the sheet of glass, the object whose disposition is in question. But the bona fide exercise of a disposition often depends on extrinsic factors, such as the air injected with the petrol into a cylinder so that a spark will cause the petrol to ignite. So (C) cannot be fixed by excluding extrinsic factors wholesale. If we add a *ceteris paribus* clause or one requiring the process from *s* to *r* to be 'non-deviant' or 'normal', the result is plausible, since we have the leeway to decide whether other things *were* equal, or whether the process from the stimulus to the response *was* normal.

(C*) A substance *x* is disposed at time *t* to give response *r* to stimulus *s* iff *x* would give response *r* if *x* were to undergo stimulus *s* at time *t*, *other things being equal.*

(C**) A substance *x* is disposed at time *t* to give response *r* to stimulus *s* iff *x* would give response *r via a normal process* if *x* were to undergo stimulus *s* at time *t*.

But a reductive definition of a disposition will need to be specific: it will need to specify *which* other things have to be equal, and *what* kind of process is normal. And while we can say in general terms that other things *relevant to x's disposition to give response r to stimulus s* have to be equal, and the process has to be *the kind of process that occurs when x manifests the disposition to give response r to stimulus s*, these will differ in each case. Thus, other things are *not* equal so far as conductivity is concerned when a wire is attached to the kind of safety device described above, and the process from *s* to *r is* deviant where fragility is concerned when dropping a sheet of toughened glass attached to an explosive device detonates the device.

So far, this is not a fatal blow to the reductionist programme. Powers could still be 'congealed hypothetical facts or states of affairs', even if no general formula covered every power. But if we cannot specify precisely when other things are equal and what counts as a normal process *for each particular case*—fragility, conductivity, the desire to please one's mother, etc.—then we are in effect still saying that so far as disposition *D* is concerned, other things are equal, or the process is normal, *if, and only if, D is manifested*. And this *is* tantamount to an admission that the reductionist programme is stymied, because (C*) and (C**) cannot be serviceable templates for reductive definitions if the left-hand side explains the right-hand side, instead of the other way around.

The debate about deviant causal chains between desires and acts, and the so far less protracted debate about physical dispositions, suggest that this is how things are turning out. Several clever philosophers have tried to show how to eliminate the deviant causal chains between triggers and manifestations, but it looks increasingly as if the concepts of substance, cause, and event are inadequate to account for the exercise of a disposition. Be that as it may, while the debate about dispositions is contentious, it is acknowledged on all sides that in every case where the manifestation of a disposition involves a process running from a stimulus to a response, the stimulus can cause the response *without the disposition being manifested*, since the relation between a disposition and its manifestation is process-specific, whereas the causal relation between events is process-unspecific.

This is all that concerns us for present purposes, because it shows that the point on which Anscombe and Davidson are agreed, namely, that philosophers who insist that desires are causal factors 'can do no more than postulate a "right" causal connexion' between a desire and an act, is simply a corollary of this larger claim about disposition and powers in general. Hence, it has nothing specifically to do with normativity or teleology, and it has no tendency to show that when a desire explains an act, it does not do so as a causal factor. So there is no need to show how to eliminate the deviant causal chains between desires and acts in order to defend the claim that explanations of intentional action are causal explanations, as long as we do not insist that the exercise of a disposition is reducible to a specific kind of sequence or concatenation of events.[49]

5.6 Aims and intentions

I conclude that Davidson's view that desires are causal factors is not cast into doubt by the impossibility of eliminating the 'deviant' causal chains, but the price of showing this is a much more radical departure from the Humean theory of causation than Davidson was prepared to contemplate. But if we leave the topic here, we shall miss the significance—both for the topic itself and for the twentieth-century debate—of the fact that desires are manifested in goal-directed behaviour.

As we have seen, Davidson argues that desires are causal factors by
pointing out that while it is true that an explanation such as 'James went
to church because he wanted to please his mother' attributes a justification
to the agent, it must do more than this, because it is possible to see a certain
kind of value in doing something without doing it for that reason.[50] How,
Davidson asks, can we turn the italicized 'and' into a 'because' in 'James
went to church *and* wanted to please his mother (and knew or believed that
going to church would please her)'?

The answer he favours is that 'James went to church because he wanted
to please his mother' explains why James went to church causally. But he
does not claim to have *proved* this. His argument is in effect a challenge:

> One way we can explain an event is by placing it in the context of its cause;
> cause and effect form the sort of pattern that explains the effect, in a sense of
> 'explain' that we understand as well as any. If reason and action illustrate a
> different pattern of explanation, that pattern must be identified.
>
> Hampshire rejects Aristotle's [conception] of wanting as a causal factor
> [. . .] But I would urge that, failing a satisfactory alternative, the best argument
> for a scheme like Aristotle's is that it alone promises to give an account of the
> 'mysterious connection' between reasons and actions.[51]

I agree that wants *are* causal factors and that 'James went to church because
he wanted to please his mother' is a causal explanation, but we should not
find it surprising that Davidson's challenge failed to convince his opponents,
not only because his solution faces the problem of deviant causal chains, but
also because there are other patterns of explanation that apply to intentional
action apart from cause-and-effect, in particular, act-and-aim.

An agent's *aim* in doing an intentional act is, by definition, the content
of the desire manifested by the act, in other words, the content of the
desire because of which she does it. For example, Judas's aim in kissing
Jesus was to betray him if, and only if, he kissed him because of his desire
to betray him. (Remember: desire includes the whole gamut of wanting or
valuing, as well as what we would normally call 'desire'.) If one begins an
act because one wants to ϕ and continues it because one wants to ψ, then
one's aim in doing it changes; and if one does an act both because one
wants to ϕ and because one wants to ψ, or partly because one wants to ϕ
and partly because one wants to ψ, one's aim is compounded or divided in
the same way.

As for *intentions*, philosophers tend to conceive of them as attitudes, rather
than contents of attitudes, but both conceptions are equally legitimate. Like

other names of speech acts or mental states, such as 'desire', 'belief', and 'assertion', we use 'intention' to refer both to a case of someone's intending something and to what someone intends. For example, 'Judas's intention in kissing Jesus was to betray him', like 'Tom's belief is that the minister will resign', refers to a content; whereas 'Judas stated (revealed, abandoned) his intention to betray Jesus', like 'Tom stated (ditto) his belief that the minister will resign', refers to an attitude.

Now, when we refer to someone's *intention in doing something*—e.g. Judas's intention in kissing Jesus or James's intention in going to church—we are referring to a content, again, the content of the desire manifested by the act. There is no distinction between an agent's aim in doing something and his intention in doing it. Hence,

(1) James went to church because he wanted to please his mother

as this would normally be meant and understood, and

(2) James's aim (intention) in going to church was to please his mother

contain precisely the same information, so if wants are causal factors, (2) contains non-redundant causal information about James's going to church, and there is a perfectly good sense in which it is a causal explanation. However, the content of an attitude is an intensional object, an object of thought, and therefore *not* a causal factor; and the pattern that ostensibly explains James's churchgoing in (2) is not cause-and-effect but act-and-aim. So a philosopher like Anscombe, who doubts whether wants are causal factors, will not find it difficult to explain the difference between 'and' and 'because' without conceding that they are. She will simply point out that if James's *aim* or *intention* in going to church was to please his mother, it follows that he went to church because he wanted to please her—*because*, not merely *and*.[52]

So the act-and-aim scheme is quite capable of explaining the 'mysterious connection' between reasons and actions, and Davidson's challenge can be met. Anscombe's dismissive comment about Davidson quoted above—'the solution lacks acumen', etc.—seems to pursue this line of thought:

> True, not only must I have a reason, it must also 'operate as my reason': that is, what I do must be done *in pursuit* of that end and *on grounds* of the belief.[53]

Her point seems to be that '*in pursuit* of that end and *on grounds* of the belief' explains the difference between the *and* case and the *because* case perfectly well without mentioning causation.

That is why I said we should not find it surprising that Davidson's challenge failed to convince his opponents. But Anscombe's exclusive attachment to the act-and-aim scheme does not seem any more astute than Davidson's to the cause-and-effect scheme. In effect, they agree that (1) and (2) contain the same information, but he prefers to explain (2) in terms of (1), and therefore claims that both explanations rely on the cause-and-effect scheme applied in (1), whereas she prefers to explain (1) in terms of (2), and therefore believes that both explanations rely on the act-and-aim scheme employed in (2).[54] But if a desire is a disposition to pursue an aim, and an aim is the content of a desire, then both explanations apply both schemes.[55]

On the one hand, (1) explains an act by identifying the desire because of which the agent did it. So if a desire is a disposition, and a disposition is a causal factor, and an explanation that identifies a causal factor applies the cause-and-effect scheme, then (1) applies the cause-and-effect scheme. But a disposition is defined by its manifestation, and a desire is manifested in the pursuit of an aim. So unlike explanations that mention simple physical dispositions such as solubility and fragility, (1) implicitly applies the act-and-aim scheme as well.

On the other hand, (2) evidently applies the act-and-aim scheme, because it explains an act by identifying the agent's aim in doing it. But if the agent's aim in doing an act is the content of the desire because of which he does it, then (2) implicitly applies the cause-and-effect scheme as well.

In sum, an explanation of an intentional act that refers to the desire the act expressed or to the intention with which it was done is both causal and teleological. It is causal because it refers to a disposition, and it is teleological because the kind of disposition it refers to is a disposition to pursue an aim, in other words, a disposition that is manifested in goal-directed behaviour.[*]

Let me add a final comment about the act-and-aim scheme and the cause-and-effect scheme. Ginet defends a way of explaining the 'mysterious connection' between reasons and actions without conceding that wants are causal factors, in which the explanatory scheme they are supposed to illustrate involves intentions considered as attitudes, rather than as aims.[56] He argues that the 'and' can be turned into a 'because' in 'James went to church *and* he wanted to please his mother' by adding the following

---

[*] Although desire can also be expressed in behaviour that is not goal-directed, e.g. crying with frustration (see 5.2).

condition, which mentions a *de re* intention concurrent with the action it explains:

(I) When James went to church, he intended the act to please his mother.

Notice that the intention Ginet postulates must be *de re*, because if James went to church *because* he wanted to please his mother, then pleasing his mother was not merely something he was conscious of aiming or intending to do when he set off for church, like getting home in time to watch the football on TV. It was the aim *at which his act was directed*, or *what he intended it to achieve*.

Ginet denies that (I) mentions a 'causal condition'. He says (i) that it 'does not entail that the accompanying intention it mentions caused the action'; and then, amplifying this, (ii) that it does not 'entail anything at all about what, if anything, caused the action'.[57] But whereas (i) is clearly true, since accompanying does not imply causing, (ii) is question-begging. For if Ginet is right in thinking that (I) implies that James went to church *because* he wanted to please his mother, then whether it entails something about what caused the action depends on whether desires are causal factors. In other words, the explanation-scheme that (I) applies explicitly is not the cause-and-effect scheme. It is a variant of the act-and-aim scheme, which differs from it in referring to an intention-attitude instead of an intention-aim. But Ginet is not entitled to assume that (I) does not implicitly apply the cause-and-effect scheme as well.

So, instead of concluding that we *can* explain an intentional act without implying anything about its causal history, Ginet should have concluded that Davidson's challenge does not prove we *cannot*. Like Davidson and Anscombe, he seems to assume that *either* explanations of intentional action apply the cause-and-effect scheme (as his 'causalists' maintain) *or* they apply the act-and-aim scheme (as his 'non-causalists' maintain), but not both.

5.7 Summary

The argument in this chapter can be summarized as follows.

Intentional action does not fit the theories of causation and causal explanation that held sway in the mid-twentieth century. Desires are not causes as the Humean theory conceives of them; our knowledge about motives and reasons—especially our own motives and reasons—is not causal knowledge as the Humean theory conceives of it; and explanations of intentional acts do not subsume them under laws. Wittgenstein and his followers were right to point these things out.

Davidson's minimal adjustment to the Humean theory of causation and Hempel's theory of causal explanation proved to be too minimal when it was faced with the problem of deviant causal chains. And his defence of the Aristotelian doctrine that desires are efficient causes was ineffective—I mean the argument about turning 'and' into 'because'—because it failed to take another Aristotelian doctrine into account, namely, that final causes play as indispensable a role in our explanations of intentional action as efficient causes.[58]

Nevertheless, Davidson's principal claims about the explanation of intentional action were right: desires are causal factors and rationalizations are causal explanations. But, as Anscombe put it in *Intention*: '[T]his sort of causality [...] is so far from accommodating itself to Hume's explanations that people who believe that Hume pretty well dealt with the topic of causality would entirely leave it out of their calculations.'[59]

Finally, we do not have to choose between the view that explanations of intentional action refer to final causes and the view that they refer to efficient causes. For if desires are dispositions that are manifested in goal-directed behaviour, explanations that identify the desires our acts are intended to satisfy will inevitably do both.

6

Reason and Knowledge

6.1 Reasons, justifications, and explanations

If we survey the literature from the last fifty years there appears to be a wide divergence of opinion about what reasons are. For instance, Davidson says that reasons consist of mental states or dispositions, in particular, beliefs and desires; von Wright says that a request can be a reason; Kenny and Audi both say that goals are reasons; Dancy says that grounds (whether true or false) are reasons; and Raz says that a reason is a fact.[1] These are all opinions about reasons of a specific kind, namely, a person's own reasons for doing an intentional act. But before attempting to assess them, we should remind ourselves about the intellectual functions of reasons in general, in other words, what we use them to do.

There may be a divergence of opinion about what reasons are, but there is broad agreement that we use reasons to do two closely related things, namely, to justify and to explain. The sense of 'justify' in play here is the OED's broad sense 6: 'to furnish adequate grounds for, warrant.' It is not the narrower sense 3: 'to prove or maintain the righteousness or innocence of; to vindicate (from a charge).'

These two things, justifying and explaining, are closely related. On the one hand, to justify doing, believing, or feeling something—e.g. reducing the sauce, believing it will snow, or feeling angry—is to explain why it is just or right to do it, believe it, or feel it. (Not necessarily morally right, as these examples show; and not necessarily obligatory or required.) And on the other hand, in some cases, if one explains why something is the case—e.g. why the price of oil will fall—one also justifies believing that it is the case; and in some cases, if one explains why someone does, believes, or feels something, one also justifies their doing, believing, or feeling it. For example, one

might explain that someone feels angry because a legitimate goal was disallowed. But one can also explain why something is the case *without* justifying
the belief, since what one is explaining is a datum rather than a prediction—
e.g. why the price of oil has fallen—and one can explain why someone did,
believed, or felt something *without* offering a justification, either because it is
not the sort of thing that can be just or right, such as when one explains why
Keats contracted tuberculosis, or because it is evidently unjust or wrong,
such as when one explains why Stalin believed that Molotov was a spy or
why Dr Crippen killed his wife.

It therefore seems plausible that the basic function of a reason is to
explain something—in other words, to make something intelligible or
understood—and more particularly to explain why something is the case.
That is why there are reasons why but no reasons how, what, which, when,
where, or who. But the idea of something's being the case does not involve
a contrast between facts and values, or the past and the future, or necessary
and contingent, or probable, possible, and actual, or any other curtailment
of the kind of fact or truth we use reasons to explain. I am not contrasting
the idea that something *is* the case with the idea that it *ought to be* or *was* or
will be or *must be* or *can be* or *is probably* the case. For example, if the price of
oil has fallen, and James will go to church, and Lucy must or can or will
probably or ought to get home before dark, then each of these things is the
case, and the reason or reasons for its being the case explain why. Nor am
I downplaying the importance of justification in the use of reasons. The
relationship between explanation and justification is not major versus minor
or original versus derivative; it is simply general versus particular.

Now it may seem as if the justificatory use of reasons is the primary one
where a person's own reasons for doing an intentional act is concerned,
because when we explain a person's conduct by giving his own reasons for
it, we explain it in terms of his own assessment of what he would be justified
in doing, and why.[2] So, one might think, his own reasons for his conduct
explain it *because* they justify it, or seem to justify it, at least to him; and so
explaining is not the primary function of a reason that explains an intentional act in this way. But this would be a mistake.

Consider the statement

(1) James went to church because it would please his mother.

It is true that (1)—as it would normally be meant and understood—implies
that the *explanans* is part of James's own assessment of what he would be

justified in doing, and why. In other words, (1) implies that James thought that the fact that it would please his mother justified his going to church, or at least would justify it in the absence of countervailing reasons—that it 'spoke in favour' of his going to church, as we might say. But it does not follow that the explanatory use of reasons is not the primary one, because a justification *is* an explanation, and so a potential justification is a potential explanation, a potential explanation of why something is just or right.[3]

Since explanations like (1) are normally meant to give an agent's own reasons for his behaviour, they complicate the relationship between justification and explanation. Basically, they illustrate the fact that since an agent's assessment of what he would be justified in doing influences his behaviour, we refer to the assessment when we explain the behaviour. So far, this is perfectly straightforward. If the temperature of a gas affects its behaviour, we refer to its temperature when we explain the behaviour of the gas. The complication arises from two facts. First, while explanations like (1) are not necessarily intended to justify the conduct they explain, they attribute a potential justification to the agent. Second, they include explanations of our *own* conduct, so *these* explanations attribute potential justifications *to ourselves*.

It does not follow that we always mean to justify our own conduct when we explain it in this way, but we often do, especially when the behaviour is in the recent past or the present or the future. This also applies to explanations which give our reasons for feelings or beliefs. For example, 'I shall vote Tory because the Tories have pledged to cut taxes', 'I feel proud to be a Tory because...', and 'I believe the Tories will win because...' would all normally have this dual function. They would normally explain why I intend to do something, or why I feel something or believe something, by attributing a justification for doing, feeling, or believing it to me; and at the same time they would *also* normally purport to justify doing, feeling, or believing the thing in question.

Evidently, the relationship between justification and explanation can be complex, especially when the one doing the explaining or justifying is also the one whose thought or conduct is being justified or explained. But even in these cases, the primary function of a reason is, as it always is, to explain why something is the case.[*]

---

[*] Raz objects to an attempt to '[explain] reasons independently of value' that it cannot 'preserve the normativity of reasons', 'account for the fact that defying reasons is irrational', or explain

We can support this conclusion about what we do *with* reasons by considering what we do *to* them. We do not cook them, chew them, or swallow them. In fact the range of things we do to them is quite small. Like explanations, we find (discover, identify) them or find them out, state (render, give, offer, supply, or provide) them, consider (assess, weigh, or compare) them, accept (endorse) and reject (challenge, dispute) them. No doubt this list can be extended, but not in ways that would cast doubt on the idea that reasons are explanations. But the fact that it includes assessing and weighing reasons reminds us that justification is an important kind of explanation, because it implies that reasons can be good (strong, convincing, conclusive, or decisive) or bad (weak, unconvincing, inconclusive, or indecisive). Of course, explanations in general can be good or bad, but it is arguments or justifications in particular that can be conclusive or decisive or the opposite, because we rely on them when we conclude or decide that this or that is the just or right thing to do or feel or believe, in view of our other beliefs, and our aims and values; and when we take a practical step—in other words, act *for* a reason—as a result.

A reason, then, explains why something is the case, but we need to be aware of the complexity that our talk about explanation involves. There are four points to note.

First, to explain something to someone is to make it clear to them, to make them understand it. But what makes something clear to one person may not make it clear to another. Hence, when we use the verb 'explain' with a *to*-complement, as in 'Justin explained to the children why the kitten had died', we imply that the explanation took into consideration, or at any rate did not exceed, the knowledge and the powers of comprehension of the audience for whom it was intended. (The same applies to the verb 'prove'.) By contrast, when we use the verb without the complement, the explanation is no longer explicitly related to a specific audience, but explanations still vary greatly in how explicit and precise they are, and in the knowledge and intellectual maturity or sophistication required to understand them. Every explanation qualifies as such relative to a standard, which is generally set by the presumed knowledge and intellectual ability of the intended audience.

why 'one may disregard a reason only to follow a more stringent one' (Raz, *Engaging Reason*, p. 28). These remarks support the view that the idea of a *justification* cannot be explained 'independently of value', but they do not count against the view that reasons in general are explanations, and that a justification is a particular kind of explanation, namely, an explanation of why something is just or right.

Second, we can use the word 'explanation'—like the words 'statement', 'question', 'answer', 'announcement', etc.—to refer either to a communicative act (an act of asking or saying something), or to what the act communicates (what is asked or said). So we can describe an explanation as patient or evasive, or alternatively as true or false; but it is the act of saying something, or the person who says it, that may be patient or evasive, whereas it is what the person says that may be true or false. A communicative act is not the right sort of thing to be true or false. No behaviour is. If it were, it would also be the right sort of thing to be proved, disproved, or contradicted. Since reasons can be stated (rendered, given, offered, etc.) they can only be explanations in the sense of things said or communicated, not in the sense of the saying or communicating of these things.

Third, the use of 'explanation' has a further kink, because we can call the whole of what is communicated an explanation, or just part of it. For example, if someone explains that the price of oil will fall because growth in China will slow down, what he says as a whole is an explanation; but we also distinguish between the *explanandum* (i.e. what is explained) and the *explanans* (i.e. what explains it), and use the word 'explanation' to refer to the latter part alone.[4] If we describe one fact as explaining, or being the explanation of another, this is the way in which we are using the word. Thus, in the example just mentioned, the presumed fact that the price of oil will fall is presented as an *explanandum* and the presumed fact that growth in China will slow down is presented as an *explanans*. A reason—for example, the reason why the price of oil will fall—is evidently an explanation in the sense of an *explanans*.

Finally, if a picnic was cancelled because the weather was bad, the *explanans* is the fact that the weather was bad and the *explanandum* is the fact that the picnic was cancelled. So the fact that the weather was bad is the reason why the picnic was cancelled. But it would be quite normal to say that the weather, or the bad weather, explains why, or is the reason why, the picnic was cancelled, although the weather is not itself the *explanans*. It is what the *explanans* is a fact about. It may be surprising to find that we use the word 'reason' to describe such different things as facts and fog. But it is no stranger than the fact that we use the word 'explanation' to describe both sayings and things said. In any case, as Strawson points out, there are distinctions we need to draw in order to understand philosophically our non-philosophical thought and talk that we do not need to draw in our non-philosophical thought and talk itself.

Now one such distinction (Strawson explains) is between the natural relation of causality, 'which holds in the natural world between particular events or circumstances', just as spatial and temporal relations do, and the 'intellectual or rational or intensional relation' which holds between two facts or truths, when one explains the other.[5] The relata now are not events or circumstances in the natural world, but 'obstinately intensional objects, not assignable to a place in nature'. It is true that we sometimes speak as if facts have a location in space and time, as when we ask where a certain fact can be found, or when a certain fact emerged, but what these idioms really show is that a fact can be recorded in a particular place, or be discovered at a particular time. Again, when we think of or state a fact or a truth, these mental and communicative acts *are* assignable to a place in nature, as are the things—such as fog and picnics—that the facts we think of or state are generally about. But facts themselves can only be objects of thought. (Regarding facts and truths, see 7.2.)

Our willingness to call such different things as facts and fog 'reasons' is one indication that we sometimes ignore the distinction between causing and explaining in our non-philosophical thought, and that we fail to mark it explicitly and consistently in our use of words. And there are others. We use the same kind of nominalization to refer to the terms of both relations (e.g. 'the picnic's being cancelled'), we use the same verbs and verb phrases to express both relations themselves (e.g. 'causes' and 'due to'), and we readily combine terms referring to events and facts in an explanation, without finding the result jarring. For example, if someone says that the picnic was cancelled because of bad weather, which relation should we assume he has in mind? The answer is not one or the other, or both, or even that we cannot tell. There is no point in trying to tell, because he is ignoring the distinction, and he is ignoring it because there is no need to attend to it in order to explain why the picnic was cancelled.

But if there is no need to attend to the distinction between reasons and causes for *this* purpose, it is vital to attend to it if we want to understand the various claims about reasons with which we began. For Raz's view that reasons are facts is evidently about reasons as opposed to causes—in other words, it is about the *explanans* or *reason why* itself; whereas Davidson's claim that reasons consist of mental states or dispositions, von Wright's claim that a request can be a reason, Dancy's claim that grounds are reasons, and Kenny's and Audi's claims that goals are reasons: all these are about factors that the *explanans* in an explanation of a person's conduct must or may, explicitly or implicitly, introduce.

For example, if Felicity packs her bags because she wants to leave, her desire to leave *causes* her to pack her bags—the act *manifests the desire*—but while her desire to leave is a mental state, the *reason why* she packs her bags is *the fact that she wants to leave.*

Equally, if Sybil feeds James oysters because she believes oysters are aphrodisiac, the *reason why* she feeds James oysters is *the fact that she believes this*: her believing it is a mental state, and *what* she believes—namely, *that oysters are aphrodisiac*—is the *ground on which* or *reason for which* she feeds James oysters, or her *justification* for doing so. (It is more idiomatic to speak of the ground on which someone believes something than the ground on which she does something, but the latter use of the phrase is common in philosophy and law, and I shall use it freely.)

Again, if Peter passes Paul the salt because Paul asks him to, Paul's request—by which I mean the communicative act, rather than what it communicates—*causes* Peter to pass Paul the salt. But the *reason why* Peter passes Paul the salt is neither the act nor its content—namely, *that Peter pass him the salt*—it is *the fact that Paul asks him to pass the salt.*

Finally, an agent's *goal, aim,* or *intention* in doing an act is the *content* of the desire the act manifests, for example, *to die with dignity* or *to get home before dark.* So if Lucy's goal in calling a taxi is to get home before dark, then the *reason why* she calls a taxi is *the fact that she wants to get home before dark.*

Evidently, the word 'reason' is not reserved by philosophers, any more than by others, for an *explanans* or *reason why.* It also used to refer to various explanatory factors, including both mental states, such as believing X and desiring Y, and their contents—that is, justifications or grounds and aims or intentions, respectively. Some, including the present author, have expressed their disapproval, not because they deplore laxity in the use of words as such, but because it causes confusion in this case, as we shall see. But if we want to avoid unnecessary contention, the best strategy is to be intensely relaxed about how words are used, and intensely vigilant about the different ideas they are used to express. I shall adopt the policy of calling causes 'causes', grounds and justifications 'grounds' and 'justifications', goals, aims, and intentions 'goals', 'aims', and 'intentions'. I shall sometimes refer to a ground as a 'reason for', but I shall reserve the term 'reason why' for an *explanans.* This is policy, not dogma.

6.2 Reasons, grounds, and intentions

Grounds and intentions are both contents of mental states, but they are contents of different mental states. For the *ground on which* or *reason for which* one does an act is something one believes (e.g. *that oysters are aphrodisiac*), whereas the *intention with which* one does an act is something one desires (e.g. *to get home before dark*). Hence, doing something for a reason is not the same as doing it intentionally, and many things are done for a reason that are not done intentionally, such as weeping at sad news or laughing spontaneously at a joke.

When philosophers think of desires and beliefs as explanatory factors, they tend to think of them in combination, for the good reason that explanations of action that refer explicitly to desires normally involve assumptions about beliefs, and explanations that refer explicitly to beliefs normally involve assumptions about desires. Geach mentions a nice example. We cannot explain why Dr Johnson stood bare-headed in Uttoxeter marketplace by saying that he expected rain unless it is understood that he wanted to do penance, and we cannot explain it by saying that he wanted to do penance unless it is understood that he expected rain.[6] Neither the desire to do penance nor the expectation of rain explains the deed alone. So there are good reasons for thinking about desires and beliefs as explanatory factors in combination. But it is important to remember that they are distinct, particularly if we want to understand the relationship between intentional action and action done for reasons. And it is also important to remember that this symmetry between them is balanced by an asymmetry, since a rational person's beliefs affect his desires, whereas his desires do not affect his beliefs.

Intentional action and action done for reasons are commonly equated. Indeed, both Davidson and Anscombe claim that intentional action can be defined in terms of reasons. Davidson acknowledges that we sometimes say we did an act 'for no reason', but he claims this really means that we did it for no *further* reason, no reason 'besides wanting to do it', adding that this 'defends the possibility of defining an intentional action as one done for a reason'.[7] Anscombe is more circumspect. She allows that in some cases the statement that one did an intentional act for no reason may be literally true. But she still claims that intentional action can be defined in terms of reasons:

What distinguishes actions which are intentional from those which are not? The answer that I shall suggest is that they are the actions to which a certain sense of the question 'Why?' is given application; the sense is of course that in which the answer, if positive, gives a reason for acting.[8]

She does not say straight out here that she is defining intentional action, but she makes it clear in §47 that this is what she has in mind:

> the term 'intentional' has reference to a form of description of events. What is essential to this form is displayed by the results of our enquiries into the question 'Why?' . . . I have defined intentional action in terms of language— the special question 'Why?'.

What does the claim that intentional actions 'are the actions to which a certain sense of the question "Why?" is given application' mean? It does not mean that every intentional act *is* done for a reason, only that every intentional act is *either* done for a reason *or* done for no reason. But, Anscombe explains, one does not reject the question 'Why?' by answering 'No reason', as one would reject it if one said, 'I wasn't aware of doing it.' So intentional acts can, she believes, be defined as acts to which the question 'Why?' properly applies. She compares saying one did an intentional act for no reason to answering the question 'How many coins do you have in your pocket?' by saying 'None'.[9] The idea is that the question 'How many coins do you have in your pocket?' is refused application if one does not have a pocket, but not if one has an empty pocket.

Davidson's and Anscombe's views about the relationship between intentional action and reasons are unsatisfactory for three reasons. First, regarding Anscombe's proposal, the comparison between 'Why?' and 'How many coins do you have in your pocket?' suggests that we are dealing with a presupposition, in other words, that 'Why?' is predicated on the assumption that one did the act intentionally in the way that 'How many coins . . . ?' is predicated on the assumption that one has a pocket. But in that case we cannot *define* an intentional act as one about which the 'Why?' question can sensibly be raised, any more than we can define a pocket in this way. It may be true that a pocket is the part of a garment of which we can sensibly ask 'How many coins do you have in it?', but if so, the reason for this is that a pocket is a small bag or pouch sewn into clothing, and one can put coins in a small bag or pouch. One cannot *define* a pocket by stating that the question 'How many coins . . . ?' can be raised about it. The fact that the question can be raised is *explained* by the definition. In the same way, it may be true that intentional acts are the ones of which we can sensibly ask 'Why?' in the relevant sense, but if so, the definition of an intentional act needs to explain why.

Second, some acts that are *not* intentional are done for reasons. For example, someone who laughs at a joke or swears because he drops a hammer on his foot may not laugh or swear intentionally. But it would be absurd to insist that he cannot be laughing or swearing for a reason, or that the 'Why?' question cannot 'be given application'. For the relevant sense is 'that in which the answer, if positive, gives a reason for acting', and 'Because it was funny' or 'Because I dropped the hammer on my foot' certainly *can* give reasons for laughing or swearing. Of course, they may be poor or insufficient reasons, say, because the joke was offensive, or children were present, or one was in a church. But equally, they may be perfectly good reasons, which fully justify laughing or swearing.

Third, we do not only *act* for reasons; we believe and feel and want for reasons too. Indeed the very fact that is someone's reason for doing an act can also be their reason for believing or feeling or wanting something. For example, the fact that the azalea died can be Margaret's reason for sacking the gardener, believing the soil is limey, feeling at the end of her tether, and wanting to get drunk. But believing, feeling, and wanting are not intentional. So even if it were true that only intentional acts are done for reasons, the involvement of a reason could not be what being intentional consists in, or how it should be defined. And the same applies to the proposal that being intentional should be defined in terms of the applicability of the 'Why?' question. For whatever the fact that we can raise the 'Why?' question about it *can* explain about an act, it can explain about things (beliefs, desires, etc.) that are not intentional as well.

For these reasons, it is a mistake to equate intentional action and action done for reasons, or to imagine that one can be defined in terms of the other. An intentional act is an act done with an intention, and the *intention with which* one does an act is the content of a desire because of which one does it. So by definition an intentional act is a manifestation of desire. Whereas the *reason for which* or *ground on which* one does an act is the content of a belief because of which one does it. So by definition an act done for a reason is a manifestation of belief. For example, if Sybil feeds James oysters with the intention of seducing him, feeding him oysters is a manifestation of her desire to seduce him; and if she feeds him oysters *for the reason*, or *on the ground*, that oysters are aphrodisiac, feeding him oysters manifests her belief that oysters are aphrodisiac. It is true that both kinds of explanation are possible in most cases of intentional action, because desires and beliefs normally explain an intentional act in combination. But the idea of a *reason for which* or *ground on which* one does an act is a particular application of an idea with a much broader scope than the idea of an *intention with which* one does an act, because reasons do not just inform our conduct, but also the elements of our mental lives—the desires, beliefs and feelings—from which it flows.

6.3 Reasons, grounds, and explanations

As we saw in 6.1, the word 'reason' can be used to refer either to an *explanans* or to an explanatory factor, whether the latter is a mental state, such as a desire or a belief, or the content of a mental state, such as an intention or a ground, and theories of explanation are likely to go wrong if the distinction between these things is not properly understood. Probably the most confusing feature of our licentious use of 'reason' is that we employ it both to refer to a *ground* or *reason for* and to refer to an *explanans* or *reason why*. In this section, I shall explain the idea of a ground and the distinction between an *explanans* and a ground in more detail (in (A) and (B)), and discuss a view about the explanation of intentional action which has attracted support because they are confused (in (C)).

(A) If one does an act because one believes that *p*, the ground on which one does it is that *p*. (I shall return to this rule, and discuss an exception to it, in (B).) What about the reverse? If the ground on which one does an act is that *p*, does it follow that one believes that *p*? It is commonly assumed that it does follow, but what is wrong with the view that we can act on grounds we do not believe, just as we reason from premises we do not believe when we argue by *reductio*? For example, suppose a meeting clashes with a game Charles wants to watch on TV, and he pretends there is a lecture on the Stoic theory of happiness that he cannot afford to miss. Grace may choose to accept his excuse and reschedule the meeting, even if she knows full well that he is planning to watch the game. ('Accept' here does not imply the slightest degree of credence: it simply means that she proceeds on the assumption that it is true, for instance, to avoid a confrontation.) Is this not a case of acting on a ground one does not believe?

The answer is that we can if we wish call a premise someone accepts and acts on her ground, regardless of whether she believes it, and say that the ground on which Grace rescheduled the meeting was that Charles had to the attend the lecture. Alternatively, we can define a ground as the content of a belief because of which someone does (believes, feels, etc.) something, thereby retaining the principle that believing that *p* is a necessary condition for acting on the ground that *p*, and say that the ground on which Grace rescheduled the meeting was that it was better to accept Charles's excuse, so as to avoid a confrontation. I am not aware of a decisive reason to prefer one option or the other. But the second is generally preferred by philosophers, and I shall follow that convention here, noting only that it is exactly that, a convention.

(B) It is worth underlining the fact that if someone does an act because she believes that *p*, the ground on which she does it is not normally that she believes that *p*, but that *p*. Compare

(1) James went to church because it would please his mother

and

(2) James went to church because he believed it would please his mother.

In both cases, the explanation cannot be true unless the *explanans* is a fact: (1) cannot be true unless James's going to church would in fact please his mother, and (2) cannot be true unless James did in fact believe that it would please his mother. But whereas the *explanantia* are different, the ground (1) and (2) attribute to James—the thought, whether true or false, which they imply seemed to James to speak in favour of going to church— is the same. In both cases, it is the thought *that going to church would please his mother*. This is obvious in the case of (1). But it is also true in the case of (2). The *explanans* in (2) is the fact, or supposed fact, that James *believed* his going to church would please his mother, but the ground (2) attributes to James is *what* he is said to have believed, and not the fact that he believed it.

Thus, explanations like (2) split the agent's ground from the explanation of his behaviour. The utility of being able to do this should be obvious. Since explaining is a relation between facts or truths, the *explanans* in an explanation of someone's behaviour must be a fact or truth, but the *ground* on which he acted may be false. (2) allows for this possibility by prescinding from the implication carried by (1) that James's going to church *would* please his mother, while attributing the same ground or justification for going to church to James himself.

We can confirm that this is how (2) works by comparing a case where the explanation of a person's conduct looks superficially like (2), but the justification attributed to the agent is *not* what he is said to have believed, and *is* the fact, or supposed fact, that he believed it. For example, suppose Roger believes he is being pursued by MI5. There are various things he could do, such as fly to Brazil, or destroy his hard drive, or complain to his MP. But suppose instead that he sees his doctor. If we explain that Roger saw his doctor because he believed he was being pursued by MI5, we are probably envisaging a different justification from the one we would be envisaging if we said that this was why he destroyed his hard drive. One way to describe the difference is to say that it was not *what* Roger believed that informed his decision to see his doctor, but the fact that he believed it. In other words, Roger's justification for seeing his doctor was not that he was being pursued by MI5, but that he *believed* he was. Again, suppose Ruth reasons as follows: 'People who believe that property is theft should stand up and be counted; I believe that property is theft; so I should stand up and be counted.' And so she stands up, and is counted. The fact that she believes that property is theft is part of her justification, but the fact, or supposed fact, that property is theft is not.

Now, returning to (2),

(2) James went to church because he believed it would please his mother,

it should be clear that the justification it attributes to James is not like Roger's justification for seeing his doctor or Ruth's justification for standing up. It is *what* (2) says James believed, namely, that going to church would please his mother, and not the fact, or supposed fact, that he believed it. So if we imagine James reasoning *sotto voce*, (2) tells us we should imagine him saying, 'It will please Mother; so I shall go to church.' The premise is his justification, and it is about his mother rather than himself. So, as I said earlier, the *explanans* in (2) is the fact, or supposed fact, that James *believed* his going to church would please his mother, but the *ground* (2) attributes to James is *what* he is said to have believed.

Similarly, the ground that

(3) James went to church because he wanted to please his mother

attributes to James is again that his going to church would please his mother, and not that he *wanted* to please his mother. The ground on which a man blinds himself or sees an analyst may be that he wants to sleep with his mother, but if (3) is true, the ground on which James went to church is not that he wanted to please his mother, although the fact that he wanted to please her does explain why he did so.

Our lax use of the term 'reason' can make us lose sight of the fact that if someone does an act because he believes that p, the ground on which he does it is not that he believes that p, but that p. But if we bear in mind that 'His reason for doing it' can mean *either* the *ground on which* he did it or the *reason why* he did it, it should be possible to avoid confusion.

(C) The confusion between a ground and an *explanans* accounts for a claim Dancy defends in several publications, that when we give a true explanation of an intentional act by stating the agent's reasons for doing it, the *explanans* need not be a fact. He writes as follows:

> The explanations we give when we specify the agent's reasons for acting [. . .] are unusual in being non-factive. What this means is that for the explanation to be correct as an explanation, it is not required that what is offered as *explanans* in fact be the case. [. . .] A perfectly correct explanation of an act might be:
>   His reason for doing it was that it would increase his pension.
> But such an explanation cannot be factive, in the sense given above, since it can perfectly well be expanded thus:
>   His reason for doing it was that it would increase his pension, but he was sadly mistaken about that.[10]

Dancy acknowledges that we may prefer to use what he calls a 'factive turn of phrase' such as 'He did it *because* it would increase his pension'. But 'the difference between the factive and the non-factive [turns of phrase] cannot be of any real significance', because either way we explain the act by 'laying out the considerations in the light of which the agent acted', and these considerations do not need to be true:

> We can phrase our explanation as we like, and that is the end of the matter. [. . .] a thing believed that is not the case can still explain an action.[11]

What exactly is factivity? The term 'factive', in the relevant sense, was originally applied to verbs whose object in a true sentence must state a true proposition or a fact. Fac*tive* verbs are therefore a sub-class of fac*tual* verbs, verbs that take finite clauses as direct objects—such as 'admit', 'agree', and 'say'—most of which refer to a kind of speech act or a kind of knowledge or belief. For example, 'know' and 'believe' are both factual verbs, but 'know' is factive, since what is known must be a fact, whereas 'believe' is not factive, since what is believed may be either true or false. But philosophers have also described the mental state of knowing as factive, and believing as non-factive. Dancy claims that some explanations are factive while others are not, and that the concept of knowledge is factive, but he also mentions a 'factive turn of phrase' and 'the factive pressure of the word "because"'.[12] This is problematic in two ways.

First, it is true that the belief that doing X will increase one's pension can be mistaken; but the belief that two is the square root of four cannot. Does this mean that the verb 'believe' (or believing) is factive in some cases and not in others? We could choose to say this, but it would be an unnecessary departure from the conventional idea of factivity, so it is better to say that 'believe' is not factive because what someone believes may be either true or false. Similarly, we *could* ask whether 'explains why' and 'is the reason why' are non-factive in some cases (or whether some explanations are non-factive), but it is better to ask whether they are factive or non-factive *tout court*, and to say that they *are* factive if and only if the *explanans* and the *explanandum* in a true explanation must both be facts.

Second, verbs, mental states, turns of phrase, explanations, concepts, and connectives form a bewilderingly heterogeneous group. Let us say that a sentence-forming operator O on one or more sentences or *that*-clauses, (that) $s_1 \ldots$ (that) s_n, is factive if and only if the statement 'O(that) $s_1 \ldots$ (that) s_n' cannot be true unless the statements 's_1' $\ldots$ 's_n' are true. Accordingly, 'explains why' is factive if and only if 'that s_1 explains why s_n' cannot be true unless 's_1' and 's_n' are both true; 'His reason for doing it was' is factive if and only if 'His reason for doing it was that s' cannot be true unless 's' is true; and so on.

If we define factivity in this way, 'explains why' is certainly factive. For if a's being F explains why b is G, b is G because a is F; if a's being F explains why b is not G, b is not G because a is F; if a's not being F explains why b is G, b is G because a is not F; and if a's not being F explains why b is not G, b is not G because a is not F.[13] But 'because' must be factive, for if 's_1 because s_2' is true, then 's_1' and 's_2' must also be true. So 'explains why' must be factive too.

But *why* is 'explains why' factive? Dancy says, 'knowledge is factive, because "He knows that it is raining but it isn't" is uninterpretable', but this gets things the wrong way round. On the contrary, 'He knows that it is raining but it isn't' is uninterpretable—or at any rate cannot be true—

because 'He knows that' is factive; 'He knows that' is factive because one cannot know (whereas one can believe) that something is the case if it is not the case; and one cannot know that something is the case if it is not the case because knowing (unlike believing) that something is the case is a relation between knowers and facts or truths.

Similarly, 'explains why' is factive because nothing can explain why something *is* the case if it is *not* the case, and if something *is* the case, a fiction or falsehood cannot explain why; and the reason for *this* is that explaining why something is the case is a relation between one fact or truth and another—the relation of making intelligible or understood. For example, neither the fact that growth in China will slow down nor any other fact can explain why the price of oil will fall if in fact it will *not* fall. And if the price of oil *will* fall, but growth in China will not in fact slow down, then that growth in China *will* slow down cannot explain why the price of oil will fall, although of course it can seem to, if it seems to be a fact.

Is 'His reason for doing it was' factive? Dancy says that 'His reason for doing it was . . . , but he was mistaken' does not sound self-contradictory to him, adding 'not everyone's ears agree with me about this'.[14] But many sentences can be interpreted in more than one way, depending on context and priming, and a sentence that is, and therefore sounds, contradictory when it is interpreted in one way may not be, or sound, contradictory when it is interpreted in another way. So if intuitions about 'His reason for doing it was' differ, we should expect to find that it can be interpreted in more than one way.

And of course it can. For as we have seen, the word 'reason' is not used exclusively to mean an *explanans*. It is also used to mean an explanatory factor, including a *ground*. Thus, if 'His reason for doing it was that it would increase his pension' is meant to imply that this—i.e. *that it would increase his pension*—explains why or is the reason why he did it, then 'His reason for doing it was' *is* factive, whereas if it is only meant to imply that this was the ground on which he did it, then it is *not* factive, because an *explanans* must be a fact, whereas a ground may be either true or false. Evidently, Dancy interprets it in the second way. He writes:

> I suggest that locutions such as
>> His reason for doing it was that it would increase his pension
>> The ground on which he acted was that she had lied to him
> are not factive

using 'his reason for doing it' and 'the ground on which he acted' as synonyms, and of course he is perfectly entitled to do this. His mistake is to confuse a ground and an *explanans*, and the comment, 'We can phrase our explanation as we like [...] a thing believed that is not the case can still explain an action', is a result of this confusion. For example, if Marcus married, but marrying was never going to increase his pension, what explains Marcus's marrying is not the thing he believed, namely, *that marrying would increase his pension*. Stating his ground—the thing believed—is a way of explaining why he did it, and his ground need not be true. But when we explain an act in this way, the *explanans* is not the ground, the thing believed, but the fact, or supposed fact, that he believed it.

This kind of mistake is easy to make when statements are studied out of context. But when we are actually explaining conduct, instead of explaining how conduct is explained, we generally make it clear how 'His reason for doing it was...' should be understood.

6.4 Reasons, grounds, and knowledge

In the remainder of this chapter, I shall focus on a simple kind of explanation of intentional action, exemplified by

(1) James went to church because it would please his mother.

I shall argue that explanations of this kind, as they would normally be meant and understood, attribute knowledge of the *explanans* to the agent and not merely belief. This argument will lay a foundation for the final chapters of the book, in which I shall defend the idea that knowledge is the ability to be guided by facts, and then show how this conception of knowledge provides a new solution to the problem posed by Plato in the *Meno* about whether knowledge is a better guide to acting the right way than true belief.

There are various kinds of *because*-explanations of intentional acts. In what I shall call the standard case, *the explanatory clause as a whole also expresses, or purports to express, the ground on which the agent did the act.*[*] (1) is

---

[*] If a fact is a true proposition, the standard case is one in which the explanation as a whole implies that the *explanans* is the agent's ground; whereas if (as argued in 7.2) a fact is the truth of a proposition, it is one in which the explanation as a whole implies that the *explanans* is the truth of the agent's ground. The formulation in the main text is designed to avoid relying on either view about the relationship between facts and propositions at this stage.

an example. For it implies *both* that the fact that it would please his mother explains why James went to church, *and* that the ground on which he went to church was that it would please his mother. Hence, it also implies that the ground on which James went to church was true, regardless of whether it was a reason, or a good reason, to go to church.

Compare (1) with

(1)

(2) James went to church because he believed it would please his mother

(3) James went to church because he wanted to please his mother

and

(4) James went to church because he knew it would please his mother.

Like (1), they identify the ground on which James went to church: (2) and (4) do so explicitly, since they contain the finite clause 'it would please his mother', whereas (3) also does so, but implicitly, since it contains instead the non-finite clause 'to please his mother'. But by contrast with (1), the ground is not expressed by the explanatory clause *as a whole* in (2), (3), or (4). (2) and (3) are therefore consistent with James's being mistaken about whether his going to church would please his mother, and although (4) implies that he was *not* mistaken, in this case the implication is due to the factivity of 'he knew' rather than the factivity of 'because'.

As I mentioned in 5.1, there are also *because*-explanations of intentional action that do not even identify a ground implicitly, or suggest that the agent had one, such as

(5) Sally bit a policeman because she was drunk

and

(6) Sally bit a policeman because she had had too much to drink.

In *this* kind of explanation, the *explanans* refers to the agent's state of mind, or a factor that affected it.

My topic now is standard *because*-explanations, such as (1), as it would normally be meant and understood, where the explanatory clause as a whole expresses or purports to express the agent's ground. But I am not exclusively interested in action. Belief, desire, and feeling are just as much in the frame. Unlike (1), standard explanations of *these* phenomena are not even implicitly teleological, for we do not normally explain why someone *believes* X, or *wants* Y, or *feels* Z, by saying what her *aim* in believing or wanting or feeling these things is, or what *goal* her belief, desire, or feeling was meant to achieve. But that only goes to show that we should not associate grounds too closely with aims (as we saw in 6.2), and the question I shall pursue now applies in the same way to every *because-explanation* in which the explanatory clause as a whole expresses the agent's ground.

The question is what these explanations imply about the subject's cognitive state, about what she knows or believes. In particular, do they imply that the subject knows the *explanans*? For example, does (1) imply that James *knew* that his going to church would please his mother? Or does it only imply that he *believed* this? Or does it imply neither of these things?

Consider first the idea that it implies neither knowledge nor belief. There is nothing to prevent us from setting aside the principle that a ground must be something the agent believes, and calling a premise on which he decides to act his ground, whether or not he believes it to be true. For example, in the case described in 6.3, where a meeting clashes with a game, we can choose to say, if we wish, that the ground on which Grace rescheduled the meeting was *that Charles had to attend a lecture*. But we do not have the same freedom of manoeuvre with standard *because-explanations*, because of the factivity of 'because'. For example, if someone explained that Grace rescheduled the meeting *because Charles had to attend a lecture*, but added the disclaimer 'mind you, she knew full well that he was planning to watch the game', this would have the effect of putting the original explanation in scare-quotes; in other words, it would signal that it had been meant ironically, as if to add the qualification 'or so she said'.

So we are left with the belief view and the knowledge view.

The belief view will seem plausible if we assume that a standard *because-explanation* simply adds 'the factive pressure of the word "because"' to a statement of the agent's ground. On this assumption,

(1) James went to church because it would please his mother

implies that James *believed* going to church would please his mother, because it implies that this is the ground on which he went to church, and it implies that James's going to church *would* please his mother, because the *explanans* in a true explanation must be a fact. But it does not imply that James *knew* that it would please his mother. And the same applies to standard *because*-explanations of beliefs and feelings. On the same assumption, 'Sebastian believes that he will be cured because the doctor said so' implies that Sebastian believes truly that the doctor said he would be cured; and 'Eleanor felt angry because a goal was disallowed' implies that Eleanor believed truly that a goal was disallowed. But again, these explanations merely add the factive pressure of the word 'because' to the identification of a ground: they do not attribute knowledge of the *explanans* to Sebastian and Eleanor, only true belief.

The knowledge view was first explicitly defended by Unger.[15] But Prichard expressed it in passing in 1932, apparently without thinking that it needed to be defended:

> [According to a certain view about duties] we can never, strictly speaking, do a duty, if we have one, because it is a duty, i.e. really in consequence of knowing it to be a duty [. . .] At best, if we have a duty, we may do it because we think without question, or else believe, or again think it possible that the act is a duty.[16]

The 'i.e.' signals the idea: one cannot do something *because* it is a duty unless one *knows* it is a duty, since doing something because it is a duty and doing it 'really in consequence of knowing' that it is a duty are one and the same thing.

I shall argue that the interpretation of standard *because*-explanations associated with the belief view is mistaken, and that the knowledge view is right: *a 'standard' because-explanation of action, thought or feeling, i.e. one in which the explanatory clause expresses or purports to express the agent's ground, implies that the agent knows the explanans.*

Consider the following examples:

(A) Suppose Jim made some truffles in the belief that Anna loves them, but he did not *know* that Anna loves truffles. (Perhaps he had overheard Anna's sister saying how much 'Anna' loves truffles without realizing that this was another Anna.) The *ground* on which Jim made truffles is evidently *that Anna (i.e. his Anna) loves them*. We can imagine him muttering *sotto voce* 'Anna loves truffles; so I shall make some'. But if in fact she does not love truffles, the *reason why* he made them cannot be *that Anna loves them*, because an *explanans* or *reason why* must be true. So in this case, he did not make truffles *because* Anna loves them. (This is common ground between all three views.)

Presumably, he made truffles because he *believed* Anna loves them. But if that is the reason, if his belief was false, then it is also the reason if it happened to be true. For comparison: if Meno took the left fork because a malevolent passer-by who wanted to lead him astray told him that that was the road to Larissa, then this remains the reason even if the passer-by was confused and gave Meno the right directions by mistake. The reason does not become the fact that the left fork *was* the road to Larissa, although we can register the fact that the directions were right by saying that Meno took the left fork because someone told him that that was the road to Larissa, *which happened to be true*. In the same way, we can register whether Jim's belief that Anna loves truffles was true or false by saying that he made truffles because he believed *truly* that Anna loves them or because he believed *falsely* that Anna loves them, but not by referring to his belief in the *explanans* if it was false and referring directly to Anna's love of truffles if it happened to be true.*

We need to be careful when we pronounce on what people would say in a given situation, not least because there are different ways speakers can expect what they say to be understood. But it is fairly clear that no one who understood this story would *say* that Jim made truffles because Anna loves them, and this cannot be explained by 'the factive pressure of the word "because"', because it still holds if we assume that Jim's belief was true. Nor is this a quirk of English. Every language in which it is possible both to explain intentional conduct and to distinguish between knowledge and true belief has a way of registering that if the *ground on which* an agent does an act is X, and X happens to be true, it does not follow that the *reason why* she does it is X. I would guess this means every language that is known. Scholars used to claim that the distinction between intentional and unintentional conduct was not recognized or understood in biblical or Homeric times, but this myth was demolished years ago.[17] Similarly, Plato drew attention to the distinction between knowledge and true belief, but it was already implicit in the way people thought and spoke.

---

* Bernard Williams comments that 'the difference between false and true beliefs on the agent's part cannot alter the *form* of the explanation which will be appropriate to his action' ('Internal and External Reasons', repr. in *Moral Luck*, p. 102). The purpose of the remark is to support the view (which Williams ultimately rejects) that if someone who wants to drink gin and believes that some stuff is gin has a reason to drink it *if his belief is true*, then he has a reason to drink it *if his belief is false*—if the stuff is actually petrol, for example.

(B) The insufficiency of true belief is especially obvious if we consider a case where there can be no question of someone's knowing something because it is not a thing which *can* be known. For example, it was impossible to know in 1997 which team would win the 1998 World Cup. But suppose Marianne had unshakeable faith in the French team and bet 1000 francs that France would win. We know now that France *was* in fact going to win, but we also know that Marianne did not know this when she placed the bet. So why did she do it? Her *ground* may have been that France was going to win. We can imagine her murmuring (presumably in French) 'France *will* win; so I shall place a bet'. But the fact that France was going to win cannot be the reason why she placed the bet. Perhaps the reason is simply that she was convinced that France was going to win, or perhaps the story was more complicated than that. Perhaps Joan of Arc appeared to her in a dream and told her that France would win. But whatever the right answer is, it is certainly *not* simply that France *was* going to win.

(C) These two examples make it clear that if the ground on which someone does something is X—i.e. the content of the belief/because of which she does it is X—and X happens to be true, it does not follow that the *reason why* she does it is X. And if we consider some of the cases that pack the literature about knowledge, in which true belief is supplemented by a particular kind of cause or justification, or by another condition, but still falls short of knowledge, it appears that nothing short of knowledge will suffice. I shall mention three familiar examples, and leave it to the reader to test this claim against others. Like disco music and the laminated wooden racquet, the first example belongs to a time when the debate about Gettier cases was livelier than it is today:

> Henry is watching the television on a June afternoon. It is Wimbledon men's finals day, and the television shows McEnroe beating Connors; the score is two sets to none and match point to McEnroe in the third. McEnroe wins the point. Henry believes justifiably that (1) I have just seen McEnroe win this year's Wimbledon final, and reasonably infers that (2) McEnroe is this year's Wimbledon champion. Actually, however, the cameras at Wimbledon have ceased to function, and the television is showing a recording of last year's match. But while it does so McEnroe is in the process of repeating last year's slaughter. So Henry's belief (2) is true, and surely he is justified in believing (2). But we would hardly allow that Henry knows (2).[18]

Now suppose Henry, recalling that his brother backed McEnroe and stood to win £100, infers that his brother has won £100. It should be obvious that the fact that McEnroe is this year's champion is not the reason why Henry believes that his brother has won £100. The reason is that Henry *believes* that McEnroe is this year's champion. Hence, 'Henry believes that his brother has won £100 because he believes that McEnroe is this year's champion' is true; but 'Henry believes that his brother has won £100 because McEnroe *is* this year's champion' is false.

(D) Next, consider a case described by Goldman:

> A newspaper reporter observes p [say, that Assad has fled Damascus] and reports it to his newspaper. When printed, however, the story contains a typographical error so that it asserts not-p. When reading the paper, however, S[eb] fails to see the word 'not', and takes the paper to have asserted p. Trusting the newspaper, he infers that p is true. Here we have a continuous causal chain leading from p to S[eb]'s believing p; yet S[eb] does not know p.[19]

This example was originally designed to disprove a simple causal theory of knowledge, for the deviance in the causal chain prevents Seb from knowing that Assad has fled Damascus. But what concerns us now is whether it also prevents the *explanans* in a standard *because*-explanation of Seb's believing or feeling or doing something from being the fact that Assad has fled Damascus. For instance, suppose he infers that the Sunnis will come to power, or cancels a business trip to Beirut. Could it be true that he makes the inference or cancels the trip *because* Assad has fled?

It seems obvious that no one would *say* this—at least without qualification or elaboration—perhaps because causal explanation is not a transitive relation. For if the *explanans* in a true causal explanation must raise the probability of the *explanandum* to a point or by a degree that is above a certain threshold, then explanatoriness is not transmitted along sufficiently improbable or chancy sequences of events. Owens illustrates the point with a well-known nursery rhyme:

> For want of a nail the shoe was lost,
> For want of a shoe the horse was lost,
> For want of a horse the rider was lost,
> For want of a rider the battle was lost,
> For want of a battle the kingdom was lost,
> And all for want of a horseshoe nail.

He comments: 'It requires a succession of accidents in order to keep the chain going and the first element can do little more than explain the second.'[20] The application of this point to the story about the newspaper report should be obvious, the accidents in this case being the errors in printing and reading, the second reversing the effect of the first.

But if we set aside the question of whether causal explanation is transitive, and assume that there is a way of interpreting 'Seb cancelled the trip because Assad had fled' in which it *is* validated simply by the existence of a 'continuous causal chain' connecting the two events, the question whether standard *because*-explanations of intentional acts implicitly attribute knowledge of the *explanans* to the agent is not affected. For if we interpret 'Seb cancelled the trip because Assad had fled' in this way, it ceases to be the kind of explanation the knowledge view and the belief view are in contention over, because the explanatory clause 'Assad had fled' no longer purports to express Seb's ground.

Recall the ambiguity of 'Sally bit a policeman because she was drunk', which *might* be intended to identify the ground on which Sally bit a policeman, but is more likely not to be. The kind of *because*-explanation the knowledge view and the belief view are in contention over is the kind that *is* meant to identify a ground, whereas the kind that is made true by the existence of a causal chain—e.g. from drinking to biting, or from one man's flight to another man's cancellation—is the kind that is not.

(E) Finally, the following is adapted from a well-known case attributed to Ginet:

> George is touring the countryside in upstate New York. Delighted by the picturesque barns dotting the landscape, he photographs them one by one. Unbeknownst to him, most in fact consist only of façades, which the local tourist authority has arranged to look like barns from the road, but by chance one of the photographs he takes is of a real barn.

There is general agreement among philosophers who have thought about this kind of case that the one time George photographs a real barn, he believes truly, but does not know, that that is what he is doing. Their reasons differ. Some say it is because the processes that result in him believing he is photographing a barn are unreliable in this situation; others say it is because he believes mistakenly that he is photographing a barn in close counterfactual situations; and the reasons proposed by others are different again. But whatever the right explanation is, it seems clear that George does not know that he is photographing a real barn, and equally clear that he does not take the photograph *because the structure is a barn*, even though he can be expected to give this reason, should he be asked. Presumably, the reason why he takes this photograph is the same as the reason why he takes the others, namely, that he *believes* it is a barn, or that it looks like one.

These five examples do *not* prove that standard *because*-explanations imply that the agent knows the *explanans*. A series of examples could never prove this, because however many examples we examined it would always remain possible that a set of conditions falling short of knowledge which we had not considered would be sufficient to make the explanation true. But they do prove that true belief (cases (A) and (B)), true belief plus justification (case (C)), and true belief plus causation (cases (D) and (E)) are insufficient to make a standard *because*-explanation true. Whereas knowledge is sufficient. For if Jim made truffles because he *knew* that Anna loves them, and not merely because he believed truly that she loves them, the ground on which he made them remains the same, namely, *that Anna loves truffles*, but we can now say *either* that Jim made truffles because he knew Anna loves them *or* that Jim made truffles because Anna loves them, and there can be no objection to saying that the reason why Jim made truffles was simply *that Anna loves them*. And the same applies to Marianne, Henry, Seb, and George. In every case, *if we can explain the act (belief, desire, feeling, etc.) in terms of the agent's knowledge of a fact, then we can also explain it directly in terms of the fact known*. Knowledge, unlike belief, is transparent: we can look straight through it to the fact.

The evidence is not conclusive, but it is hard to explain unless Prichard's equation is right, unless doing something because of a fact and doing it really in consequence of knowing the fact are one and the same thing. The orthodox view is that intentional action is explained by identifying the beliefs and desires that jointly caused it. But it turns out that the mental state that standard *because*-explanations invoke as an explanatory factor is knowledge rather than belief. Standard *because*-explanations do not mention knowledge explicitly, so this is easy to miss. But whereas 'The ground on which he acted was that she had lied to him' purports to identify the content of a *belief* because of which the agent did the act, standard *because*-explanations purport to identify a fact the agent knew.

We do not have a special word for a fact known considered as an explanatory factor—for what stands to knowledge as a ground stands to a belief and as an aim or intention stands to a desire—presumably because the transparency of knowledge lets us call it a 'reason why'. But it is not *merely* a reason why, for there are reasons why people do intentional acts that are not grounds, such as being drunk. It is a fact, as we sometimes put it, *in the light of which* the agent did the act being explained, a fact that *guided* her when she did it. The conclusion we have reached is in effect that the idea of being guided by a fact is not the same as the idea of doing, or believing, or feeling something on certain grounds, and it is not a compound of that idea together with truth, or truth and justification, or truth and causality, or any of the other agglomerations of ideas that were proposed as definitions of knowledge, and proved to be inadequate.

6.5 Conclusion

I first defended the idea that some explanations of intentional action that are generally thought to attribute belief to the agent actually attribute knowledge in my article 'How Knowledge Works'. Since then, some have agreed that if one's reason for doing an act is that *p*, then one knows that *p*, while others have disagreed.[21] But as far as I know, all those who have disagreed have interpreted 'one's reason for doing the act' as referring simply to the *ground on which* one did the act, regardless of the *reason why* one did it.[22] The exposition here is designed to make the principal idea easier to accept by removing this reason for disagreement. As we shall see in the next chapter, this connection between knowledge and reasons offers the prospect of a new theory of knowledge.

7

Knowledge as an Ability

7.1 Introduction

The question, 'What is individual factual knowledge?' is quite narrowly focused in three respects. First, there is communal knowledge as well as individual knowledge. Second, a distinction is often drawn between factual knowledge and practical knowledge, or between knowledge that something is the case and knowledge how to do something. Third, as well as asking what knowledge is, it is also possible to ask whether or how knowledge of one kind or another can be acquired. Before attempting to answer the question, I shall dwell briefly on each of these three points.

First, we can distinguish between the possession of knowledge by an individual and the possession of knowledge by a community or group. For example, if we speak or enquire about the state of knowledge in a particular field of biology or history, we are not concerned with what anyone in particular knows about, say, the genetics of fruit flies or the Hundred Years War, but with what the scientific or academic *community* knows. We commonly describe the state of scientific or historical research with the impersonal construction 'It is known that . . .', but although there is a close connection between individual and communal knowledge, this does not simply mean 'Someone or other knows that . . .'. If we imagine that it does, we are ignoring the role of documents, archives, and libraries in the economy of knowledge. For the invention of writing means that each of us can cease to remember without all of us, collectively, ceasing to know. That is why Thamus, the mythical king of Egypt whom Socrates talks about in the *Phaedrus*, was right to say that writing is a recipe for reminder, and not for memory, but wrong to infer that it cannot extend knowledge, but only a semblance of it.

Second, there is sometimes said to be a distinction between practical knowledge and factual knowledge, a distinction that Ryle introduced under the rubric 'knowing how and knowing that'. As many commentators have pointed out, these labels are misleading, since 'that' is not the only pronoun we combine with 'know' to attribute factual knowledge to someone. For example, the statements that Tom knows whether it will rain tomorrow, when and where Alexander was born, what time the match begins, and how sponges reproduce all attribute items of factual knowledge to Tom. The moot questions are, first, whether knowing how to do something is the same as being able to do it or being skilled at doing it, as Ryle is widely thought to have claimed; and second, whether knowing how to do something and knowing that something is the case are essentially different kinds of knowledge. These questions have been studied intensively in recent years, but they require more patient treatment than I can give them here, and I shall not address them.[1]

Third, and most importantly for present purposes, the theory of knowledge is concerned not only with the question of what knowledge is, but also with the questions of whether and how knowledge of various kinds can be acquired. This quick formulation embraces many difficult and contentious matters, but the point I should like to emphasize is that the question of what knowledge is and the question of how it can be acquired are quite different, even though they are connected. A recent article by a distinguished British philosopher includes the extraordinary claim that we can 'explain what it is to know that A by identifying different possible means of knowing [i.e. coming to know] it'. At a minimum, he says, 'to understand what it is to know that A, all one needs is an open–ended list of means of knowing that A, perhaps together with some indication of whether some means of knowing that A are more basic than others'.[2] But this cannot be right.

Take the fact that Tunis is west of Pisa. An open-ended list of the means of knowing this might be: *being told by someone who knows; consulting a map; measuring the longitude of each city with a sextant; and so on.* How could anyone imagine that this list explains *what it is* to know that Tunis is west of Pisa, whether or not it is supplemented by an indication of which of these means, if any, is more basic than the others? Surely it is one thing to explain how knowledge can or cannot be acquired, and hence how knowledge-claims can be tested, and quite another to explain what knowledge is, just as it is one thing to explain how a right or a duty can be acquired, and hence how it is possible to decide whether someone has a certain right or duty, and quite another to explain what a right or a duty is.

Consider the ownership of a house. An open-ended list of the means of acquiring a house might be: *buying it, either by private treaty or in an auction; inheriting it; occupying it for a sufficient period, if it has been abandoned; and so on.* But the list does not begin to explain what owning a house *is*. On the contrary, buying and inheriting are, by definition, ways of acquiring property, ways in which title can be transferred, and we cannot hope to understand what it is to acquire something unless we already know what it is to own it, or what it is to transfer title unless we already know what it is to have title. The same is true of knowledge. We cannot explain what it is to know something by explaining how we can learn it. On the contrary, we cannot understand what it is to learn something unless we already know what it is to know it. A list of ways of learning is no more a theory of knowledge than a list of ways of forgetting.

Why do philosophers confuse or amalgamate the question of what knowledge is and the question of how knowledge can be acquired? There seem to be two main reasons. First, the principal aim of modern epistemology was to refute the sceptical doctrine that we do not in fact know various things that we commonly take ourselves to know. But the claim that we *do* know these things—about causes, about the past or the future, about other people's thoughts and feelings, and so on—can only be vindicated by showing that there is a satisfactory answer to the question of *how* we know them.* Consequently, when, in the 1960s, defining knowledge assumed the same importance in philosophy as refuting scepticism, there was a tendency for philosophers to fold the question about how knowledge can be acquired into the question of what it is. But it is a mistake to imagine that a definition of knowledge can refute scepticism. If it could, it would be tantamount to an ontological proof of the existence of knowledge, which is absurd. The only concept whose definition proves that it has instances is the concept of definition itself.

This is not to say that there are no limits on how someone can learn something. Clearly there are such limits. That is why we can test someone's claim to know something by asking how he found out, or decide that someone does not know something because he wasn't in the right place at the right time, because he reasoned from a mistaken premise, or because the

---

* That is why sceptical claims (e.g. I do not know that I am not a brain in a vat) are commonly supported by claiming that that there is no satisfactory answer to the question of how we know what the sceptic denies that we know (viz. that I am not a brain in a vat). See for example, DeRose, 'Solving the Sceptical Problem', p. 2.

man who informed him didn't know it himself. Equally, we can conclude
that someone does not own something because he never had the opportunity
to acquire it, because the man he paid did not own it in the first place, or
because the document was not properly drawn up. But to repeat, it does not
follow, and it is not true, that understanding how property or knowledge of
various kinds can be acquired is the same as understanding what it is.

The second main reason why philosophers have confused the question of
what knowledge is and the question of how knowledge can be acquired is
that it is still commonly assumed that knowledge is a species of belief. But
whereas there are limits on how someone can acquire knowledge, there are
no similar limits on how someone can acquire belief. For example, one can
acquire belief but not knowledge about the outcome of tomorrow's battle
by examining the entrails of a sheep. So if we assume that knowledge is a
species of belief, it is tempting to think that deciding whether A's belief that
p qualifies as knowledge is a matter of deciding whether it was acquired in
the right way. And so the question of how knowledge can be acquired is
commonly regarded as part of the larger question of what it is.

For these reasons, and perhaps others, there is a tendency in epistemology
for what the press corps calls mission creep. We start out wanting to say
what knowledge is, but we quickly get embroiled in the question of how it
can be acquired. I shall focus exclusively on the question of what knowledge
is in this chapter, and on the question of why we value knowledge in the
next. Questions about the limits and sources of knowledge have bulked
larger in the last four centuries, but they are best devolved to the branches of
philosophy that study different kinds of knowledge—philosophy of science,
philosophy of mathematics, moral philosophy, and so on—and I shall
mostly ignore them here. There is no reason a priori to expect that the
ways of acquiring knowledge, or its limits, can be defined informatively in a
topic-neutral way, and there is no encouragement to believe this from the
record of general epistemology during the last fifty years.

7.2 How knowledge gets expressed

I shall defend the theory that individual factual knowledge (from now on,
I shall refer simply to knowledge) is the ability to be guided by the facts, in
other words, to take the facts into consideration or account, in what we
think or feel or do.

Most philosophers still think that knowledge is, in Ryle's sardonic phrase, an '*élite* suburb' of belief.[3] But it is doubtful whether this can be right. First, the simple fact that philosophers have failed to explain what kind of belief knowledge is, despite (one would guess) more hours of work being devoted to the problem during the past sixty years than were spent philosophizing in the whole history of ancient Greece, suggests that it is not any kind of belief at all.

Second, knowledge does not seem to have the same kind of object as belief. A fact, in the relevant sense of the word, is simply a truth; the facts about something are simply the truth about it, and knowledge of a fact is knowledge of a truth. But what is a truth? One might think *either* that a truth is simply a true proposition *or* that it is the truth *of* a proposition, and these are evidently not the same. For the truth of a proposition is not a true proposition, any more than the beauty of a place is a beautiful place, or the goodness of a man is a good man.[4] But there are several reasons for preferring the view that a fact is the truth *of* a proposition. One reason that is often canvassed is that facts and propositions have different counter-factual conditions for their existence. For example, if France had won the 2006 World Cup instead of Italy, the proposition that Italy won would still have existed, but the fact would not.[5] Second, facts are discovered, learned, known, communicated, forgotten, and ignored. But the discovery (etc.) of a fact is the discovery (etc.) of *the truth of* a proposition, not the discovery (etc.) of a proposition. For example, Eratosthenes is credited with discovering the fact that the Earth is round, not with discovering the proposition. Third, facts have various properties relating to the effect of learning or recalling them, such as being shocking or surprising. But to be shocked or surprised by a fact is to be shocked or surprised by the truth of a proposition, rather than the mere proposition, even if some propositions are shocking or surprising in themselves.

If these points are right, what a person knows, when she knows that *p*, is the truth of the proposition that *p*. But what a person believes, when she believes that *p*, is the proposition that *p* itself. Hence, the object of knowledge 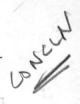 is not the same as the object of belief. It might be objected that if this were true, statements like 'I always believed Philby was a traitor; now I know it' would be false. But in fact this does not follow. For 'it' can be used simply to avoid the repetition of a clause or phrase, as in 'Tom is longing for the war to end and Lucy is praying for it'. 'I always believed Philby was a traitor; now I know it' is true if, and only if, I always believed Philby was a traitor, and now I know Philby was a traitor, i.e. if, and only if, I now know the truth of the proposition that Philby was a traitor, and this is a proposition I always believed.

Third, and most importantly for our purposes, Ryle himself points out several ways in which knowledge seems like an ability or skill, while belief seems like a tendency or disposition.[6] Among them: belief, like love or trust, can be foolish, passionate, obstinate, fanatical, or whole-hearted, whereas knowledge, like the ability to solve quadratic equations or cast a fly, cannot be any of these things. We can ask or urge someone to believe or not believe something, but we cannot ask or urge someone to know or not know something, but only to remember or forget something, or to find something out. We ask *why* rather than *how* someone believes something, wanting a justification; whereas we ask *how* rather than *why* someone knows something, wanting to be told the means by which the knowledge was acquired. ('How *can* you believe...' and 'How are you *able* to believe...' are of course perfectly in order.)

As these remarks suggest, the main alternative to the '*élite* suburb' picture of knowledge is that it is an ability.[*] This general idea originates with Plato, but in the twentieth century it was particularly associated with Wittgenstein and Ryle. Wittgenstein claims that 'the grammar of the word "knows" is evidently closely related to that of "can", "is able to"', and Ryle asserts that '"know" is of the same family as skill words'.[7]

The idea that knowledge is an ability or skill is important, because it transforms the task of defining knowledge. For instead of asking what we need to add to belief to get knowledge, we are forced to ask how knowledge gets exercised or expressed, since this is invariably how abilities and skills are defined. What is the ability to multiply, and how does it differ from the ability to divide? What is the ability to play tennis, and how does it differ from the ability to play squash? The whole answer is given by explaining what multiplying or playing tennis is, and how it differs from dividing or playing squash.

But Wittgenstein's and Ryle's remarks are studiedly imprecise, and neither of them pursues the idea that knowledge is an ability or skill far enough

---

[*] Another alternative, proposed by Williamson, is that 'knowing is the most general factive stative attitude' (*Knowledge and its Limits*, p. 34). I discuss this proposal, and its relationship with the definition of knowledge defended here, in my article, '"The most general factive stative attitude"'.

to make it seem convincing, because they do not attempt to explain what someone who knows something—e.g. that Tunis is west of Pisa—is able to do that someone who does not know it is unable to do, or what skill or skill-like trait he has that the other lacks. Nor did their followers succeed in developing the idea that knowledge is an ability into a convincing theory of knowledge, partly because of a tendency to associate knowledge too closely with the use of language to express knowledge or to communicate information.[8]

For example, White argues that knowledge is the ability to produce the correct answer to a possible question.[9] But on the most natural interpretation, to produce the correct answer to a question is to state it, and, in this sense, it is possible to know that p without being able to produce the correct answer to the question whether p. For example, there are circumstances in which we might want to say that a dog knows that it is time for a walk, but it cannot say so. White explicitly acknowledges that 'there is no reason why young children and animals should not be said to know many things [e.g.] that it is time for a walk', and he denies that having the ability to produce the right answer to a possible question 'implies [. . .] manifesting it in any verbal way', but he does not explain how, exactly, the exercise of this ability is to be defined.[10]

Perhaps what White had in mind is that to produce the correct answer to a possible question is merely to enable someone to state it; for a dog certainly can make its owner aware of the fact that it is time for a walk, and thereby enable him or her to state it. But this definition would be too liberal, because in this sense, a piece of litmus paper, which cannot know anything, can produce the correct answer to the question whether a solution is acidic. Alternatively, it may be that to produce a correct answer is to *intentionally* enable someone to state it.[11] But this would not be liberal enough. For even if it is plausible that a dog intends, by leaping towards the door, to get a walk underway, or to get someone to get a walk underway, it is surely *not* plausible that it intends to enable anyone to state that it is time for a walk. White's definition of knowledge therefore seems to be unhappily poised between tautology and falsehood: to know whether p is, tautologically, to know the answer to the question whether p, but it is not *to be able to answer* the question whether p.

It might be objected that what we are inclined to say about animals is not a convincing reason for rejecting a theory of knowledge. Animals without language have an attenuated awareness of facts, and we should philosophize about knowledge with competent speakers in mind, and allow our conception of the cognitive powers of animals to be decided by our epistemology, and not vice versa. This objection has some force, despite the fact, noted above, that White's theory of knowledge was meant to be consistent with attributing knowledge to animals. But in any case, knowledge has a far more extensive role in our lives than the ability to provide answers to questions does, and a satisfactory definition will have to reflect this. Bernard Williams points out that the traditional definition of knowledge as justified true belief is too narrowly tailored to what he calls the *examiner's situation*, where 'informed questioners are concerned with someone's credentials with regard to a piece of knowledge', which he points out is far from typical in practice.[12] White's theory of knowledge is tailored to what might be called the *expert witness situation*, where uninformed questioners are concerned to establish whether *p* from someone who is presumed to know. Of course, both of these situations arise, but it is difficult to see why either of them should be thought capable of providing the key to explaining what knowledge is.

Kenny proposes a different definition of knowledge as an ability, which avoids the pitfall of thinking that knowledge is primarily expressed in speech. Knowledge, Kenny says, is 'an ability of a unique kind', but he doubts whether it is possible to say precisely what it is an ability to do:

[T]here is no simple way of specifying how knowledge gets expressed in behaviour, and indeed some pieces of knowledge may never affect behaviour at all. The most that we can say is that to know is to have the ability to modify one's behaviour in indefinite ways relevant to the pursuit of one's goals.[13]

Two things are right about this definition, and two things are wrong with it. The first point in its favour is that if knowledge is an ability, then defining knowledge will, as Kenny implies, be a matter of specifying how it is exercised, manifested, or expressed. This is a perfectly general point about powers of every kind. Dispositions, abilities, and liabilities are all powers; and, as I pointed out earlier, powers are always defined in terms of their exercise, in other words, what they are powers to do. Second, Kenny is right to emphasize the peculiar flexibility of knowledge, in other words, that it can be expressed in indefinitely many ways. For example, Tom's awareness of the fact that the rouble has collapsed can be expressed in his booking a holiday in Russia, buying shares in Gazprom, or sending dollars to a friend in Moscow.

On the other hand, Kenny seems to equate the question of how know-ledge gets expressed in behaviour and the question of what knowledge is an ability to do. But this is a mistake. For if knowledge is an ability, it can be exercised in thought and feeling no less than in behaviour. Performing a calculation in one's head, making an inference, conceiving a desire or forming an intention, believing, doubting, hoping, fearing: all these things can express knowledge just as much as behaviour can. For example, Tom's awareness of the fact that the rouble has collapsed can be expressed in his *forming an intention* to take a holiday in Russia, whether or not he takes any practical steps to do so; or *hoping* that his friend in Moscow has his savings in dollars, instead of supplementing them. Furthermore, while performing a calculation in one's head is something we do in pursuit of our goals, at least for the most part, believing, doubting, hoping, and fearing are not. We do not do these things intentionally or on purpose, and so the scope of knowledge, the extent to which it affects human life, is much larger than the scope of purposes or aims. If we recall the distinction between doing things for reasons and doing things with intentions, knowledge matches reason in its scope (see above, 6.2).

The second weakness in Kenny's account of knowledge is that he fails to explain what unites the heterogeneous variety of things that can express the knowledge that *p* as opposed to the knowledge that *q*. To know, he says, is to have the ability to modify one's behaviour in indefinite ways relevant to the pursuit of one's goals. But if this is the most we can say about how knowledge is exercised, the difference between knowing one thing and knowing another is bound to remain obscure.

But is this a weakness? Naturally, the answer depends on what form an explanation of the difference between knowing that *p* and knowing that *q* is supposed to take. But if what is being sought is a formula connecting specific kinds of thought and action with the possession of specific pieces of knowledge, it may be objected that this is unfeasible. There is a trivial sense in which the various modifications to a person's thought or conduct that express her knowledge that *p* have something in common, for they are all informed by her knowledge that *p*. Hence, if Tom's knowledge that the rouble has collapsed is an ability, there can be nothing wrong with saying that its exercise will consist in thought and conduct informed by the knowledge that the rouble has collapsed. But it is not very illuminating. And it becomes positively misleading if it makes us think that we can say specifically what acts Tom is able to perform if and only if Tom knows

[handwritten margin note: but able to do those things under your control]

that the rouble has collapsed. For if A knows that *p*, it does not follow that A is able to do *all* the things that could be informed by the knowledge that *p*. For example, if Tom knows that the rouble has collapsed, it does not follow that he is able to arrange a loan from the World Bank. And if A is able to do *at least one* of the things that can be informed by the knowledge that *p*, it does not follow that A knows that *p*. For example, an investment in Gazprom can be informed by the knowledge that the rouble has collapsed, but there is no need for Tom to know that the rouble has collapsed in order to buy shares.

The reply to this objection is that the difference between knowing one thing and knowing another *cannot* be explained by saying specifically what thoughts and acts can express the knowledge that *p*. But it does not follow that we cannot explain what knowing that *p* is an ability to do. Compare the question 'What is enthusiasm?' Enthusiasm isn't a tendency to do specific things. For instance, enthusiastic sportsmen do not invariably hop from foot to foot and punch the air. But it is, in part, a tendency to do a range of things in an enthusiastic manner. We can call it an *adverbial* tendency, if the phrase is acceptable: a tendency to do things enthusiastically. Similarly, unpunctuality is a tendency to do things such as arriving for meetings, submitting tax returns, and answering correspondence later than the appointed time. But there is no other way of classifying unpunctual acts except by saying that they are done late, which is about how they are related to clocks, not about which acts they are. So being unpunctual can also be described as an adverbial tendency, although in this case the adverb is an adjunct of time, rather than of manner.

The lesson of these examples is that while enthusiasm and unpunctuality are not tendencies to perform specific acts, this does not prevent us from explaining what they are tendencies to do. But is it possible to say what knowing that *p* is an ability to do in a similar way, by specifying an adverbial clause which we can introduce into a sentence to indicate that the act or thought it mentions was informed by the agent's or thinker's knowledge of a particular fact?

In fact this is a relatively simple thing to do. For we can convey exactly the same information by saying either that an act was informed by the agent's knowledge that *p*, or that the agent did the act in view of, or in the light of, the fact that *p*. And a fact in view of which, or in the light of which, an agent does an act is a fact *because of which* she does it, not in the general sense of a reason why, but in the particular sense of a fact she was guided by,

Adjunct / contingency

or took into consideration or account. For example, 'James went to church *because it would please his mother*', as this would normally be meant and understood, implies that in going to church James was guided by the fact that doing so would please his mother. The adverbial clause 'because it would please his mother' is not of course an adjunct of time or manner, but what is called an adjunct of contingency, like 'He called *in order to warn her*', or 'He bought a magazine *in case she was delayed*'.

So the idea that knowledge is an ability not only transforms the task of defining knowledge, it makes it tractable. For while philosophers have been unable to say what kind of belief knowledge is, or what needs to be added to belief to get knowledge, short of knowledge itself, it is quite easy to say how knowledge gets expressed. To take another example, my knowledge of the fact that Hampstead is on the Northern Line gets expressed whenever I am guided by the fact that Hampstead is on the Northern Line, in what I think or do. This happens when I head for the Northern Line at King's Cross to get home, or when I merely deduce from the fact that Balham is on the Northern Line that one can travel from Hampstead to Balham without changing lines.

Talk of being guided by a fact is metaphorical of course, but the phrase is familiar to English-speakers—the OED records it in the fifteenth century—and it is not hard to explain. To be guided by a fact is to take it into consideration or account.[14] So the metaphor is dispensable, but it is helpful, because it draws attention to the similarity between being aware of facts and being aware of things. Think of a cat stalking a bird. The cat expresses its awareness of the bird when it modifies its behaviour in response to way the bird modifies *its* behaviour. The bird hops this way, the cat turns this way; the bird flutters across the courtyard, the cat advances a few paces; and so on. The cat's movements are responsive to, are guided by, the bird. Or think of a traveller following a guide. The guide takes the left fork, so the traveller takes the left fork; the guide pauses, so the traveller pauses; and so on. Being guided by facts is similar. Whether one is guided by facts or by things, one is responsive to what one is guided by. But, as Wittgenstein pointed out, this is not like a train being guided by the rails, because the way knowledge gets expressed depends on one's aims or purposes, by one's desires and values, and because being guided by the facts is not passive or constraining, any more than reading is, although the reader's thought (if she is reading silently) or speech (if she is reading out loud) is guided by the words she sees on the page.

Hence, if we conceive of knowledge as an ability, and approach the problem of defining knowledge by asking how it gets expressed in our mental lives and in our conduct, instead of asking how it can be certified or acquired, we can define it as the ability to be guided by the facts. But the word 'fact' must be understood in the broadest possible sense, so that does not involve a contrast between facts and values, past and future, contingent and necessary, or a posteriori and a priori. For example, if Sheldon believes that the circumference of a dime is more than an inch and a half because its diameter is more than half an inch and π is greater than three, the view defended here implies that he knows that π is greater than three in just the same way as it implies that he knows that the diameter of a dime is more than half an inch. Even if mathematical truths are rules, as Wittgenstein argued, it is still a fact that π is greater than three, in this broad sense of 'fact', just as it is a fact that a driver must stop at a red light.

How does this definition compare with Kenny's and White's? First, it is flexible, in the sense that it allows knowledge to be expressed in indefinitely many ways, and it is precise, in the sense that it reveals precisely what the difference is between knowing one fact and knowing another. For one knows that p if and only if one's thought and conduct can be guided by the fact that p, and one knows that q if and only if one's thought and conduct can be guided by the fact that q. White's definition is precise but inflexible, whereas Kenny's is flexible but imprecise. The definition proposed here has the advantage of combining both virtues.

Second, it also subsumes both Kenny's and White's definitions: Kenny's, because the ability to be guided by the facts in general includes the ability to modify one's behaviour in the pursuit of one's goals, and White's, because the ability to be guided by the fact that p in particular includes, in the case of competent and uninhibited communicators, the ability to give the correct answer to the question whether p. Kenny's definition is, in effect, the result we obtain if we apply the idea of being guided by the facts to the particular case of goal-directed behaviour, as opposed to believing, wanting, hoping, fearing, or any other kind of thought or feeling that knowledge can inform. As for White's definition, we saw earlier that giving the right answer to a question is only one of the ways in which knowledge can be expressed, but of course it need not be an expression of knowledge at all. For it would be absurd to suggest that someone knows that p if he happens to give the right answer to the question whether p for *whatever reason*, for instance, because it is the answer he thinks the person asking will be glad to hear. What competent and uninhibited communicators who know whether p can do that others cannot do is give the right answer to the question whether p *because it is the right answer*—that is, either give an affirmative answer *because p* or give a negative answer *because not-p.* So White's definition is the result we obtain if we apply the idea of being guided by the facts to the particular case of answering the question whether or not something is the case.

In sum, if we pursue Wittgenstein's idea that the verb 'knows' is closely related to 'can' and 'is able to', or Ryle's idea that 'know' is a skill word, we can define knowledge as the ability to be guided by the facts. This explains why competent and uninhibited communicators who know that p can give the right answer to the question whether p, and more generally why knowledge allows us to modify our behaviour in the pursuit of our goals. But our beliefs and desires and doubts and hopes and fears can be guided by facts, no less than our deeds. So defining knowledge in this way also reflects the fact that knowledge does not only get expressed in our conduct, but also in the elements of our mental lives from which it flows.

7.3 Objections and replies

Philosophers have objected to the claim that knowledge of a fact is the ability to be guided by it on various grounds, which may be summarized as follows: knowing a fact is not (1) necessary, or (2) sufficient, for being able to be guided by it; (3) there is no such ability as the ability to be guided by a fact; (4) knowledge is not an ability but a state; (5) a person's knowledge of a fact explains her ability to be guided by it, so the knowledge and the ability cannot be identical. I shall comment on these objections in turn.

7.3.1 Knowing a fact is not necessary for being able to be guided by it

I argued in 6.4 that one cannot be guided by a fact one does not know. Readers may find it helpful to review the argument there now. Instead of recapitulating it in detail, I shall add some comments about the relationship between explanations of thought and action that refer to knowledge, and ones that refer to belief.

The argument in 6.4 made use of several cases of true belief without knowledge, including ones that were invented when the project of defining knowledge in terms of belief was in full swing. For the same examples that were used then to show that knowledge cannot be equated with justified true belief, or justified true belief with no false lemmas, or true belief caused by the right event, can be used to show that if one has the justified true belief that *p*, or the justified true belief with no false lemmas, or the true belief caused by the right event, it does not follow that one can be guided by the fact that *p*. Something one believes but does not know can be the ground on which one does something, but cannot be guided by a fact one does not know, any more than one can follow a guide one cannot see. In fact, the relationship between knowledge and true belief is like the relationship between perception and veridical hallucination. For if a traveller sees the guide taking the left fork and follows him, then he is guided by the guide; whereas if he cannot see the guide, but he hallucinates him taking the left fork, and takes it himself for that reason, he is not guided by the guide. A fact that guides one is not merely a ground one acts on, and one can only be guided by a fact one knows.*

When philosophers assumed that knowledge is a species of belief, they naturally also assumed that explaining thought and action in terms of knowledge is essentially the same as explaining it in terms of belief. For whatever part belief plays in causing thought and action, it surely plays the same part whether or not it has the characteristics that were thought to make it qualify as knowledge, such as having the right kind of justification or the right kind of cause. But it turns out that they were wrong. Explanations involving knowledge are quite different from ones involving belief, because an agent can only be guided by the facts he knows.

Of course, it can seem to someone who merely believes something to be the case just as if he knows it to be the case, and it can be impossible to tell belief from knowledge in another. For believing something tends to influence thought and behaviour in the same way as knowing it for a fact. In some cases, the influence of a belief can be diminished by the subject's knowledge that his evidence is weak or that he is affected by prejudice. In this sort of case, the extent to which he is influenced by the belief will depend on the extent to which he controls what he thinks and does by

---

* Guidance by a rule is similar, for, as Quine points out, behaviour *fits* any rule it conforms to, but it can only be *guided* by a rule the behaver knows ('Methodological Reflections on Current Linguistic Theory', p. 386). Interestingly, Wittgenstein draws the contrast between following and conforming to rules in terms of reasons (*BB*, pp. 13–15).

reminding himself of such facts. But even so, if someone would do X or believe Y or feel Z if he knew that *p*, then he will be disposed to do X or believe Y or feel Z if he believes that *p*. It is sometimes claimed that to believe that *p* is to be disposed to act (think, feel) 'as if *p*' or 'as if *p* were true'. But this must mean that to believe that *p* is to be disposed to act (think, feel) *as one would if one knew that p*, or *as one would if one were guided by the fact that p*, since the mere fact that something is the case need not have any influence on us at all. How would I be disposed to act if there were an odd number of stars in the galaxy? Exactly as I *am* disposed to act. Yet I do not believe this, or believe the opposite.[*]

Hence, one can do or think or feel something that the facts would justify one in doing or thinking or feeling if one knew them, without being guided by the facts. And this is exactly what conceiving of knowledge as an ability rather than a species of belief leads us to expect. For many performances that normally display an ability or skill can also be done occasionally by luck. For instance, a bad speller might spell 'accommodate' correctly from time to time, and a novice fly fisherman might cast a perfect fly. If knowledge is the ability to be guided by the facts, this is exactly what happens when someone who does not know a certain fact acts in a way that seems to express knowledge of it, because he happens to have the right opinion: e.g. when a guide who believes that the left fork is the road to Larissa and happens to be right, but has never been there and does not really know, points a traveller in the right direction, or gives him the right advice.

In sum, belief mimics knowledge, so it can be difficult to tell them apart. But the fact that it can be difficult to distinguish between belief and knowledge in practice is not an obstacle to explaining the difference between them in theory, and the root of the difference is that one cannot be guided by a fact one does not know. Of course it does not follow that an act that expresses belief and not knowledge is done aimlessly, or for no reason. For example, if Sybil feeds James oysters because she believes they

---

[*] The phrase 'disposition to act as if *p*' is widely used without the gloss Braithwaite gave it when he introduced it. He explains that it is to be treated as an abbreviation for 'disposition to act in ways that would be conducive to the satisfaction of one's needs if *p* were true' ('The Nature of Believing', p. 134). But this is not a plausible theory of belief, since plants and primitive animals have the disposition to act in ways that are conducive to satisfying their needs without having beliefs. The phrase is now generally treated as an abbreviation for 'disposition to act in ways that would be conducive to the satisfaction of one's desires if *p* were true'. Velleman is rightly critical of the idea that belief can be defined purely in terms of its effect on behaviour (*The Possibility of Practical Reason*, pp. 255f.).

are aphrodisiac, it is fairly obvious what her aim is, and her reason for doing it—that is, her *ground*—is the content of her belief. But she is not guided by the facts about the effect of eating oysters, and as the analogy between false belief and veridical hallucination suggests, and the argument in 6.4 confirms in detail, this would remain the case if her belief happened to be true.

Hence, explanations that involve knowledge, such as 'He took the left fork because he knew that it led to Larissa', are quite different from ones that involve belief, such as 'He took the left fork because he believed that it led to Larissa'. The *ground* on which the man is said to have acted is the same in both cases, but the knowledge-involving explanation refers to a feature of his situation he was aware of and took into account, whereas the belief-involving explanation merely refers to his state of mind.

7.3.2 Knowing a fact is not sufficient for being able to be guided by it

It might be objected that knowledge cannot be the ability to be guided by the facts, because knowing a fact is not sufficient for being able to be guided by it, either on the grounds that some facts it is possible to know are too recondite to guide anyone in doing anything at all, or on the grounds that knowledge requires less intellectual sophistication than being guided by facts. The first argument does not merit extensive comment. Every fact, however insignificant or obscure, is potentially someone's reason for doing or for not doing something, for believing or wanting something, or for hoping or fearing something. It would be tedious to illustrate this with examples, and besides, it is easily proved. For at a minimum, the fact that *p* is self-evidently a reason for believing that the proposition that *p* is true, or that the proposition that not-*p* is false, or that if *p* implies *q*, then *q*. The second argument may seem more convincing. For example, I mentioned earlier that there are circumstances in which we might want to say that a dog knows it is time for a walk. But it could be argued that since dogs cannot give reasons for their actions, they cannot act for reasons, and so the fact that it is time for a walk cannot be a dog's reason for doing anything. If that is right, then knowledge requires less intellectual sophistication than the ability to be guided by reasons, and so they cannot be identified or equated.

Evidently, dogs cannot give reasons for their actions, at least if giving a reason means stating it, because they cannot speak. But the objection is a weak one, for two reasons. First, it is not obvious that animals cannot do

KNOWLEDGE AS AN ABILITY

something for a reason unless they can give reasons for doing something, and, as a matter of fact, there are well-known examples of animals doing things which seem to depend on reasoning, such as the story about Chrysippus's hunting dog. In hot pursuit, it reached a place where the path branched into three; it sniffed one path, but didn't detect its quarry's scent; it sniffed the second, but drew a blank again; and then it took the third path *without* sniffing. Annas and Barnes comment on the story as follows:

> How is its action to be explained? Chrysippus argues that it must have engaged in some simple reasoning: it said to itself, in effect: 'Either A or B or C; but not A, and not B: therefore C.' [...] It is the fact that the dog selects the third track without further experiment which requires explanation—and the explanation which Chrysippus offers is highly plausible.[15]

If Annas and Barnes are right, and Chrysippus's explanation *is* plausible, then the syllogism sets out the dog's reason for taking the third path, despite the fact that the dog could not have stated this or any other reason, for this or any other act.

Annas and Barnes are unusual for philosophers. For although the ethological literature is widely believed to provide copious evidence of reasoning by dogs, primates, and some birds, philosophers have tended to be more sceptical than non-philosophers about the intellectual abilities of animals without language. But—and this is the second reason why the objection is weak—suppose there are compelling arguments to show that the evidence from studies of animal behaviour has been misinterpreted, and Chrysippus's dog only engaged in some *quasi*-reasoning, and only *quasi*-acted for the reason set out in the syllogism. Still, the objection will not have been made out if these arguments (or other ones) also prove that it only *quasi*-knew that its quarry had taken the third path. Certainly, the terms we use to describe the exercise of rational powers by human beings apply only in an attenuated or analogical sense to many animals. Which animals these are is a matter of dispute, but the general proposition is not. But the same is true where cognition is concerned. So if the objection is to bite, it has to be shown that when guidance by facts has become attrited, knowledge remains intact. But the arguments which have persuaded philosophers that only human beings can act for reasons do not show this. They do not drive a wedge between knowledge and the ability to be guided by the facts. On the contrary. Davidson, for example, argues that only members of a speech community can act for reasons, because a creature cannot act for reasons if it cannot have beliefs, and only a member of a speech community can have beliefs.[16] But a creature cannot be incapable of having beliefs and yet be capable of knowledge. (This is true whether or not knowledge implies belief, simply because we are fallible.)

Davidson's reason for claiming that only a member of a speech community can have beliefs is that an animal cannot have a belief 'unless it understands the possibility of being mistaken'; but this 'requires grasping the contrast between truth and error', a contrast Davidson claims can only emerge within a speech community.[17] But it is not self-evident that an animal cannot have a belief unless it understands the possibility of being mistaken. A dog can be hungry or lustful or want to bury a bone, whether or not it can understand the possibility of being frustrated or disappointed, and whether or not it can grasp the contrast between success and failure, and if the analogy between belief and desire is misjudged, Davidson does not say why this is so. But the cogency of Davidson's argument is beside the point. What matters for present purposes is that his sceptical conclusion about animals does not cast doubt on the claim that knowledge that p is sufficient for being able to be guided by the fact that p. Indeed, far from weakening the link between cognition and reason, Davidson reinforces it, for he also claims that attributing beliefs and desires to a creature only makes sense to the extent that doing so reveals a broadly rational pattern in its behaviour.

The argument here neither supports nor contradicts the sceptical view about animals which Davidson and, for different reasons, Aristotle, Aquinas, and Descartes all recommend. But it does support the proposition, on which their arguments converge, that knowledge and the ability to be guided by facts are either co-present or co-absent. If the theory of knowledge defended here is right, the reason for this could not be simpler: they are identical.

7.3.3 There is no such ability as the ability to be guided by a fact

Hacker argues that knowledge of a fact cannot be the ability to be guided by it because there is no such ability. Abilities, he claims, correspond to 'act descriptions':

'To ϕ', one might say, is the general form of an act description. But 'to ϕ for the reason that p' is no more a different act description from 'to ϕ for the reason that q' than 'to ϕ for A's sake' is a different act description from 'to ϕ for B's sake'.[18]

For example, 'to marry for the sake of money' and 'to marry for the sake of love' are not different act descriptions, they are the same act description, namely 'to marry', combined with different adverbial clauses. Hence, there is no such ability as the ability to marry for money, or the ability to marry for love: there is simply the ability to marry, which one can exercise for different reasons, or in the light of different facts.

This argument has three main weaknesses. First, Hacker does not say what verb phrases he regards as admissible substitutions for the variable ϕ in an 'act description'; second, he does not explain how we are to decide whether or not two phrases are the same 'act description', and correspond to the same ability; and third, the comparison between doing an act for one reason rather than another and doing an act for A's sake rather than B's sake does not support his case. I shall comment on these points in turn.

(A) Abilities are generally attributed in English with the auxiliary verb 'can' or the auxiliary construction 'is able to', followed in both cases by an infinitive verb or verb phrase. But the verb or verb phrase need not signify an act in the sense of a deed. Thus, 'walk', 'run', 'play tennis', and 'play squash' signify activities as opposed to acts, while 'fall asleep' and 'stay awake' signify neither. Furthermore, a verb phrase used to attribute an ability will commonly include an adverbial phrase as a constituent. For example, a multi-talented man may be able to run a mile *in four minutes*, fall asleep *on a crowded train*, remain calm *under fire*, and sing *in tune*. Hence, one cannot argue that there is no such ability as the ability to do an act for a particular reason on the ground that 'for the reason that p' is an adverbial phrase. But Hacker does not say which adverbial clauses can be used to specify an 'act description', and which cannot.

(B) How are we to decide whether the ability to ϕ and the ability to ψ are identical or distinct? For example, is the ability to run a mile in four minutes a different ability from the ability to run a mile in five minutes? Or are they the same ability, i.e. the ability to run a mile, which can be exercised at different speeds? What about the ability to fall asleep on a crowded train? Does this specific ability exist, or is there just the ability to fall asleep, which can be exercised in different places?

We can assume that for all ϕ and for all ψ, the ability to ϕ and the ability to ψ are different abilities if it is possible to have one without having the other.

It follows that the ability to run a mile in four minutes and the ability to run a mile in five minutes are different abilities, since it is possible to have the second without having the first, even though it is not possible to have the first without having the second. Again, the ability to fall asleep on a crowded train cannot be the same as the ability to fall asleep on a crowded bus, because someone could have one, in this case either one, without having the other. (The different noises and rhythms could be the reason, or just a hatred of buses and a love of trains.)

Similarly, if p and q are different reasons, the ability to ϕ for the reason that p cannot be the same as the ability to ϕ for the reason that q, regardless of whether the theory of knowledge defended here is right, because it is always possible that someone should be able to do a certain act for one reason but not for another. For instance, it is possible that a sports fan should be able to stay awake until three in the morning because a match is being broadcast on TV, but not because she needs to finish a chapter of *Syntactic Structures*, or that a man should be able to marry for the sake of money and unable to marry for the sake of love, because he is unable to love.

This is not to say that the abilities to marry for money and to marry for love are unrelated. It is obvious that they *are* related, since someone who marries for money and someone who marries for love both marry, just as someone who runs a mile in five minutes and someone who runs a mile in four minutes both run a mile. But this is not because marrying for money (or running a mile in five minutes) and marrying for love (or running a mile in four minutes) are the same act, and correspond to the same ability. It is because they are both species of the generic act of marrying (or running a mile), and the corresponding abilities are related in the same way. Compare dispositions. Tin melts at 232°C, silver at 961°C. Are 'to melt at 232°C' and 'to melt at 961°C' different 'act descriptions', in Hacker's terminology, or are they the same 'act description' with different adverbial clauses attached? I would not venture to say. But the disposition to melt at 232°C and the disposition to melt at 961°C are evidently different dispositions, although of course they are both species of the generic disposition to melt.

(C) Finally, the example of marrying for the sake of money and marrying for the sake of love shows that Hacker's comparison between doing an act for one reason rather than another and doing an act for A's sake rather than B's sake does not support his case, for here too we have distinct species of the same generic act, and, corresponding to them, distinct species of the same generic ability.

7.3.4 Knowledge is not an ability but a state

The use of the term 'state' is partly stipulative, and so we find different conceptions of a state in philosophical writings. Some philosophers contrast states with abilities or dispositions, while others include an object's abilities and dispositions among its states, and of course this difference can lead to apparently conflicting claims. For example, some philosophers prefer to say that being gaseous is a state, whereas being volatile is not; or that being depressed is a state, but being prone to depression is not. Others prefer to say that all these conditions are states and to distinguish between states of different kinds. But these apparently conflicting claims may only reflect a terminological disagreement, a disagreement in the use of the term 'state'.

One common approach to defining a state is to contrast states with processes, and to explain the distinction between them by distinguishing between verbs that have progressive tenses, corresponding to processes, and verbs that do not have progressive tenses, corresponding to states. For example, 'kill', 'knit', 'learn', and 'prove' have progressive tenses: 'is killing', 'was knitting', etc.; whereas 'know', 'believe', 'be able', and 'be blue' do not. We can say that a child is learning how to multiply or that a cat is killing a bird; but not that a child is knowing how to multiply or that a cat is being able to kill a bird. So on this approach, killing and knitting are held to be processes, whereas knowing and believing are held to be states.

In fact, this way of drawing the distinction between states and processes needs fine-tuning, because many verbs that are generally acknowledged to signify states as opposed to processes have an idiomatic progressive tense. This is true especially of psychological verbs. Thus we have, 'I am hoping', 'I am intending', and so on. What distinguishes these verbs from ones that signify processes is that for them the rule holds that A is ϕing if and only if A ϕs. Thus, I am hoping that Lucy will arrive soon if and only if I hope that Lucy will arrive soon, I am intending to give up whisky for Lent if and only if I intend to give up whisky for Lent, and so on. Hence, hoping and intending are states. By contrast, memorizing is a process, since I can spend all morning memorizing *Kubla Khan* without completing the task.[19]

With or without this qualification, knowledge is certainly an intellectual state, in this sense of the term 'state', but it is not a state as opposed to an ability, because by these criteria abilities are states. But what distinguishes abilities from other kinds of states? I shall not attempt to define an ability here, I shall confine myself to the following observations.

An ability is a power, and therefore an actual property of the substance that possesses it, and not merely the possibility that the kind of act or event that manifests it should occur. For example, if *aqua regia* is able to dissolve gold, this does not mean merely that it is possible for gold coming into contact with it to dissolve. The point applies to every ability, but there is an additional reason for refusing to classify powers as possibilities in those cases where their exercise involves some physical or intellectual skill. For, as I pointed out earlier, many tasks that can be performed by agents with the relevant skills can also be performed occasionally by luck by those without them, as when a novice casts a perfect fly. If he does so, it follows that it is possible for him to do so, but not that he has the ability to do so. So the possibility and the ability are not the same.

However, abilities are sometimes confused with certain kinds of possibilities for which we also use the auxiliary verb 'can', specifically, circumstantial possibilities (opportunities) and epistemic possibilities (cases of consistency with known fact). As Kenny points out, both these distinctions are marked linguistically in English.[20] We refer to epistemic possibilities but not abilities with the word 'may'. For instance, 'Peter may still be in Rome' does not mean that he is able to remain there, it means that for all we know he is still there. And we refer to abilities and opportunities differently in the future tense. Kenny's own example is that 'I can speak Russian tomorrow, we have guests coming from Moscow' is correct, whereas 'I can speak Russian next spring; I shall be taking a beginner's course this fall' is incorrect. We refer to future opportunities either with 'can' or with 'will be able', but we refer to future abilities only with 'will be able'.

Both Hume and Ryle confuse abilities with epistemic possibilities, but the distinction between abilities and opportunities is the easier one to lose sight of in this context.[21] But it is important not to lose sight of it, for, if we do, we may imagine that a person is able to take a fact into account without knowing it, as long as it is a fact he can easily ascertain. 'Surely,' we may say, 'Tom could easily have taken the fact that it was going to rain into account: all he had to do was check the forecast.' Fair enough. But the phrase 'could have' here refers to an opportunity: it means that Tom's circumstances allowed him to do the thing in question, i.e. to take the fact that it was going to rain into account. That is why we can also say that Tom could have taken (i.e. would have been able to take) the fact that it was going to rain into account *if only* he had checked the forecast.

The distinction between an ability and an opportunity is not affected by how easily the ability is acquired. Some abilities can be acquired easily and in moments—for example, the ability to pronounce the name 'Luigi' or to spell the word 'fruit'. Even in these cases, possessing an ability is not the same as being in circumstances in which it is easy to acquire it. An ability is internal to the agent, and a positive factor in accounting for an act, whereas an opportunity is external, and may amount to no more than the absence of circumstances that would prevent the act from being done or interfere with it. As Kenny points out, it is difficult to make the intuitive truth that abilities are internal whereas opportunities are external precise.[22] But it does not seem necessary to argue that acquiring knowledge enlarges our abilities rather than altering our circumstances.

7.3.5 A person's knowledge of a fact explains her ability to be guided by it, so the knowledge and the ability cannot be identical

However, it is possible to agree that knowledge enlarges our abilities because it enables us to be guided by facts, without agreeing that knowledge of a fact *is* the ability to be guided by it. Williamson and Setiya both take this position. They argue, independently, that a person's knowledge of a fact explains her ability to be guided by it, so the knowledge and the ability cannot be the same state. I shall comment on their arguments in turn.

Williamson agrees that someone who believes truly that *p* without knowing that *p* cannot do X because *p*, cannot do Y because *p*, cannot do Z because *p*, and so on:

> But a single failure to know explains all these incapacities. If the incapacities constituted the failure to know, the correlation between the incapacities would be an unexplained coincidence.[23]

This objection is surely unconvincing. Of course, explanations vary depending on the context in which they are given and the purpose for which they are required, with what is assumed to be common knowledge, and so on. But it simply is not true that if someone could not do X because *p*, could not do Y because *p*, etc., and these incapacities constituted her failure to know, the correlation between them would be an unexplained coincidence. Clearly, it would be explained by whatever explains her failure to know, such as the fact that she did not see this morning's paper. Similarly, if the inability to do crawl, or breaststroke, or doggy paddle, . . . constitutes the inability to swim, it does not follow that someone's inability to do crawl, or breaststroke, or doggy paddle, . . . is an unexplained coincidence. It is explained by whatever explains her inability to swim. Williamson says that 'a single failure to know explains all these incapacities'. And in a sense it does. It explains them by including them, in the way that a person's inability to ride a bicycle explains why she cannot cycle from X to Y, from Y to Z, from Z to W, and so on.

Setiya's argument is similar. He writes as follows:

> [The theory that knowledge of a fact is the ability to be guided by it] cannot be right. For the relation of knowledge to this capacity is not symmetric. When someone lacks knowledge, they cannot act because p because they do not know that p. Compare the converse claim: S does not know that p because he cannot do things because p. That explanation is false. [. . .] On Hyman's view, there should be no asymmetry: the explanations should be on a par.[24]

The argument is not quite accurately expressed. First, 'the relation of knowledge to this capacity is not symmetric' cannot be exactly what Setiya means. For things are not related by a single relation, but by many, and it is possible for things to stand in both symmetric and asymmetric relations, e.g. two siblings, one taller than the other. Perhaps he means that nothing can stand in an asymmetric relation to itself. But that brings us to the second point, which is that the asymmetry Setiya detects is not between a person's knowledge of a fact and her ability to be guided by it, it is between two *facts*: the fact that a person does not know a fact, and the fact that she cannot be guided by it. Setiya holds that the first fact explains the second, but the second does not explain the first. But if he is right about this, it merely follows that these are different facts. It does not follow that knowledge of a fact and the ability to be guided by it are different states. Similarly, if you park on a double yellow line, you contravene section 238 of the Highway Code *because* you do so, and not the other way around: you do not park on a double yellow line because you contravene section 238 of the Highway Code. So these are two facts asymmetrically related to each other. Still, parking on a double yellow line and contravening section 238 are one and the same act.[25]

Hence, if 'S cannot be guided by the fact p because he does not know it' sounds right, while 'S does not know the fact that p because he cannot be guided by it' sounds wrong, this does not refute the theory that knowledge of a fact is the ability to be guided by it. If it did refute it, many philosophical theories would be easier to dismiss than in fact they are. For example, some philosophers hold that to have a certain colour is to look that colour to normal observers in normal conditions. I do not myself believe this theory is correct, but it would be too quick to dismiss it on the grounds that 'Her hair looks blue because it *is* blue (and not because of a trick of the light)' is perfectly intelligible and may be true, whereas 'Her hair is blue because it looks blue (and not because of the shampoo she uses)' scarcely makes sense.[26]

Presumably, the fact that one statement sounds right and the other sounds wrong reflects the fact that there are different ways of interpreting the 'because'—i.e., there are different kinds of explanations—and if we interpret the 'because' in the wrong way, a valid explanation can seem false.[27] Thus, we can expect a philosopher who accepts this theory of colour to say that 'Her hair looks blue because it is blue' is potentially a valid causal explanation of why someone's hair looks blue, whereas 'Her hair is blue because it looks blue' is part of a valid explanation of the kind of property being blue is. It is likely to sound baffling if we are expecting a causal explanation, such as '. . . because of the shampoo she uses', because it is not that kind of explanation. But we cannot infer from this that the theory of colours it illustrates is false.

Similarly, 'S does not know the fact that p because he cannot be guided by it' will sound baffling if we are expecting a causal explanation—e.g. 'Tom does not know that I'm here because I didn't tell him', or 'Anne does not know who won because she didn't hear the news'—for the same reason. But this has no bearing on whether it is part of a valid explanation of the kind of mental state knowing a fact is, i.e. on whether knowledge is the ability to be guided by the facts.

But if neither Williamson's argument nor Setiya's is convincing, it does not follow that knowledge *is* the ability to be guided by the facts, as opposed to a state that explains why we have the ability, as they suggest. Consider the soporific power—the *virtus dormitiva*—of a drug. The drug has a particular internal structure, which explains why it has the ability to cause sleep. Having this internal structure is a matter of how it *is*, specifically, how its parts are arranged in relation to each other, whereas being able to cause sleep is a matter of what it *does*, when it is ingested. The drug has the power because it has the structure, the structure is the 'ground' or 'basis' of the power. Might knowledge be analogous to the drug's structure rather than its power?

To answer this question we need to recall the distinction between possessing knowledge and containing information. We can assume that the state that 'grounds' a person's ability to be guided by a fact is an informational state, which is realized in the synaptic connections and neural firing patterns in her brain. Philosophers and neuroscientists have sometimes assumed that knowledge itself is an informational state, but containing information is not the same as possessing knowledge. For instance, an old vinyl record does not know the songs recorded on it, but it contains the information that enables a record-player to play them, because it was stamped with the right shaped groove (the information is realized in the groove). So it would be a mistake to think that knowledge is analogous to the informational state of the record, as opposed to the record-player's ability to play the song. It is the ability rather than the state that grounds it. That is why the acid test of what a person knows—as of any ability or skill—is what she says and does, for example, when she modifies her behaviour in pursuit of her goals.*

Furthermore, it is a basic rational principle that simpler empirically adequate hypotheses are to be preferred. There are certainly other theories of knowledge which imply that knowing that *p* is necessary and sufficient for being able to be guided by the fact that *p*, apart from the theory that they are the same intellectual state, such as the functionalist theory that *knowing a fact is having the second-order property of having some first-order property that grounds the ability to be guided by it*. But the theory that knowing a fact *is* being able to be guided by it is obviously the simplest explanation, hence the onus of proof must fall on those who prefer a different one. Besides, if the functionalist theory turned out to be preferable, I would regard this as more of a vindication than a defeat. For the principle I have been at pains to defend in this chapter, that the right way to define knowledge is to explain how it gets exercised or expressed in rational thought and behaviour, instead of asking how it can be certified or acquired, would be confirmed.

---

* In Wittgenstein's terms, a person's behaviour is not a *symptom* of knowledge, but a *criterion*. This is not a reversion to behaviourism; it is perfectly compatible with the point made earlier, that knowledge gets expressed in thought and feeling as well as in behaviour.

7.4 Our knowledge of our own mental states

The theory of knowledge defended in this chapter is partly inspired by Wittgenstein's claim that 'the grammar of the word "knows" is evidently closely related to that of "can", "is able to"'. But it contradicts his famous remark: 'It can't be said of me at all (except perhaps as a joke) that I *know* I am in pain.'[28] For the fact that I am in pain certainly *can* be my reason for doing, wanting, or believing something, say, for taking an aspirin, for wanting to lie down, or for believing I have spent too long in the sun. So if the theory of knowledge defended here is right, it *can* be said of me (not merely as a joke) that I know I am in pain. Is this a reason for disputing Wittgenstein's remark? Or is it a reason for rejecting or modifying the theory of knowledge?

Two preliminary points should be noted. First, Wittgenstein made less famous remarks that express a different view. For instance, in a remark about my knowledge of the disposition of my limbs, e.g. whether my arm is extended or not, he says: 'I simply *know* how it is—without knowing it *because*...Just as I also know where I feel pain—but do not know it *because*.'[29] (I have no quarrel with this.) Second, the claim that I cannot be said to know that I am in pain is an ingenious gambit to play against the philosopher who is tempted by the thought that *only* I can know whether I am in pain. It turns the tables on him in a dramatic way, and puts him on the defensive. But it is not an essential part of Wittgenstein's attack on the idea that we cannot ever really know what others think and feel, or even whether they have thoughts and feelings at all.

Wittgenstein supports the claim that I cannot be said to know that I am in pain with two arguments, or rather, with a challenge and an argument. Here is the challenge:

> It can't be said of me at all (except perhaps as a joke) that I *know* I am in pain.
> What is it supposed to mean—except perhaps that I *am* in pain?

And here is the argument: our use of the verb 'know' is coordinated with the use of a number of other verbs, and can only occur in circumstances which might also permit the use of these other verbs—verbs such as 'learn', 'doubt', 'believe', 'suspect', 'find out', and so on. But I cannot be said to learn, doubt, believe, suspect, or find out that I am in pain; hence, I cannot be said to know I am in pain either. The relevant remarks are these:

Other people cannot be said to learn of my sensations *only* from my behaviour,—for *I* cannot be said to learn of them. I *have* them.

The truth is: it makes sense to say about other people that they doubt whether I am in pain; but not to say it about myself.

'I know...' may mean 'I do not doubt...' but does not mean that the words 'I doubt...' are *senseless*, that doubt is logically excluded.

One says 'I know' where one can also say 'I believe' or 'I suspect'; where one can find out.[30]

I shall comment on the challenge and the argument in turn.

(A) So far as the challenge is concerned, there appears to be a simple answer. The difference between 'Katy knows she is in pain' and 'Katy is in pain' is that 'Katy knows she is in pain' implies that Katy can be guided by the fact that she is in pain, whereas 'Katy is in pain' does not. A fish or a new-born baby cannot be aware of the fact that it is in pain—although it can of course be in pain—because a fish or a baby cannot be guided by reasons in the way it acts. Hence, if Katy is a new-born baby, 'Katy is in pain' may be true, but 'Katy knows that she is in pain' will certainly be false. A new-born baby can *be* in pain, but she cannot *know* whether she is in pain, either that she is or that she is not.

(B) What about the argument? First, there are cases other than the contested ones about my current conscious state where some but not all of the verbs Wittgenstein mentions seem to apply happily, such as the most elementary truths of arithmetic. For example, I know, and I once learned, that $3 + 2 = 5$, but is this something I could suspect or surmise? It seems not. So the coordination of these verbs appears to be looser and more variable than Wittgenstein's remarks imply. Second, it invites the following question: why can't we concede that the use of the verb 'know' is *normally* or *generally* coordinated with the use of the other verbs Wittgenstein mentions, while insisting that facts about my present conscious experience, and possibly other facts that I can know, are anomalous cases? After all, there are plenty of anomalies of this sort in our use of words, and the verb 'know' itself provides several examples.

For example, Ryle says: 'To know a truth I must have discovered or established it', but the 'must' is rash, because there are anomalous cases.[31] I know that I live in London and that I speak French, but these are not things that I have discovered or established. In a similar vein, Wittgenstein says: 'If someone [...] knows something, then the question "how does he know?" must be capable of being answered.'[32] But must it? Elsewhere, he denies that it must:

'But how could I know that I should have reacted like this if you had asked me?'—How? There is no How. But there are indications that I am right in saying this.[33]

Again, Wittgenstein says: 'Whether I *know* something depends on whether the evidence backs me up or contradicts me.'[34] But what is the evidence that $1 + 1 = 2$ or that identity is symmetric? And yet I know these things. So Wittgenstein may have been right to deny that I can suspect or surmise that I am in pain, and to insist that the question 'How do you know that you are in pain?' is absurd. But why should we infer that I cannot know that I am in pain? He does not say.

Hence, Wittgenstein's position appears to be a weak one, unless he had a plausible conception of knowledge in mind, which draws the boundaries of what one can be said to know more narrowly than I wish to, and which supports his idea about the coordination of verbs. But it is difficult to be certain whether he did have such a conception of knowledge in mind. As far as I know, the only commentator who has addressed this question directly is Kenny. He writes as follows:

Throughout his life [Wittgenstein] thought of knowledge as involving the possession of a true description of a state of affairs. That was why in the *Tractatus* he declared knowledge of tautologies impossible, since tautologies were not pictures of states of affairs. That is why, since 'I am in pain' is not, when I am in pain, a true description in the normal sense, 'I know that I am in pain' cannot be in order if 'know' is being used in the normal sense.[35]

Wittgenstein certainly suggests that the sentence 'I am in pain' is not a description: when you say that you are in pain, he argues, you do not 'read off what you say from the facts'.[36] If he thought of knowledge as involving the possession of a true description of a state of affairs, the claim that I cannot be said to know that I am in pain would have looked like a corollary of this doctrine. But is Kenny's interpretation correct? On the face of it, it is plausible. It explains Wittgenstein's remarks about knowledge of one's own conscious state, and it also accounts for the doctrine that we ought not to speak of knowing mathematical propositions either, which some commentators have attributed to Wittgenstein, presumably on the basis of the following lines from the *Remarks on the Foundations of Mathematics*: 'If you know a mathematical proposition, that's not to say you yet know *anything*. // I.e., the mathematical proposition is only supposed to supply a framework for a description.'[37] But there are other remarks, notably in *On Certainty*, which suggest that even though he distinguished sharply between mathematical propositions and true descriptions of states of affairs, he was happy to speak of knowledge in mathematics, and which therefore tell against Kenny's interpretation. For example: 'If I say "I know" in mathematics, then the justification for this is a proof.'[38]

But whether or not Kenny's interpretation is right, the conception of knowledge he attributes to Wittgenstein is mistaken. If Rebecca knows that the angles of a triangle are equal to two right-angles, that *is* something Rebecca knows, and there is nothing wrong with saying so. We can acknowledge the differences between the ways in which mathematical knowledge and empirical knowledge are acquired, used, and tested, without drawing such narrow limits around the field of knowledge that mathematics is excluded from it. And the same goes for our own conscious states. The sort of knowledge that is expressed in what Wittgenstein thought of as a true description of an empirical state of affairs is of course one pre-eminent paradigm of knowledge. But we should not allow ourselves to become so captivated by a paradigm that no other sort of knowledge seems possible. My knowledge extends to every fact I can be guided by, be it a fact about my perceptible environment, a mathematical fact or a fact about my own conscious state. In every case, I can respond to the fact rationally, or take it into consideration or account, and that is all we need to talk of knowledge.

In sum, Wittgenstein's famous remark, 'It can't be said of me at all (except perhaps as a joke) that I *know* I am in pain', is a dramatic reversal of philosophical orthodoxy. But the arguments he offers to support it are inconclusive, and, if Kenny's interpretation is correct, its ultimate source was a mistaken conception of knowledge itself. It would be generally agreed that in normal circumstances an adult human being knows whether or not he is in pain, whereas a man in a delirium, a new-born baby, or a fish does not. The theory of knowledge defended here explains why.

7.5 Conclusion

The idea that knowledge is an ability was occasionally pursued by philosophers influenced by Wittgenstein and Ryle between the 1960s and 1990s, but it was almost completely eclipsed by the idea that knowledge is a species of belief. Gettier's influential article 'Is justified true belief knowledge?' persuaded most philosophers that knowledge is not simply justified true belief, but several decades passed before scepticism about the idea that knowledge is *some* kind of belief started to gain ground.

Some philosophers challenged the assumption that knowledge is a species of belief. In particular, Ryle pointed out several ways in which knowledge resembles other abilities and skills, while belief resembles tendencies and dispositions, and Vendler argued that belief and knowledge have different objects: what is believed is a proposition, whereas what is known is a fact.[39] (See 7.2.) But these arguments had little effect on opinion, and when the assumption that knowledge is a species of belief began to be more widely questioned, the main reason was exhaustion. Gettier instigated a vast amount of work, but no definition of knowledge in terms of belief commanded general assent; counterexamples were invented that seemed to disprove every published proposal; and inevitably, the more arcane the definitions proposed in the literature became, the more likely it seemed that even if one was devised to which no counterexample could be found, it would not be a plausible explanation of what knowledge is, because there could be no point in using such a complicated concept—in other words, because it could not matter whether someone met the conditions comprising it or not.

For these reasons, a sceptical view of the prospects for a definition of knowledge in terms of belief has become quite common, and the view that knowledge—as opposed to justified belief—does not matter has also been aired.[40] But the idea that knowledge is a kind of belief has cast such a long shadow that even those who reject it tend to equate the question of whether it is possible to define knowledge in terms of belief with the question of whether it is possible to define knowledge at all, and so the conviction that knowledge is indefinable has increased in popularity at the same time.[41]

If knowledge is the ability to be guided by the facts, the project of defining knowledge did not run into the sands because knowledge is inherently resistant to definition, but because it is an ability and not a species of belief, and so the question we need to ask in order to define it is how it gets exercised or expressed, rather than how it can be certified or acquired. We need to think about knowledge applied, employed, in the infinitely varied circumstances that arise in the course of human life. We need to think about knowledge in action, knowledge in use. Why did so few philosophers see this during the last fifty years? The main reason is probably that intentional action was invariably regarded as the effect or expression of desire and belief. Until quite recently, hardly anyone saw that the kind of explanation that refers to knowledge cannot be subsumed into the kind that refers to belief.[42]

A theory of factual knowledge is first and last a testable definition of the kind of intellectual state an individual's knowledge of a fact is. But a convincing theory will not only explain what knowledge is: it will also explain why we value it. I shall turn to this problem in the next chapter.

8

The Road to Larissa

8.1 The tree of knowledge

O sacred, wise, and wisdom-giving plant,
Mother of science, now I feel thy power
Within me clear not only to discern
Things in their causes but to trace the ways
Of highest agents deemed however wise.

These are the opening lines of the serpent's eulogy of knowledge in Book 9 of *Paradise Lost*, the speech that persuades Eve to eat the fruit from the 'wisdom-giving plant'. Milton composed his poem during the years the Royal Society was founded. He understood and admired the power and beauty of modern science, and saw as clearly as anyone had done before the problem with the orthodox interpretation of the story of the Fall. Knowledge is good for human beings, and, as the serpent says to Eve, 'God, therefore, cannot hurt ye and be just.'

The story is traditionally called the Fall of Man, or simply the Fall, but does the name reflect how it was understood by the community in which it was first told and written down? Daube thought not. He said that it should be called the Rise: 'It is only if we read [*Genesis* 3] through late Jewish rabbinical and Christian spectacles that it is about a fall.'[1] As I shall explain, I think the case for this view is compelling. But let us first recall the orthodox interpretation.

In the Christian tradition, both the name and the interpretation were made canonical by Augustine's commentary in *The City of God*.[2] We are told in the last verse of *Genesis* 2 that before they ate the knowledge-giving fruit, Adam and Eve were 'naked and not ashamed'. According to Augustine, their nakedness was not shameful because 'not yet did lust move those members [the genitals] without the will's consent'.[3]

The devil, a fallen angel, envious of man's innocent and unfallen state, chose the serpent to 'insinuate his persuasive guile into the mind of man' because 'being slippery, and moving in tortuous windings, it was suitable for his purpose'. The serpent, Augustine says, 'first tried his deceit upon the woman, making his assault upon the weaker part of that human alliance', judging that the man might be more susceptible to persuasion by the woman than by himself. God had told Adam he would die if he ate the fruit, but Eve was persuaded by the serpent that the threat was empty, and that if she ate the fruit she would herself become like a god. Adam was not persuaded, but he yielded to Eve, 'the husband to the wife, the one human being to the only other human being'.

Thus Eve was deceived, but Adam, Augustine says, 'sinned with his eyes open'. 'Although they were not both deceived by credulity, yet both were entangled in the snares of the devil and taken by sin.' What sin did Adam and Eve commit? It was the sin of pride. 'The evil act had never been done', Augustine says, 'had not an evil will preceded it. And what is the origin of our evil will but pride? And what is pride but the craving for undue exaltation?' The immediate result of their sin was that their eyes were opened, they saw they were naked, they were ashamed, and they covered the shameful parts of their bodies with fig-leaves.

Augustine acknowledges that it may not be immediately obvious to everyone who hears the story that Adam and Eve committed an act of great wickedness. But he insists that we should not think that the sin was a small and light one merely because it was committed about food. On the contrary, he explains, 'obedience is the mother and guardian of all the virtues', and preferring to fulfil one's own will instead of the Creator's 'is destruction'.

Adam and Eve, Augustine says, 'despised the authority of God', and God's punishment was that man would henceforth live 'in a hard and miserable bondage', since he had chosen obedience to his own will rather than to God's, 'doomed in spite of himself to die in body as he had willingly become dead in spirit, condemned even to eternal death (had not the grace of God delivered him) because he had forsaken eternal life'. Augustine summarizes his interpretation of the story as follows: '[Adam and Eve] committed so great a sin, that by it human nature was altered for the worse, and was transmitted also to their posterity, liable to sin and subject to death.'

This is the orthodox interpretation of the story in the Christian tradition, and the canonical interpretation in the Roman Catholic Church. The interpretation in the Jewish tradition has been similar since the rabbinic period—in other words, for the last two thousand years.

Daube's remarks about the story of the Fall occur in his lectures *Civil Disobedience in Antiquity*, Adam and Eve, he explains, being 'probably [among] the earliest heroes of civil disobedience'. Daube compares the story with the Greek myth of Prometheus. There, Zeus, the King of the Olympians, is determined to withhold from man the basic material for civilization, namely fire, but Prometheus, a being halfway between the gods and the earth-dwellers, steals fire from heaven and delivers it to man. 'Zeus cannot undo what has been done; he can only inflict dire punishment on the two conspirators, Prometheus and man.'[4]

The myth, Daube says, reflects an archaic phase in theology when man looks on the gods as being opposed to him. 'Nor can one be surprised that there should have been such a phase seeing that, before the advent of even primitive technology, it must have been very natural for man to feel himself in the midst of a largely inimical set-up.' Any gains, he adds, were to be attained in defiance of the dominant forces around him.

> In the Bible, one of the chapters representing this stage is the so-called story of the Fall [...] Stripped of subsequent interpretation, the narrative reports that Adam and Eve were in a garden, living crudely and mindlessly like the animals surrounding them. 'They were naked and not ashamed'—this, from the wisdom narrator's point of view, was not a blissful Rousseauesque state but a horrible primitivity. However, there was a tree in the garden with knowledge-giving fruit. Only God forbade the couple to eat of it, and he made sure his prohibition would be heeded by threatening them with immediate death if they disobeyed: 'On the day that you eat thereof, you shall assuredly die.' A being half-way between God and man, the serpent, informs them that this threat is empty: the fruit is not death-bringing, not fatal, on the contrary it will open their eyes and make them discerning. So they do eat of it, and indeed God turns out to have been lying. They do not die, and their eyes are opened exactly as the serpent, the Prometheus of the Biblical story, told them. They become discriminating between good and evil, aware of their nakedness— capable of shame.[5]

'Just like Zeus,' Daube concludes, 'God inflicts fearful retribution on the rebellious serpent and couple, but like Zeus, he must put up with the start of human civilization.'

Perhaps the suggestion that the story should be called the Rise is an exaggeration. The Hebrew word for fall (*nepilah*) does not occur in the story itself, or in any of the references to it in the Hebrew scriptures. Nor does the story seem to describe a change for the worse in human nature. But it does describe a dramatic change for the worse in the circumstances in which human beings live, and it explains some of the most difficult and painful aspects of human life, as well as the origin of civilization. Nevertheless, Daube's interpretation of the story must be essentially right.

First, as he points out, nakedness was considered shameful by the community in which the story was originally written down. It is extraordinary that commentators continue to miss this point. For example, one recently published commentary on *Genesis* says: '*Genesis* 2 ends in a brief notation about the innocence of the first human couple. Although they were "naked" there was no shame in it.'[6] But 'there was no shame in it' is not what the verse says. It says, 'And they were both naked, the man and his wife, and not ashamed', which is very different. The great rabbi Rashi, who died eight centuries before the naturist movement got going, did not make the same mistake. He comments on the verse: 'They were not aware of the *derech tzniut* [the rabbinic laws concerned with modest clothing and conduct], to distinguish between good and bad.'[7]

Furthermore, Augustine's explanation of why Adam's and Eve's nakedness was not shameful is unconvincing. He says, 'not yet did lust move those members without the will's consent.' But there is no evidence for this explanation in the text, and it is difficult to understand why the fact that sexual arousal can be involuntary should make it shameful. The shamefulness of an involuntary reaction (as opposed to shameful conduct) generally depends on its being observed or occurring in an inappropriate situation, as when Odysseus is ashamed to be seen weeping by the Phaeacians, and hides his face in his cloak.

The second consideration that favours Daube's interpretation over Augustine's is that there is no mention in the story of the devil. Satan first appears in Jewish writings in the post-exilic period, about four centuries after *Genesis* was composed; and there, in *Job* for example, he is clearly subordinate to God and unable to act without His permission. Satan emerges as an independent personality and the personification of evil in the first century CE, and the earliest extant statement in Jewish writings that he was responsible for the Fall is by Rabbi Eliezer, around the year 100.

Third, as for the serpent, Augustine says that he is slippery and moves in tortuous windings, but in *Genesis* he is described as *arum*, which means, crafty, shrewd, or cunning. This does not imply that he is wicked or evil, any more than the Greek word *polymetis*, which Homer uses as Odysseus's epithet, means this. What is clear is that the serpent knows that the humans will not die upon eating the forbidden fruit, but will become 'like Gods, knowing good and evil' (*Genesis* 3.5), as God himself acknowledges they have done: 'Behold,' God says, 'the man is become as one of us, to know good and evil' (3.22).

Fourth, the orthodox interpretation of the story ignores God's lie. God says to Adam: '[O]f the tree of the knowledge of good and evil, thou shalt not eat of it: for in the day that thou eatest thereof thou shalt surely die' (*Genesis* 2.17). The serpent says: 'Ye shall not surely die' (3.4). And this proves to be true. Ever since Paul, the orthodox interpretation has finessed this point by interpreting 'die' as 'become mortal' or 'become susceptible to eternal death'. But 'die' is not used to mean these things anywhere else in the Hebrew scriptures. Besides, the creation story does not say that Adam and Eve were created immortal, despite Augustine's claim that they forsook eternal life. On the contrary, it implies that they were created mortal, for God expels Adam from the Garden of Eden to ensure that he will not *become* immortal by eating from the tree of life (3.22–23).[8]

Fifth, it cannot have been wicked or sinful on the part of Adam and Eve to eat the fruit of the tree of knowledge, because when they ate the fruit they did not yet know the difference between good and evil. It is true that they knew they were disobeying God. The story implies that this is something one can know without yet understanding evil, wickedness, or sin, and no doubt this is correct. But disobedience in a state of moral innocence or ignorance, even deliberate disobedience—for example, by young children—is not evil, wicked, or sinful, regardless of whom one disobeys.

Sixth, knowledge in general, and knowledge of good and evil in particular, are good for human beings. This has always been acknowledged as a powerful reason to reject the story in its orthodox interpretation, or to deny that God's commandment not to eat the fruit was just. In *Paradise Lost*, the serpent explains the point when he advocates disobedience to Eve with consummate forensic skill. But the earliest anti-Christian polemicists were already aware of it. In *Against the Galileans*, Julian 'the Apostate' writes:

Is it not excessively strange that God should deny to the human beings whom he had fashioned the power to distinguish between good and evil? What could be more foolish than a being unable to distinguish good from bad? For it is evident that he would not avoid the latter, I mean things evil, nor would he strive after the former, I mean things good. And, in short, God refused to let man taste of wisdom, than which there could be nothing of more value for man. For that the power to distinguish between good and less good is the property of wisdom is evident surely even to the witless; so that the serpent was a benefactor rather than a destroyer of the human race.[9]

For all these reasons, Daube's interpretation of the story must be essentially correct. It is not a story of human sin and just punishment by a just god; it is a story of a deceitful god who is jealous of human progress and visits the most terrible retribution on the man and woman who take the first perilous and defiant step towards civilized human life.

Daube comments that although the story pits man against God, it is presumably modelled on precedents involving struggles of man against man, and indicates familiarity with a situation where a potentate can only with difficulty be got to concede a minimum of independent life to his subjects. He adds: 'There may be a reminiscence, too, of a helpful role of persons who, while connected with the ruler, side with the oppressed—and pay the price.'[10] This is surely plausible, but what is certain is that the story is the earliest affirmation in our culture of the value of knowledge for human beings, and its indispensible place in human life.

8.2 The *Meno* puzzle

Several centuries after *Genesis* was written down, Plato presented the following puzzle about knowledge in the *Meno*:

> SOCRATES: If a man knew the way to Larissa, or any other place you please, and walked there and led others, would he not be a good guide?
> MENO: Certainly.
> SOCRATES: And a person who had the right opinion as to which was the way, but had never been there and did not really know, might also be a good guide, might he not?
> MENO: Certainly.
> SOCRATES: And presumably as long as he has the right opinion, he will be just as good a guide as the one who knows—if he believes the truth instead of knowing it.

MENO: Just as good.

SOCRATES: Hence true opinion is as good a guide to acting the right way as knowledge is. (*Meno* 97a–c)

The puzzle is this. Knowledge is not the same thing as true belief. For example, no one can know now which team will win the next World Cup. But across the world there are people who fervently believe their team will win, and some of them will turn out to be right. They will not turn out to have *known* which team would win, but to have had the right opinion. (One can say 'I *knew* it!' meaning 'I was certain!' or 'I was right!') So knowing has to be distinguished from having the right opinion, that is, believing something that happens to be true. But while the superiority of knowledge over ignorance—which the author of *Genesis* took for granted—is not hard to explain, it *is* hard to explain why knowledge is superior to true belief. True belief seems to be as good a guide to acting the right way as knowledge is, since the one who knows the truth and the one who merely believes the truth will pursue the same course of action, or offer the same advice. So why does it matter what we know?

I shall argue that Plato's own solution to the puzzle fails, but that it can be solved if we accept the theory of knowledge defended in Chapter 7.[11] However, the solution I envisage steers a path between opposing views about the value of knowledge. For some philosophers claim that we simply value the truth, and it does not matter whether we achieve the peculiar kind of relation to it we call 'knowing' it—however exactly that should be defined—as long as we are guided by the truth, while others hold the opposite view. But I maintain that being guided by the truth and being guided by knowledge are one and the same thing, so both of these opposing views are partly right and partly wrong.

Three other preliminary remarks:

(A) On the one hand, the idea that knowledge is a better guide to acting the right way than true belief does not imply that knowledge is always preferable to ignorance, that every fact is worth the expense of learning or remembering it, or that the advance of science has benefits but no costs. On the other hand, if none of these things is true—as most people believe—it does not follow that knowledge is ever worthless, but only that its value is in many cases outweighed by the value of other things, such as survival, or peace of mind.

Is some knowledge absolutely worthless? Sosa thinks so:

At the beach on a lazy summer afternoon, we might scoop up a handful of sand and carefully count the grains. This would give us an otherwise unremarked truth, something that on the view before us is at least a positive good, other things equal. This view is hard to take seriously. The number of grains would not interest most of us in the slightest. Absent any such antecedent interest, moreover, it is hard to see any sort of *value* in one's having that truth.[12]

But two points count against this view. First, it is always possible that, at some stage, one will be invited to bet on the number of grains of sand in a handful. It's the kind of thing that can happen on a lazy summer afternoon at the beach. So it would presumably be worth preparing for the eventuality, say, by averaging a thousand carefully conducted trials, if the cost of doing so were nil. And if that counts as having an antecedent interest, then we have an antecedent interest in knowing any fact that can be the subject of a bet, which means any fact that can be known at all. Second, as Horwich points out, the view that all knowledge has some value accords with the conventional idea that a perfect being would be omniscient.[13] Luke says that God knows the number of hairs on each person's head. Whether it interests Him does not seem to the point.

However, neither of these arguments is conclusive. Regarding the first, perhaps it is always possible that an item of knowledge will prove useful, but the chance of it doing so can be negligible—i.e. so small that it can be ignored—and hence the value of knowing it can be negligible as well. Regarding the second, the idea of a perfect being may be a guide to what we value, but not in the simple way Horwich implies. For it is essentially the idea of a being without limits rather than a being that realizes human values to the highest degree. For example, a perfect being is traditionally held to be omnipresent, but this does not imply that every location has some value. Besides, it is not obvious that the idea of a perfect being, as opposed to the idea of a perfect specimen of some kind of being, makes perfect sense, and if it does not, then it is an imperfect guide to what we value for that reason alone.

The right answer, I suggest, is that the value of knowledge can be negligible. Whether this is closer to Sosa's view or Horwich's is debatable.

(B) I am not concerned, at least directly, with the value of the concept of knowledge, as opposed to the value of knowledge itself. These topics are not always sharply distinguished, but they are distinct. For there can be a positive value in having a concept of something that is itself of negative value, such as crime or sin, or of no value positive or negative, such as the number π.

(C) Various questions have been discussed by philosophers under the general heading 'The Value of Knowledge', but I shall focus narrowly on a single question. I shall talk throughout in general terms about the value of knowledge, but this should always be read as referring to the question raised by the passage in the *Meno*: is knowledge a better guide to acting the right way than true belief, and if so why?

8.3 Plato's solution to the puzzle

Here is Plato's own answer. Knowledge, Socrates explains, is more valuable than true belief, because true beliefs are like the statues made by Daedalus, which were so life-like that they ran away unless they were tied down:

> So long as they stay with us, [true beliefs] are a fine possession, and effect all that is good; but they do not care to stay for long, and run away out of the human soul, and thus are of no great value until one ties them down by working out the cause [*aitias logismō*]. That process, my dear Meno, is recollection, as we agreed earlier. (97e–98a)

The interpretation of this passage is controversial, especially the phrase *aitias logismō*, which I have translated as 'working out the cause'. However, Socrates appears to be saying that what makes a true belief more durable, more stable, is understanding why it is true; and he is certainly claiming that the stability of knowledge is what makes it more valuable than true belief:

> Once they are tied down, they become knowledge, and are stable. That is why knowledge is more valuable than true opinion. What distinguishes one from the other is the tether. (98a)

In sum, Plato's idea appears to be that knowledge involves *understanding why* the things we know to be true are true; and that understanding this makes us able to hold fast to the truth, and avoid lapsing into falsehood. And that explains why knowledge is more valuable than true belief.[14]

The solution is ingenious, but it is not convincing, for four main reasons. First, beliefs that do not have a rational foundation are not necessarily unstable. Some of our most stable beliefs are inculcated in us as children, without being tied down by 'working out the cause'—moral and religious beliefs, for example. The prophets and preachers who offer to guide us on the road to salvation generally tell us that they know the way; but even if they are mistaken, their beliefs tend to be stable, perhaps because the stabilizing effect can be achieved by merely believing that one has 'worked out the cause'.

Second, neither the stability of knowledge, nor its status as knowledge, is invariably due to evidence or rational support. Russell and Whitehead complete their proof of the proposition that $1 + 1 = 2$ on page 86 of *Principia Mathematica*, volume 2, and perhaps this counts as 'working out the cause'. But it is doubtful whether the proof transformed a belief into knowledge, or made it more stable and less liable to 'run away'.

Third, knowledge is not uniformly more stable than belief. Since we are forgetful, we lose a good deal of the knowledge we acquire: trivial knowledge, such as the number of coins I have in my pocket, much of the knowledge we acquire when we read a newspaper, and much of the knowledge we acquire at school. Some philosophers maintain that whether the beliefs we acquire by testimony—for example, when we read the papers—count as knowledge or mere opinion can depend on the reliability of the source. And that may be right. But the reliability of the source—as opposed to what we believe about it—will not normally affect how securely we hold on to these beliefs, or how easily they are forgotten and slip out of our minds.

Fourth, as Craig has pointed out, the stability of a person's beliefs is important in some cases but not others. 'Many beliefs', he writes, 'are required for the guidance of single, "one-off" actions under circumstances that will not recur, and once the particular occasion is past there is no obvious value at all in their persistence.'[15] For instance, it is important for me to have a true belief now about the time I am due to meet a visitor this afternoon, and the time when I promised to call a friend in Los Angeles tonight. But by next Wednesday, it probably won't matter whether I have retained either of these beliefs. So the idea that stability is what makes knowledge more valuable than mere true belief suggests that it is *not* more valuable in cases where its usefulness is short-lived.

For these reasons, Plato's own solution to his problem is unconvincing. And this may make us wonder whether the problem is real. Perhaps the idea that knowledge is more valuable than true belief is an illusion. Perhaps it is part of the mystification of knowledge Wittgenstein criticized in *On*

Certainty: '...a queer and extremely important mental state...a state of affairs which guarantees what is known, guarantees it as a fact.'[16] Perhaps it is a nostalgic tribute to a conception of knowledge—Plato's, Descartes's—we can no longer share.[17]

Whatever one may think about these diagnoses, a sceptical attitude to Plato's problem—in other words, the thought that perhaps knowledge is *not* more valuable than true belief—has become quite widespread in the last forty or fifty years, since the publication of Gettier's article 'Is Justified True Belief Knowledge?', for four main reasons.[18]

First, Gettier showed that justified true belief is not sufficient for knowledge, from which it follows that knowledge is not necessary for justified true belief. But in that case, why should we care about knowledge? Wright expresses this thought as follows: 'We can live with the concession that we do not, strictly, *know* some of the things we believed ourselves to know, provided we can retain the thought that we are fully justified in accepting them.'[19]

Second, if we seek knowledge, and justified true belief is insufficient for knowledge, how can we seek the extra element knowledge requires? We can seek fresh evidence supporting the hypothesis we favour, and test and interrogate the evidence we believe we already have. But we could not seek the elusive ingredient that distinguishes knowledge from justified true belief, even if we could say exactly what it is. Kaplan makes this point as follows: 'All we can do by way of seeking knowledge is seek justified belief and hope that this justified belief will satisfy whatever other conditions a justified belief must satisfy in order to qualify as knowledge.'[20] It seems to follow that whatever the difference between knowledge and justified belief may be, scientific research, and rational inquiry in general, can simply ignore it. It *can* ignore it, because it *must*.

Third, many of the analyses of knowledge proposed during the decades that followed the publication of Gettier's article made it difficult to understand why knowledge should be more valuable than true belief.

In some cases it is their sheer complexity. For example, Swain proposed that S knows that *p* if and only if

(1) *p*,
(2) S believes that *p*,
(3) there is a set of reasons, *A*, such that
    (a) S's belief that *p* is based on *A*,
    (b) S's believing that *p* on the basis of *A* is justified,

(c) S has A as a result of at least one non-defective causal ancestry,
(d) if S has any other reasons, B, that are relevant to S's justifiably believing that p, then S would be justified in believing that p on the basis of $A \cap B$.[21]

But if this is what knowledge is, should it matter to us whether our choices are informed by knowledge or by true belief? Should we care whether we take the left fork because we know that it is the road to Larissa, all three conditions being satisfied, or because we merely have a justified true belief that it is the road to Larissa, (3)(d) not being satisfied? It is difficult to see why.

In other cases it is the specific content of the analysis that makes it hard to understand why knowledge matters. For example, Nozick's initial proposal is that S knows that p if and only if

(1) p,
(2) S believes that p,
(3) if p weren't true S wouldn't believe that p,
(4) if p were true in slightly different circumstances, S would believe that p and wouldn't believe that not-p.

In fact this analysis cannot be quite right, as Nozick himself points out.[22] But, using the terminology of possible worlds for illustrative purposes, suppose we succeeded in defining sets of worlds $\mathbf{W_1}$ and $\mathbf{W_2}$ that made an analysis of this kind watertight: S knows that p if and only if

(1) p,
(2) S believes that p,
(3) in $\mathbf{W_1}$, if p is false then S doesn't believe that p,
(4) in $\mathbf{W_2}$, if p is true then S believes that p and doesn't believe that not-p.

If this were what knowledge is, it would be hard to see why it is more valuable than true belief. For it is obvious that I want the beliefs I rely on in the actual world, e.g. about which road leads to Larissa, to be true. But why should I mind whether my beliefs in possible but non-actual worlds are true as well? Why should I mind whether the journeys I *could* take to Larissa but *don't* take end in the right place? For all I care, they can take me to Crawford, Texas, or Guantanamo Bay. It might be objected that if I don't know which of several worlds *is* the actual world, then I shall want the beliefs I rely on in all of them to be true. But this is not quite right. My only concern is that I believe the truth in the actual world, but, being imperfectly informed, there are many respects in which I cannot say which world this is.[23]

Compare Williamson's suggestion that we value knowledge because it is a state 'whose essence includes a matching between mind and world'.[24] A similar objection applies. Why is a mental state that essentially involves a matching between mind and world preferable to one that non-essentially involves a matching between mind and world? Why is the simple fact of a matching between mind and world—i.e. simply being right—not all that counts? Philosophers disagree about whether water is essentially H_2O, or whether water on twin earth might be XYZ, but the properties, and hence the value, of the water we earthlings know and love does not depend on which view is right.

The fourth reason why epistemology since Gettier has encouraged the thought that knowledge may not be more valuable than true belief is that most of the extensive literature addressing Gettier's puzzle about knowledge sought to capture the idea that, if we know the truth, we do not believe the truth fortuitously or by luck. But benefits are not worth any less because they were gained fortuitously or by luck. We may admire a man more for inventing the bagless vacuum cleaner than for winning the lottery, but pound for pound their fortunes are worth the same.[25]

8.4 An elaboration of Plato's solution

To summarize the main points covered in 8.2 and 8.3:

First, Plato's proposal is that 'once [true beliefs] are tied down, they become knowledge, and are stable. That is why knowledge is more valuable than true opinion. What distinguishes one from the other is the tether.' But this is unconvincing for four reasons:

- Beliefs that do not have a rational foundation are not necessarily unstable.
- The stability of knowledge is not invariably due to evidence or rational support.
- Knowledge is not uniformly more stable than belief.
- Whether the stability of someone's belief is of value depends on what the belief is, and the circumstances.

Second, Gettier's article 'Is Justified True Belief Knowledge?', and the literature it generated, cast doubt on the idea that knowledge is more valuable than true belief, for four reasons:

- If knowledge is not necessary for justified true belief, justification cannot be the reason why we should value knowledge more.

- We cannot seek knowledge as opposed to justified true belief, so whatever the factor is that distinguishes between them, scientific research or rational enquiry can ignore it.

- Many of the definitions of knowledge devised to deal with Gettier-type cases make it hard to see why knowledge should be more valuable than true belief, either because of their complexity, or because of their specific content.

- Believing the truth fortuitously or by luck does not diminish the advantage it confers.

I shall make one further observation about Gettier. It is implicit in what I have already said about the impact of his article, but it is worth making it explicit. As we have seen, Gettier's article showed that justification cannot be the factor that makes knowledge more valuable than true belief. And this makes the puzzle in the *Meno* more difficult to solve. Ever since Plato, it has been clear that we cannot explain why we seek knowledge simply by explaining why it is preferable to ignorance: we need to explain why it is preferable to ignorance *or* true belief. But since Gettier, it is no longer enough even to explain why it is preferable to ignorance or true belief. We now need to explain why it is preferable to ignorance or *justified* true belief. I do not mean to imply that Gettier moved the goalposts, but he did raise the bar. And as we have seen, that makes it more tempting to duck the challenge, and deny that knowledge is a better guide to acting the right way than true belief is.

Let us return now to Plato's own solution to his puzzle, the idea that knowledge is more durable, more stable than true belief. I have explained why this solution is unsatisfactory, as it stands. But Williamson defends a qualified version of it, which does not depend on the claim about an essential matching between mind and world, which I commented on in 8.3.

Knowledge, Williamson explains, is less likely to be lost than mere true belief is when new evidence comes to light:

> One can lose a mere true belief by discovering the falsity of further beliefs on which it had been essentially based; quite often, the truth will out. One cannot lose knowledge in that way, because a true belief essentially based on false beliefs does not constitute knowledge. For example, I might derive the true belief that this road goes to Larissa from the two false (but perhaps justified)

beliefs that Larissa is due north and that this road goes due north; when dawn breaks in an unexpected quarter and I realize that this road goes south, without having been given any reason to doubt that Larissa is due north, I abandon the belief that this road goes to Larissa.[26]

It is true, of course, that some beliefs are adhered to dogmatically, whatever evidence comes to light. But Williamson claims that *if we are rational*, then knowledge is more durable than mere true belief:

> Present knowledge is less vulnerable than mere present true belief to *rational* undermining by future evidence [...] Other things being equal, given rational sensitivity to new evidence, present knowledge makes future true belief more likely than mere present true belief does.[27]

This is an ingenious elaboration of Plato's own solution to his puzzle, but it is unsatisfactory for three reasons.

First, on Williamson's account, as on Plato's, the advantage of knowledge over true belief varies depending on how probable it is that the belief concerned will be undermined by the discovery of another truth; and the greater value of knowledge is sometimes negligible, because the probability of discovering such a truth is sometimes negligible.

Second, on Williamson's account, again like Plato's, the advantage of knowledge over true belief only concerns the future, because of course that is what durability is all about. So knowledge that does not have a shelf life is no more valuable, as a guide to acting the right way, than true belief.

Williamson concedes the second point, but he argues that it does not represent a shortcoming in his account: 'The present argument concerns only delayed impact, not action at the next "instant". We do not value knowledge more than true belief for instant gratification.'[28] But this is unconvincing. It is true that we do not value knowledge for instant gratification; but we do not value it for deferred gratification either. Knowledge is sometimes gratifying and sometimes painful, and the value we attach to it does not normally depend on which it is. But we do value a great deal of knowledge, especially knowledge gained without inference by perception, because we can put it to immediate use. Hence, an account like Williamson's or Plato's, which makes the advantage of knowledge over true belief contingent on what may happen in the future, remains open to the charge that it is unsatisfactory or incomplete.

One might respond to these two points, on Williamson's behalf, by denying that knowledge is more valuable than true belief regardless of the future, by accepting that the difference in value between knowledge and true belief can be vanishingly small, and by insisting that, if we are rational, knowledge is *normally* more durable than true belief. In other words, one might simply insist that this is the best that we can do, or that it is all that it makes sense to attempt. After all, if someone claimed that a Fiat is better than a Ford because it is more durable, their argument would not be invalidated by pointing out that this is normally, but not invariably, the case. But a third objection shows that even on these limited terms, Williamson's solution to Plato's puzzle fails.

Remember: Williamson's solution is that if we are rational, knowledge is less likely to be undermined by future evidence than true belief. Knowledge, he says, is relatively robust. Here again is the example I cited earlier:

> I might derive the true belief that this road goes to Larissa from the two false (but perhaps justified) beliefs that Larissa is due north and that this road goes due north; when dawn breaks in an unexpected quarter and I realize that this road goes south, without having been given any reason to doubt that Larissa is due north, I abandon the belief that this road goes to Larissa.

But what does this example really show? According to Williamson, it shows that knowledge is less vulnerable to rational undermining by future evidence than true belief. But this is not quite right. The claim it really supports is that knowledge *or true belief whose justification does not include a falsehood (NFL)* is less vulnerable than *true belief whose justification does include a falsehood (FL).*[*] Williamson is right that a true belief essentially based on false beliefs does not constitute knowledge. But a true belief that is *not* essentially based on false beliefs may not constitute knowledge either. So the example supports the claim—which no doubt is true—that *either* knowledge *or* true belief NFL is more valuable than true belief FL. But it does not support the claim that knowledge is more valuable than true belief regardless of how the belief is justified.

We have already seen that Gettier made the *Meno* puzzle harder to solve, because he showed that we cannot solve it just by explaining why knowledge is more valuable than true belief. We need to explain why knowledge is more valuable than *justified* true belief. As I put it earlier, he raised the bar.

---

[*] In fact we need to add the qualification: *as long as there is some chance that the falsehood will come to light.* There may be falsehoods that can never come to light. For example, if Goldbach's conjecture, that every even number is the sum of two prime numbers, is true but unprovable, its contradictory is an undiscoverable falsehood.

Then, when epistemology after Gettier gathered pace, each time a more exacting set of conditions for knowledge was shown to be insufficient, the bar was raised by another increment.

One of the times this happened was in the early 1970s, when several philosophers pointed out that Gettier's counterexamples to the thesis that knowledge is justified true belief are cases where a falsehood happens to justify a truth, and proposed on the strength of that observation that knowledge is true belief NFL. But examples showing that true belief NFL is not sufficient for knowledge sprung up in the literature like mushrooms, so the proposal failed.[29]

This development made the puzzle even more difficult to solve than it had been for Gettier, because it showed that we can't even solve it by explaining why knowledge is more valuable than *justified* true belief: we need to explain why knowledge is more valuable than true belief NFL. As we have seen, Williamson's example sets knowledge on a par with true belief NFL. So of course it fails to explain why knowledge is a better guide to acting the right way than true belief, *whatever* kind of justification for the belief we may have.[*]

In sum, the solutions to the *Meno* puzzle proposed by Plato and Williamson fail for similar reasons. First, they both imply that the advantage of knowledge over true belief depends on how likely it is that a truth that would undermine the belief will come to light. Second, neither solution explains why knowledge without a shelf life is more valuable than true belief. Third, Plato fails to explain why it is better to know than to have the right opinion, however stubborn the opinion is, whereas Williamson fails to explain why it is better to know than to have the right opinion, however free from the taint of falsehood the justification for the opinion is.[30]

8.5 A new solution

The puzzle in the *Meno* is surprisingly hard to solve, and this makes it tempting to abandon the idea that knowledge is more valuable than true

---

* The same argument applies *pari passu* if we compare knowledge with true belief in circumstances where the subject does not have knowledge because of the presence of counter-evidence. Cases like Ginet's story about barn façades (see above, 6.4) only support the claim that present knowledge *or mere present true belief in the absence of counter-evidence* is less vulnerable than present true belief *in the presence of counter-evidence* to rational undermining by future evidence.

belief. The conviction that knowledge—fruit of the 'sacred, wise, and wisdom-giving plant'—is a precious thing is an ineradicable part of human culture. But on our journeys to Larissa, and on our longer journeys to our various Ithacas, perhaps it is simply the truth that we value and desire, and it does not matter whether we attain the specially privileged relationship to it we call 'knowledge', as long as we are guided by the truth.

I want to suggest first that we do indeed want to be guided by the truth, when this is possible, no less and no more; and second, that this fact alone explains why we value knowledge above true belief. So I want to reconcile the sceptical sentiment expressed in the last paragraph with Plato's conviction that knowledge is a better guide to acting the right way than true belief, and do justice to both. If this is the right approach, the mistake made by philosophers on both sides of the debate—both those who accept Plato's view that knowledge is the better guide and those who reject it[31]—is to force a choice that does not exist, between being guided by knowledge and being 'merely' guided by the truth.*

The solution I propose is a corollary of the theory defended in Chapter 7, that knowledge is the ability to be guided by the facts. As I explained in 7.2, the idea that knowledge is an ability transforms the task of defining knowledge, because instead of asking what we need to add to belief to get knowledge, or how knowledge can be acquired, we are forced to ask how knowledge gets exercised or expressed, since this is invariably how abilities are defined. And it is quite easy to say how knowledge gets expressed. For example, the traveller's knowledge that Larissa is due north gets expressed whenever he is guided by the fact that Larissa is due north, in what he thinks or does, say, when he takes the road that leads north to get to Larissa, or when he merely deduces that he is heading in the wrong direction from the fact that he is heading south.

Of course, a traveller who merely believes that Larissa is due north, without knowing it, can take the road that leads north on the *ground* or *assumption* that Larissa is due north. We can imagine him murmuring, 'Larissa is due north; so I shall take that road.' But doing an act on a ground or assumption is different from being guided by a fact, and one cannot be guided by a fact one does not know, any more than one can follow a guide

---

* The next three paragraphs repeat material from 7.2 and 7.3.1, so that this chapter can be read through without jumping back to those sections. I apologize to readers who remember these points well.

one cannot see. If the traveller sees the guide taking the left fork and follows him, then he is guided by the guide; but if he hallucinates him taking the left fork, and takes it himself for that reason, then he is not guided by the guide, even if the hallucination happens to be true.

The difference between the two cases is reflected in the difference between explanations that refer to knowledge and ones that refer to belief. Thus, compare 'He took the road that leads north because he knew that it leads to Larissa' and 'He took the road that leads north because he believed that it leads to Larissa.' Only the knowledge-involving explanation is equivalent to one in which the fact about the road is itself the *explanans*: 'Why did he take the road that leads north?' 'Because it leads to Larissa.' Why are these explanations equivalent? Because the knowledge-involving explanation cites (or purports to cite) a fact about his situation that he was aware of and responded to, whereas the belief-involving explanation merely refers (or purports to refer) to his state of mind. (Compare: 'Why did he go to the door?'—'Because he heard the bell ring' *or* 'Because the bell rang.')

This provides a simple solution to the puzzle in the *Meno*. For we not only care about *what* we do, and think, and feel, we also care about *why* we do it, think it, and feel it, and we want our deeds and thoughts and feelings to be guided by the truth.* Believing something tends to influence thought and behaviour in the same way as knowing it, but thought and behaviour influenced by belief are not guided by the truth, regardless of whether the belief is true. The man who has the right opinion about the way to Larissa, but has never been there and does not really know, will lead us in the right direction, as Socrates points out. So if all we cared about was getting to Larissa, we would not, or at least should not, prefer knowledge to mere true belief. But if we want to be guided by the truth, then we are bound to value knowledge above true belief.

But why does it matter to us whether we are guided by the truth? As we saw earlier, the stability and durability that Socrates said makes knowledge a better guide than true belief to acting the right way can be achieved if we merely believe we have 'worked out the cause'. Similarly, if a traveller on the road to Larissa *believes* he knows which road to take, it will seem to him as if he is guided by the truth, whether he is really knows it or not. Why isn't this enough for us? Why do we want more? As Hume once put it, these

---

* I make no distinction between being guided by the facts and being guided by the truth (see 7.2).

questions seem to throw us back into the same uncertainty from which we have endeavoured to extricate ourselves.

But in fact it isn't the same uncertainty at all. The question of why it matters to us whether we are guided by the truth is interesting, but it is different from the question we began with, and it has a different answer. The answer, presumably, is similar to Nozick's answer to his question about the experience machine he describes in *Anarchy, State and Utopia*.[32] As he points out, the fact that most of us would not choose to plug in to the machine suggests that there are things that matter to us other than how our lives feel 'from the inside': 'Perhaps what we want is to live [. . .] ourselves, in contact with reality', he says, and machines cannot do these things for us. Nozick's remark is partly about our desire to lead an active life and partly about our desire for reality rather than illusion, both of which seem to be basic values shared by most human beings, however difficult they are to explain.

My aim in this chapter was not to discover the roots of these values in the human psyche. I have simply tried to show three things. First, Plato's conviction that knowledge is a better guide than true belief to acting the right way is consistent with the ostensibly sceptical thought (for that is how it initially appeared) that all we care about, or can reasonably care about, is being guided by the truth. Second, the reason why Plato's own solution to the puzzle in the *Meno* and Williamson's elaboration of it both fail is that the resources they deploy are too limited. In fact they are limited to two elements only: what we do, will do, or may do; and what we believe, will believe, or may believe. Only action and belief. And this is too limited a range of factors to explain why knowledge is a better guide to acting the right way than true belief. And finally, the reason why it is too limited is that the explanation lies beyond what we do and believe; it lies in the reasons why we do it and believe it.

I do not mean to suggest that we always care about being guided by the truth in every aspect of our lives. But to the extent that we care about the truth, we care about knowledge. For seeking the truth *is* seeking knowledge, as we saw earlier. And being guided by the truth *is* being guided by knowledge, as we can see now. We cannot hope to be guided by a pillar of cloud, and illuminated by a pillar of fire, like the children of Israel crossing the desert to the promised land. The truth no longer announces itself in quite this way. But we can be guided by the truth, as long as we know it. And that is a sufficient reason to value knowledge more highly than belief.

Appendix
The Modern Theory of the Will

This appendix contains a brief historical digest of the modern theory of the will for
readers unfamiliar with the historical sources. It is not by any means a substitute for
reading them, but it includes the key ideas to which the argument in Chapter 1 refers.

The Aristotelian philosophers of the Middle Ages and the Renaissance held
that the mind is a combination of two great faculties or powers, the intellect
and the will. The intellect was the faculty of understanding, which enables
us to think thoughts only human beings are capable of thinking, such as
when we believe or doubt the existence of God; while the will was the
faculty that enables us to want things only intellectual animals are capable of
wanting, such as knowledge or power. These twin powers divided human
nature from the rest of nature, and defined our special place in the natural
world. For we share the capacity for sensation with other animals. For
example, dogs and horses can see colours and hear sounds, taste sweetness
and sourness, and feel pleasure and pain. In some cases, the senses of other
animals are more acute than ours. But only human beings can think abstract
thoughts and pursue abstract goals.

Descartes introduced a profoundly different conception of the mind. He
held that the mind is an immaterial substance rather than a system of powers,
and that its defining characteristic is consciousness rather than the ability to
think abstract thoughts. But his distinction between intellect and will also
differs from that of his predecessors, since he counts sensations—e.g. of pain
or pleasure, hunger or thirst, sound or colour—as perceptions of the
intellect, and he regards belief and doubt as acts of the will: the intellect,
he claims, perceives the object of judgement, but it is the will that gives or
withholds assent. (Attributing sensations to the intellect might seem to

endow non-human animals with minds, but Descartes notoriously denied that they experience sensations.)

Accordingly, in the *Principles of Philosophy* (1.32), Descartes attributes 'sensory perception, imagination and pure understanding' to the intellect; and 'desire, aversion, affirmation, denial and doubt' to the will. But in his treatise *The Passions of the Soul*, his last philosophical work, he divides the functions of the mind according to a different principle, distinguishing between the *actions* and the *passions* of the soul (§§17–19). He identifies the will as the active faculty of the mind and the intellect as the passive faculty, but in fact his distinction between the actions and passions of the soul either cuts across or modifies the distinction he draws in the *Principles* between the intellect and the will, since desire is attributed there to the will (1.32), as it had been traditionally, but he treats it as a passion in *The Passions of the Soul* (§86).

The actions of the soul, Descartes explains, are 'all our volitions' (*toutes nos volontés*) (§17), the conscious thoughts that cause our voluntary passions and imaginings, and set our limbs in motion when we act. 'Our volitions', he continues, 'are of two sorts':

> Some are actions of the soul that terminate in the soul itself, as when we will to love God or in general to apply our thought to an object that is not material. The others are actions which terminate in our body, as when our merely willing to walk has the consequence that our legs move and we take steps. (§18)

He explains how the latter kind of volition operates as follows:

> The soul has its principal seat in the small gland located in the middle of the brain. [...] The mechanism of the body is so constructed that simply by this gland's being moved in any way by the soul or by any other cause, it drives the surrounding spirits towards the pores of the brain, which direct them through the nerves to the muscles; and in this way the gland makes the spirits move the limbs. (§34)

He thinks that the nervous system operates pneumatically, like a pipe-organ.

Descartes's account of the will in *The Passions* is designed to explain the difference between the motion in our bodies which we ourselves cause personally, such as the motion of our legs when we walk, and the motion we do not cause, such as the contraction of the heart. In other words, it is essentially a theory of individual agency *in general*: *all* of our acts originate in our wills, not just a special class of them. But he also explains in the *Principles* that the nature of the will, its 'extremely broad scope', explains why we can be justly praised or blamed for our acts. The ability to act voluntarily, 'that is, freely', he says there, makes a man 'in a special way the author of his actions and deserving of praise for what he does' (1.37). And in *The Passions* he writes:

> I see only one thing in us which could give us good reason for esteeming ourselves, namely, the exercise of our free choice and the control we have over our volitions (*l'empire que nous avons sur nos volontés*). For we can reasonably be praised or blamed only for actions that depend upon this free choice. (§152)

In *Leviathan* (1.6), **Hobbes** distinguishes between two kinds of motion that occur in animals: *vital motion*, such as the motion of the blood, breathing, feeding, and digesting; and *animal motion*, 'otherwise called *voluntary motion*', such as speech and the movement of the limbs. He does not explain the difference between them by postulating *sui generis* acts of will, but purely in terms of the involvement of the imagination: vital motion occurs independently of the imagination, whereas voluntary motion is caused by a prior image of the movement to be performed. The imagination, he explains, is 'the first internal beginning of all voluntary motion'. Images or 'appearances'—which he describes as 'relics' of sense perception—are stored in the imagination and initiate the 'small beginnings of motion', which occur inside the body. These, he says, are called *endeavour*; and he divides them in their turn into *appetite*, which is endeavour towards its cause, and *aversion*, which is endeavour away from its cause. An act of will is simply an endeavour.

> In deliberation, the last appetite or aversion immediately adhering to the action, or to the omission thereof, is that we call the WILL, the act (not the faculty) of *willing*. [...] a *voluntary act* is that which proceedeth from the *will*, and no other. (1.6.53)

Locke follows Descartes rather than Hobbes in holding that appetites and aversions cause, and are not the same as, acts of will. But although Descartes's theory of the will is elegant, he leaves several questions unanswered. He does not define the nature of volitions or explain how they are caused; he ignores the fact that we do not only *act* voluntarily, but sometimes *refrain* or *forbear* from acting voluntarily; and he assumes that voluntary action and free action are the same thing. In *An Essay Concerning Human Understanding*, Locke tells a more elaborate story.

'Our voluntary motions', he explains, 'are produced in us only by the free action or thought of our own minds and are not, nor can be, the effects of the impulse or determination of the motion of blind matter in or upon our own bodies; for then it could not be in our power or choice to alter it.'

> For example: my right hand writes, whilst my left hand is still: what causes rest in one, and motion in the other? Nothing but my will, a thought of my mind; my thought only changing, the right hand rests, and the left hand moves. (4.10.19)

Locke is speaking loosely here, eliding the distinction between the will and the act of will, which he draws assiduously in another chapter of the *Essay*. The will, he explains there, is the *ability* or *power* to prefer or choose (2.21.17), and the exercise of the power—that is, the preferring or choosing itself—is called *volition* or *willing*. More expansively, he describes the will as the power to 'begin or forbear, continue or end several actions of our minds, and motions of our bodies, barely by a thought or preference of the mind.' (2.21.5) He adds that action or forbearance that results from a volition is called *voluntary*; 'and whatsoever action is performed without such a thought of the mind, is called *involuntary*.' But Locke is careful to distinguish between voluntariness and freedom, illustrating the difference between them with the example of a man who remains happily in a locked room, believing he is free to leave:

> Suppose a man be carried, whilst fast asleep, into a room where is a person he longs to see and speak with; and be there locked fast in, beyond his power to get out: he awakes, and is glad to find himself in so desirable company, which he stays willingly in, i.e. prefers his stay to going away. I ask, is not this stay voluntary? I think nobody will doubt it: and yet, being locked fast in, it is evident he is not at liberty not to stay, he has not freedom to be gone. (2.21.10)

Voluntary, Locke explains, is opposed to *involuntary*, not *necessary*. For if one prefers what one can do to what one cannot do, one does it both voluntarily and necessarily.*

Locke describes volition as a 'thought or preference of the mind ordering, or, as it were, commanding the doing or not doing such or such a particular action' (2.21.5). But he admits that the terms 'preference', 'order', and 'command' do not capture the phenomenon of willing precisely (2.21.15), because it is always possible to elect when the time comes either to act on a

---

* I discuss this passage in 4.6.

preference, order, or command, or alternatively not to do so; whereas a volition is supposed to be the final impulse of the mind, which initiates action without a further thought of any kind. So none of these terms can be exactly right. Locke concludes that the act of willing cannot be defined in words. Since it is 'a very simple act, whosoever desires to understand what it is, will better find it by reflecting on his own mind, and observing what it does, when it *wills*, than by any variety of articulate sounds whatever' (2.21.30).

Volitions themselves, Locke claims, are caused by 'the *uneasiness* of *desire*', whose object is something that the agent lacks: 'it is this uneasiness that determines the will to the successive voluntary actions, whereof the greatest part of our lives is made up' (2.21.33).

In both the *Principles of Human Knowledge* and the *First Dialogue Between Hylas and Philonous*, **Berkeley** distinguishes between activity and passivity in terms of dependence on or independence of the will. In the *Principles* he writes:

I find I can excite ideas in my mind at pleasure, and vary and shift the scene as often as I think fit. It is no more than willing, and straightway this idea or that idea arises in my fancy; and by the same power it is obliterated, and makes way for another. This making and unmaking of ideas does very properly denominate the mind active. (§28)

And in the *First Dialogue* he explains the dependence of activity on will in detail:

Phil. The mind therefore is to be accounted *active* in its perceptions so far forth as *volition* is included in them? *Hyl.* It is. *Phil.* In plucking this flower I am active; because I do it by the motion of my hand, which was consequent upon my volition; so likewise in applying it to my nose. But is either of these smelling? *Hyl.* No. *Phil.* I act too in drawing the air through my nose; because my breathing so rather than otherwise is the effect of my volition. But neither can this be called *smelling* [...] Whatever more there is—as that I perceive such a particular smell, or any smell at all—this is independent of my will, and therein I am altogether passive. (p. 145)

Notice that whereas Hobbes regards breathing as a kind of *vital motion*, which occurs without the involvement of the mind, Berkeley implies that breathing through the nose rather than the mouth is a kind of *voluntary motion*, in Hobbes's terms, because it results from the operation of the will.

In his *Treatise of Human Nature* (2.3.1), **Hume** ignores voluntary forbearance and discards the distinction, which Locke was careful to draw, between the will and volition, the power and the corresponding act. He defines the will as follows:

> By the *will*, I mean nothing but *the internal impression we feel and are conscious of, when we knowingly give rise to any new motion of our body, or new perception of our mind.*

Like Locke, he concedes that this impression cannot be defined in words, and in his *Enquiry Concerning Human Understanding* (7.1), he says that the operation of the will is and will always remain 'mysterious and unintelligible'.

> The motion of our body follows upon the command of our will. Of this we are every moment conscious. But the means, by which this is effected; the energy, by which the will performs so extraordinary an operation; of this we are so far from being immediately conscious, that it must for ever escape our most diligent enquiry. [...] Is there any principle in all nature more mysterious than the union of soul with body? [...] Were we empowered, by a secret wish, to remove mountains, or control the planets in their orbit; this extensive authority would not be more extraordinary, nor more beyond our comprehension.

In his *Essays on the Active Powers of Man*, **Reid** (like Locke, and unlike Descartes or Hume) defends a broadly Aristotelian conception of voluntary action as the exercise of active power. He contrasts active power with speculative powers:

> The powers of seeing, hearing, remembering, distinguishing, judging, reasoning, are speculative powers; the power of executing any work of art or labour is active power. (1.1)

But he insists that we are 'unable to conceive any active power to be exerted without will': active power is, by definition, 'an attribute in a being by which he can do certain things if he wills' (1.5). It is true that we commonly attribute active power (magnetism, gravity, etc.) to mere matter, but in reality 'matter is a substance altogether inert, and merely passive' (1.6). When we describe matter as active, we are speaking 'the language of the vulgar', in the same way as when we describe the sun as rising or setting (1.6).*

Reid calls the act of the will a 'volition', or sometimes an 'intention', and he defines it as a 'determination of the mind to do, or not to do something

---

* I discuss the origin of this conception of active power in Locke's philosophy in 2.1, and return to the subject again briefly at the end of 3.2.

which we conceive to be in our power' (2.1). But he adds that this is not a 'strictly logical definition', since 'determination' is merely another word for volition. Like Locke and Hume, he maintains that volition, like other 'simple acts of the mind', cannot be defined in words. He holds that every volition must have an object; that the immediate object of volition, unlike desire, must be an act of our own; that this act must be one that we believe to be within our power; and that a volition is invariably accompanied by 'an effort to execute that which we willed' (2.1). We tend not to notice the small efforts required for acts that are made with ease, but in fact they differ only in degree from the greater efforts we are conscious of.

Reid thinks of the will both as the source of agency and as the source of moral responsibility. He is adamant that agency as such depends on the will: 'In the strict philosophical sense, nothing can be called the action of a man, but what he previously conceived and willed or determined to do' (3.1). And he equates the idea that legitimate blame depends on agency with the idea that it depends on voluntariness: 'In morals, it is self-evident that no man can be object either of approbation or of blame for what he did not.' 'That no blame can be imputed to a man for what is altogether involuntary, is so evident in itself, that no argument can make it more evident' (2.4).

In his *Introduction to the Principles of Morals and Legislation*, **Bentham** announces that he will avoid using the terms 'voluntary' and 'involuntary', 'on account of the extreme ambiguity in their signification' (he may have had Johnson's definition of 'Voluntary' in mind):

> By a voluntary act is meant sometimes, any act, in the performance of which the will has had any concern at all; in this sense it is synonymous to *intentional:* sometimes such acts only, in the production of which the will has been determined by motives not of a painful nature; in this sense it is synonymous to unconstrained, or *uncoerced:* sometimes such acts only, in the production of which the will has been determined by motives, which, whether of the pleasurable or painful kind, occurred to a man himself, without being suggested by anybody else; in this sense it is synonymous to *spontaneous.* (8.2, note a)

Bentham's explanations of spontaneity and coercion are idiosyncratic, and he does not in fact entirely avoid use of the words he proscribes. But his diagnosis of ambiguity is important, because it signals his awareness of the need to disaggregate the agential and ethical aspects of the traditional concept of the will.

Bentham follows Hobbes and Locke in distinguishing between *positive* acts, which consist in 'motion or exertion', and *negative* acts, which consist in 'keeping at rest'. 'Positive acts are styled also acts of commission; negative, acts of omission or forbearance' (7.8). A negative act, he says, may be an act of the will no less than a positive act: 'The not revealing a conspiracy, for instance, may be as perfectly the act of the will, as the joining in it' (7.8, note d). And he accepts the orthodox doctrine that all of an individual's acts are caused by the will: '[Acts] are properly termed *involuntary* [...] in the performance of which the will has no sort of share: such as the contraction of the heart and arteries' (8.5, note b); 'If the act be not intentional in the first stage, it is no act of yours' (8.5).

Like Reid, Bentham uses the term 'intention' instead of 'volition', and he accepts the cardinal doctrine in the modern theory, that the operation of the will consists in a conscious thought that causes motion in our limbs. But the causal structure of action plays an incidental role in his philosophy, and every detail of his intricate account of the complex relations between acts, circumstances, and intentions can be separated from this idea. The reason for this is simply that his approach is governed by the practical aims of his moral philosophy and jurisprudence, on which the causal structure of action has no real bearing.

In his *System of Logic*, **Mill** describes 'volitions, or acts of the will' as 'active states of mind' (1.3.5) or 'states of consciousness' (1.3.3). He follows Bentham in also referring to the act of will as an intention. His only deviation from orthodoxy is to claim that the act of will forms part of the action itself:

> Now what is an action? Not one thing, but a series of two things: the state of mind called a volition, followed by an effect. The volition or intention to produce the effect, is one thing; the effect produced in consequence of the intention, is another thing; the two together constitute the action. [...] The intention [to move my arm], followed by the fact, or (if we prefer the expression) the fact when preceded and caused by the intention, is called the action of moving my arm. (1.3.6)

In *The Emotions and the Will*, **Bain** makes a radical departure from the empiricist mainstream in two ways: first, by dispensing with *sui generis* acts of will; and second, by thinking about voluntary movement in developmental terms. The 'foundations of Voluntary Power' (321), he claims, are the innate dispositions to make spontaneous movements, to avoid pain and prolong pleasure, and to form mental associations between movements and the feelings of pain and pleasure which they alleviate or produce.

Take the fertile theme of animal locomotion. This power is at first purely spontaneous, but certain particular modes of it soon form links of attachment with the animal's sensations; these modes are then longer sustained and oftener evoked than if there were nothing but spontaneity in the case. (340)

Further developments occur as we learn to obey commands, and as we accumulate a store of ideas of our own movements, derived from the experience of seeing them occur. But the final step, which takes us to 'the summit of voluntary control', is acquiring 'the power of acting in answer to a Wish to have a certain organ moved in a definite way, as when I will to raise my hand, to stand up, to open my mouth, and so on' (350). At this final stage in the development of voluntary power, Bain says, we learn to associate the mere idea of an action with the action itself, so that all that is necessary to make the action occur is 'a determining motive', in other words, the prospect of the increase in pleasure or decrease in pain we associate with it.

On the table before me I see a glass of liquid; the infant never so thirsty could not make the movement for bringing it to the mouth. But in the maturity of the will, a link is formed between the appreciated distance and direction of the glass, and the movement of the arm up to that point; and under the stimulus of pain, or of expected pleasure, the movement is executed. The mind is largely filled with associations of this nature, connecting every conceivable motion or position of all the organs with the precise impulse for realizing them, provided only that the proper instigator of the will is present. (350*f*)

As a result of forming these associations in the mind, 'a mere idea suffices for the guiding of the voluntary operations, if duly accompanied with the motive or prompting antecedent. What was an entire blank at the opening of the active career is now supplied; channels of communication are established where there existed only blind impulse' (351).

In *The Principles of Psychology*, **James** follows Bain. Like Bain, he explains how voluntary action occurs, at least what he calls 'perfectly simple' voluntary action, without postulating volitions or acts of will. Like Bain—indeed, like Hobbes—he postulates images or ideas of the voluntary movements we are able to perform instead. We are aware of the movements of our limbs and of various other parts of our bodies, he claims, without looking to see whether they occur, because they produce distinctive kinaesthetic feelings in our minds:

Not only are our muscles supplied with afferent as well as efferent nerves, but the tendons, the ligaments, the articular surfaces, and the skin about the joints are all sensitive, and, being stretched and squeezed in ways characteristic of each particular movement, give us as many distinct feelings as there are movements possible to perform. (2.448)

James holds that, beginning in infancy, involuntary movements produce these kinaesthetic feelings, and images of the feelings are stored in the memory. This process eventually equips us with 'a supply of ideas of the various movements that are possible', and these ideas are, when we act without prior deliberation, the only mental antecedents needed for the voluntary movements they enable us to perform:

We do not have a sensation or a thought and then have to *add* something dynamic to it to get a movement. Every pulse of feeling which we have is the correlate of some neural activity that is already on its way to instigate a movement. [. . .] The popular notion that [action] must result from some super-added 'will-force', is a very natural inference from those special cases in which we think of an act for an indefinite length of time without the action taking place. (2.526)

In *these* cases, James argues, voluntary action also involves a *fiat*, 'the element of consent, or resolve that the act shall ensue' (2.501). He claims initially that this 'constitutes the essence of the voluntariness of the act' (2.501), but later says that it only occurs 'on certain occasions' (2.522), when action is preceded by deliberation, or perhaps only when a 'volitional effort' (2.562) is required to resolve indecision. What is a fiat? Primarily, it is an effort of attention to an idea, and in some cases also 'express consent to the reality of what is attended to' (568). Hence,

The essential achievement of the will [. . .] when it is most 'voluntary', is to attend to a difficult object and hold it fast before the mind. The so-doing *is* the *fiat*; and it is a mere physiological incident that when the object is thus attended to, immediate motor consequences should ensue. (2.561)

In *The Analysis of Mind*, **Russell** follows James closely. He writes:

James maintains that the only distinctive characteristic of a voluntary act is that it involves an idea of the movement to be performed, made up of memory-images of the kinaesthetic sensations which we had when the same movement occurred on some former occasion. [. . .] I see no reason to doubt the correctness of this view. (285)

Like James, Russell acknowledges that the term 'volition' may sometimes refer to a distinctive mental event, or complex of such events, apart from a kinaesthetic idea or presentiment of the movement to be performed. But he regards the volition Descartes and Locke postulated—the conscious executive impulse of the mind—as pure myth:

> The sort of case I am thinking of is decision after deliberation. Voluntary movements are a part of this, but not the whole. There is, in addition to them, a judgment: 'This is what I shall do'; there is also a sensation of tension during doubt, followed by a different sensation at the moment of deciding. I see no reason whatever to suppose that there is any specifically new ingredient; sensations and images, with their relations and causal laws, yield all that seems to be wanted for the analysis of the will, together with the fact that kinaesthetic images tend to cause the movements with which they are connected. (286)

Endnotes

CHAPTER ONE: AGENCY AND THE WILL

1. I am indebted in this paragraph and throughout this chapter to Frede, *A Free Will*.
2. Ryle, *The Concept of Mind*, p. 63.
3. Ryle, *The Concept of Mind*, p. 67.
4. Wittgenstein, *The Blue and Brown Books*, pp. 151ff.
5. Davidson, *Essays on Actions and Events*, pp. 12, 87 ('mysterious act of the will'); p. 46 ('a person does, as agent, whatever he does intentionally under some description'); p. 47 ('mark of agency'); p. 6 ('This last point [. . .] defends the possibility of defining an intentional action as one done for a reason').
6. James, *The Principles of Psychology*, vol. 2, p. 526.
7. Reid, *Essays on the Active Powers of Man*, p. 31.
8. Hart, *Essays in Jurisprudence and Philosophy*, p. 189.
9. Ryle, *The Concept of Mind*, pp. 73f.
10. Dennett, *Elbow Room*, p. 78.
11. Aquinas, *Summa Theologiae*, 1a 2ae 6, 5.
12. Wittgenstein, *Remarks on the Philosophy of Psychology I*, §845.
13. Ryle, *The Concept of Mind*, p. 56.
14. White, *Grounds of Liability*, p. 58.
15. *Smith* v. *Stone* (1647) Style 65, 82 ER 533.
16. John Austin, *Lectures in Jurisprudence*, vol. 1, p. 411; Holmes, *The Common Law*, pp. 91f & 46; Stroud, *Mens Rea*, pp. 1f; Glanville Williams, *Textbook of Criminal Law*, second edition, §7.2; Dias, *Jurisprudence*, p. 274; Moore, *Act and Crime*, p. 39; *Placing Blame*, p. 251.
17. References to Wittgenstein's writings in the main text employ the following abbreviations: *Notebooks 1914–16*: NB; *Tractatus Logico-Philosophicus*: TLP; *The Blue and Brown Books*: BB; *Philosophical Investigations*: PI; *Zettel*: Z; *Remarks on the Philosophy of Psychology I*: RPP I.
18. Schopenhauer, *The World as Will and Representation II*, p. 36. In *The Will: A Dual Aspect Theory*, O'Shaughnessy proposes a theory of the same kind.
19. Schopenhauer, *The World as Will and Representation II*, p. 36.
20. Cf. *Blue and Brown Books*, 151ff, especially the remark 'in a large class of cases it is the peculiar impossibility of taking an observant attitude towards a certain action which characterizes it as a voluntary one.'

21. In the remarks that date from 1947, Wittgenstein still shifts back and forth between *Handlung* and *Bewegung*, without considering whether there is a difference between them (e.g. *Remarks on the Philosophy of Psychology I*, §§840, 901*f*). In Anscombe's translation of these remarks, *Handlung* is sometimes translated as 'action' and sometimes as 'movement'.
22. Ryle, *The Concept of Mind*, p. 64.
23. Ryle, *The Concept of Mind*, p. 67.
24. Cf. Lowe, *Locke on Human Understanding*, p. 127.
25. Kenny, *Will, Freedom and Power*, p. 14.
26. Hornsby, *Actions*, pp. 48*f*. Cf. O'Shaughnessy, *The Will: A Dual Aspect Theory II*, pp. 377*f*.

CHAPTER TWO: ACTION AND INTEGRATION

1. References in this style are to John Locke, *An Essay Concerning Human Understanding*.
2. See the Appendix.
3. Berkeley, *The Principles of Human Knowledge*, §28; see also his letter to Johnson, 25 Nov. 1729, in *The Works of George Berkeley*, vol. 2, p. 279.
4. This interpretation of Hume's philosophy has been contested, but what matters for present purposes is that it was accepted by his successors, notably by Reid, Kant, and Mill.
5. Anscombe, *Intention*, p. 10.
6. Strawson, *Analysis and Metaphysics*, p. 118.
7. Cf. von Wright, *An Essay in Deontic Logic and the General Theory of Action*, pp. 38*f*.
8. In *Motivation and Agency*, pp. 146*ff*, Mele argues that not doing something qualifies as a 'negative' act if and only if it is a successful instance of trying not to do something.
9. Frankfurt argues unconvincingly that one can be active without acting in *The Importance of What We Care About*, p. 58.
10. See Kenny, *Action, Emotion and Will*, p. 173.
11. Descartes, *The Passions of the Soul*, §1; Bentham, *Introduction to the Principles of Morals and Legislation*, 7.13, n. f.
12. See, for example, Hacker, *Human Nature: The Categorial Framework*, p. 155.
13. Gardner, *Offences and Defences*, pp. 70*f*.
14. Cf. Daube, *The Deed and the Doer in the Bible*, ch.1.
15. Davidson, *Essays on Actions and Events*, p. 128.
16. A thorough treatment of ellipsis can be found in Quirk et al., *A Comprehensive Grammar of the English Language*, pp. 883*ff*.
17. Parsons, *Events in the Semantics of English*, p. 116.
18. This point is argued more fully in Alvarez, 'Actions and Events: Some Semantical Considerations', pp. 235*f*.
19. Davidson advocates reducing agent-causation to event-causation in *Essays on Actions and Events*, p. 128; Lowe defends the opposite reduction in 'Free Agency, Causation and Action Explanation', p. 342.

20. See Strawson, *Analysis and Metaphysics*, p. 120.
21. Strawson, *Analysis and Metaphysics*, ch.2.
22. Davidson, *Essays on Actions and Events*, pp. 44f.
23. Reid, *Essays on the Active Powers of Man*, p. 31; Bentham, *Introduction to the Principles of Morals and Legislation*, 8.5.
24. Frankfurt, *The Importance of What We Care About*, p. 78.
25. In 'Disengaging Reason', Frankfurt claims that 'active movement' qualifies as active because the agent 'supports and thereby takes direct responsibility for his own activity', whereas 'passive movements' may be caused 'by impulse or inclination' (p. 124).
26. See List & Pettit, *Group Agency*, pp. 64ff.
27. Maynard Smith & Szathmáry, *The Origins of Life*, p. 135.
28. Mele & Moser, 'Intention', p. 39.
29. For a sceptical discussion of 'sub-intentional' action, in which he reverses his earlier view of the matter, see O'Shaughnessy, *The Will: A Dual Aspect Theory II*, ch.10.
30. Raz discusses intentional expressive action in *Engaging Reason*, pp. 39ff.
31. Shakespeare, *Henry VIII*, iii.2; quoted in Darwin, *The Expression of the Emotions in Man and Animals*, p. 37.
32. Darwin, *The Expression of the Emotions in Man and Animals*, p. 182.
33. Descartes, *Principles of Philosophy*, 1.205.
34. Descartes, *The Passions of the Soul*, §152.

CHAPTER THREE: ACTS AND EVENTS

1. See J.L. Austin, 'A Plea for Excuses', repr. in his *Philosophical Papers*, p. 127; von Wright, *Norm and Action*, pp. 35–41; Kenny, *Action, Emotion and Will*, pp. 177–82.
2. Ryle, *The Concept of Mind*, p. 51.
3. Ryle, *The Concept of Mind*, pp. 53, 54.
4. Wittgenstein, *The Blue and Brown Books*, pp. 151f.
5. Anscombe, *Intention*, pp. 12f.
6. Davidson, *Problems of Rationality*, p. 103.
7. Armstrong, *A Materialist Theory of the Mind*, p. 170.
8. Prichard, *Moral Obligation*, p. 191.
9. Hornsby, *Actions*, p. 103.
10. On the visibility of action, see the exchange between Lowe and Hornsby published in *Analysis* 41–4 (1981–4). See also Steward, 'Do Actions Occur Inside the Body?', pp. 111f. In *Simplemindedness*, Hornsby claims implausibly that acts may after all be invisible (p. 99).
11. von Wright, *Norm and Action*, pp. 35f.
12. Prichard, *Moral Obligation*, pp. 188f; see also Aune, *Reason and Action*, p. 2.
13. The concept of dependence employed here is discussed in Fine, 'Ontological Dependence', pp. 269–90, and Lowe, *The Possibility of Metaphysics*, ch. 6.

14. Quine, 'Things and Their Place in Theories', in *Theories and Things*, p. 10.
15. von Wright, *Norm and Action*, p. 39.
16. Davidson, *Essays on Actions and Events*, 56ff. Danto argues that they are related as cause and effect, while Austin and Ginet argue that they are related as whole and part. See Danto, 'Basic Actions', pp. 50f; J.L. Austin, 'A Plea for Excuses', repr. in his *Philosophical Papers*, p. 149; Ginet, *On Action*, ch.3.
17. Davidson, *Essays on Actions and Events*, p. 58.
18. Davidson, *Essays on Actions and Events*, 57f. See also Anscombe, 'Under a Description'.
19. Davidson, *Essays on Actions and Events*, p. 124.
20. Strawson, 'Doers and their Doings', p. 127.
21. Leibniz, 'Whether the Essence of a Body Consists in Extension', repr. in *Leibniz: Selections*, p. 101.
22. Kenny, *Action, Emotion and Will*, p. 152.
23. Prior, *Formal Logic*, p. 85; cf. Russell, *An Inquiry into Meaning and Truth*, pp. 35f.
24. Kenny, *Action, Emotion and Will*,, p. 156.
25. Davidson, 'Adverbs of Action', p. 232.
26. Fine, 'Neutral Relations', p. 6.
27. Fine, 'Neutral Relations', p. 4.
28. Fine, 'Neutral Relations', p. 4.
29. Williamson, 'Converse Relations', p. 255.
30. For a more detailed assessment of Fine's and Williamson's arguments, see MacBride, 'Neutral Relations Revisited'.
31. Both the point and the example are due to Kenny, *Action, Emotion and Will*, p. 169.

CHAPTER FOUR: VOLUNTARINESS AND CHOICE

1. Anscombe, *Intention*, p. 10.
2. Anscombe, *Intention*, pp. 89f.
3. Anscombe, 'Will and Emotion' repr. in *From Parmenides to Wittgenstein*, p. 107; Davidson, 'Psychology as Philosophy', p. 230 & 'Freedom to Act', passim, both in *Essays on Actions and Events*; Kenny, *Will, Freedom and Power*, p. 53; Bernard Williams, *Shame and Necessity*, p. 66.
4. Ryle, *The Concept of Mind*, p. 56.
5. *Nicomachean Ethics* 1110a; *Eudemian Ethics* 1223a.
6. Strawson, *Individuals*, p. 10.
7. Regarding ignorance, see *Iliad* 19.85ff; *Genesis* 20.2–5; *Code of Hammurabi* §227; Olivelle (ed.), *Manu's Code of Law*, pp. 224.176 & 173.120–1; Hulsewé, *Remnants of Ch'in Law*, D10 & D13, pp. 123f. Regarding compulsion, see *Odyssey* 22.351; *Deuteronomy* 22.23–27; *Code of Hammurabi* §130; Olivelle (ed.), *Manu's Code of Law*, p. 180.233; Hulsewé, *Remnants of Ch'in Law*, D126, p. 162.

8. Bernard Williams, *Shame and Necessity*, p. 8. Williams is right to argue that the concept of intention and its relevance to culpability were not absent from pre-classical ethical thought. In fact, this had already been convincingly argued in Daube's 1962 Gifford Lectures, *The Deed and the Doer in the Bible*, chs. 1–3, esp. pp. 31–8, but unfortunately these were not published until 2008.

9. Bernard Williams, *Shame and Necessity*, pp. 93f.

10. Blackstone, *Commentaries on the Laws of England*, vol. 4, ch. 2.

11. *R v. Hasan* [2005] 4 All ER 685; *EE*, 1225a.

12. *R v. Hudson and Taylor* [1971] 2 All ER 244.

13. Frankfurt, *The Importance of What We Care About*, p. 40.

14. Hart & Honoré, *Causation in the Law*, p. 157. See also Oberdiek, 'The Role of Sanctions and Coercion in Understanding Law and Legal Systems'.

15. *DPP for N. Ireland v. Lynch* [1975] AC 653, at 692ff.

16. Stephen, *A History of the Criminal Law of England*, p. 107.

17. Kenny, 'Duress *per minas* as a Defence to Crime II'.

18. For example, see Kilbrandon, 'Duress *per minas* as a Defence to Crime I'.

19. Nozick, 'Coercion', repr. in *Socratic Puzzles*, p. 38.

20. The idea derives from Bentham, *Introduction to the Principles of Morals and Legislation*, 8.2.

21. Hart & Honoré, *Causation in the Law*, p. 156.

22. Hart & Honoré, *Causation in the Law*, pp. 41 & 137f.

23. Kenny, *The Ivory Tower*, pp. 31f.

24. The confusion between 'voluntary' and 'willing' seems to have contributed to the view that Aristotle's *hekōn* and *akōn* should be translated 'intentionally' and 'unintentionally'. Thus, in *Aristotle's Ethics*, at p. 103, Bostock defends the unconventional translation on the grounds that 'willingly' and 'unwillingly' would be wrong, apparently assuming that 'voluntarily' and 'willingly' mean the same. Charles proposes the same translation in *Aristotle's Philosophy of Action*, at pp. 61f and in Appendix 2.

25. *Digest*, 4.2.21.5.

26. *Digest*, 50.17.116. The controversy reverberated in medieval and early modern jurisprudence. See du Plessis, 'Force and Fear', pp. 104ff.

27. See Aquinas, *Summa Theologiae* 1a2ae 6.4.

28. On this topic see Zimmerman, 'Moral Responsibility and Ignorance'; Rosen, 'Culpability and Ignorance'; Peels, 'What Kind of Ignorance Excuses?'

29. Kenny agrees that *EE* 1225a is 'most naturally interpreted' in this way, but he defends a different interpretation, which is consistent with Aristotle's position in *NE* (*Aristotle's Theory of the Will*, p. 43). Readers who are dissatisfied with these summaries are invited to treat 'the *Eudemian* doctrine' and 'the *Nicomachean* doctrine' as labels of the views, and not as claims about the best interpretation of Aristotle's texts.

30. Westen, *The Logic of Consent*, p. 5; Kleinig, 'The Nature of Consent', p. 11. See also J.L. Austin, *How To Do Things With Words*, pp. 9f.

31. Raz, *The Morality of Freedom*, pp. 80*ff.*
32. On the reasons why consent can fail to legitimize, see Hyams, 'When Consent Doesn't Work: A Rights-Based Case for Limits to Consent's Capacity to Legitimise'.
33. Kenny, *Will, Freedom and Power*, p. 59.
34. Simmons, *Moral Principles and Political Obligations*, p. 76.
35. As we saw in 4.1, Anscombe does mention voluntary passivity. I shall comment on her remark about it in 4.6.
36. See above, n. 13.
37. *Prosecutor* v. *Kunarac*, §440, quoted in Schomburg & Peterson, 'Genuine Consent to Sexual Violence in International Law', p. 134.
38. Atiyah, 'Economic Duress and the "Overborne Will"', p. 196; cf. Dawson, 'Economic Duress: An Essay in Perspective', p. 267 & n.36.
39. But see Bronitt, 'Rape and Lack of Consent'.
40. *R* v. *Bourne* [1952] 36 Cr App R 1251.
41. John Locke, *An Essay Concerning Human Understanding*, 2.21.10.
42. Hart & Honoré, *Causation in the Law*, p. 41; Lord Scarman, in *Universe tankships Inc of Monrovia* v. *International Transport Workers' Federation* [1982] 2 All ER 67.
43. Atiyah, 'Duress and the Overborne Will Again', p. 354.
44. Raz argues that a choice is not merely an available option or alternative, but one that is (or that the agent believes to be) supported by reasons, in *From Normativity to Responsibility*, p. 178.
45. Hart, *The Concept of Law*, p. 39. See also *Francome* v. *Mirror Group Newspapers Ltd.* [1984] 2 All ER 408 at 412.
46. I am indebted in this paragraph to White, *Modal Thinking*, pp. 130*ff.*
47. According to Kenny (personal correspondence), Anscombe said that she copied this remark, apart from the example, from Aquinas 'almost verbatim', but I have not been able to locate the exact source.
48. Some cases of this kind are discussed in Frankfurt, 'Alternate Possibilities and Moral Responsibility'.
49. Hart & Honoré, *Causation in the Law*, pp. 156f.
50. On the use of the word 'involuntary', see 1.3.1.
51. Ryle, *The Concept of Mind*, p. 67.
52. Kenny, *Will, Freedom and Power*, p. 120.

CHAPTER FIVE: DESIRE AND INTENTION

1. Mill, *A System of Logic*, second edition, 6.3.2.
2. Hempel, 'The Function of General Laws in History', repr. in *Aspects of Scientific Explanation and Other Essays in the Philosophy of Science*.
3. von Wright, *Explanation and Understanding*, p. 29; Davidson, *Essays on Actions and Events*, p. 261. The first chapter of *Explanation and Understanding* contains

an excellent account of these opposed conceptions of the human sciences and their historical roots.

4. Collingwood, *The Idea of History*, pp. 208, 214–17, 228. See also Dray, *History as Re-Enactment: R.G. Collingwood's Idea of History*, chs. 2–3.

5. Wittgenstein, *The Blue and Brown Books*, p. 15.

6. *Sunday Times*, 28 May 1961: *Sayings of the Week*, quoted in Daube, *The Deed and the Doer in the Bible*, p. 100.

7. *Nicomachean Ethics*, 1139a.

8. A dispositional conception of desires differing in significant ways from the one set out here is proposed in Smith, *The Moral Problem*, 4.6.

9. Wittgenstein distinguishes between symptoms and criteria in *The Blue and Brown Books*, pp. 24 f, and in *Philosophical Investigations*, §354.

10. Kenny, *The Metaphysics of Mind*, p. 34.

11. Cf. Schroeder, *Three Faces of Desire*, pp. 16ff; Schueler, *Desire*, p. 14.

12. Russell, *The Analysis of Mind*, p. 62.

13. Wittgenstein, *Philosophical Investigations*, §580.

14. Russell, *The Analysis of Mind*, p. 32.

15. Wittgenstein, *Philosophical Remarks*, p. 64.

16. There is an astute discussion of the idea that beliefs and desires are propositional attitudes with opposed 'directions of fit' in Alvarez, *Kinds of Reasons*, pp. 66–71.

17. Molière, *Le Malade Imaginaire*, III.iii.

18. Anscombe, *Intention*, p. 17.

19. Wittgenstein, *The Blue and Brown Books*, p. 15.

20. Hart & Honoré, *Causation in the Law*, pp. 55f.

21. Melden, *Free Action*, pp. 52ff; White, *The Philosophy of Mind*, pp. 147f.

22. Hume, *A Treatise of Human Nature*, 1.3.8.

23. Davidson, *Essays on Actions and Events*, p. 11.

24. Anscombe, 'Von Wright on Practical Inference', p. 378.

25. Davidson, *Problems of Rationality*, p. 106.

26. Davidson moves some way towards acknowledging this in 'Problems in the Explanation of Action', repr. in *Problems of Rationality*. See also Stoecker, 'Climbers, Pigs and Wiggled Ears: The Problem of Waywardness in Action Theory'. Others have argued that the idea of causation by dispositions should play a key role in solving the problem of deviant causation by desires, e.g. Setiya, *Reasons Without Rationalism*, p. 32, or pointed out that deviant causation by desires is a special case of deviant causation by dispositions in general, e.g. Armstrong, 'Beliefs and Desires as Causes of Actions: A Reply to Donald Davidson', p. 4 f. See also Arpaly, *Merit, Meaning and Human Bondage*, pp. 47 & 71.

27. In *The Will: A Dual Aspect Theory II*, O'Shaughnessy comments that 'when action occurs, it is in the final analysis [desire] that underlies all the act-generative mental machinery' (p. 541). Where intentional action is concerned, this seems to me right, in the sense that the idea of an intention

with which an act is done is explained in terms of the idea of a desire because of which it is done, and not vice versa. In *Life and Action*, Thompson claims that explanations of intentional action that explain one act in terms of another, such as 'I am mixing mortar because I am laying bricks', are 'prior' to ones that refer to desires, in the sense that we can imagine a 'form of life and thought' in which the latter kind of explanation occurs and not the former, but not vice versa (p. 92). This may be true, but it does not contradict O'Shaughnessy's claim.

28. Wittgenstein, *The Blue and Brown Books*, p. 15.

29. Anscombe, *Intention*, p. 10.

30. This is how I interpret Anscombe's remark about Hume's theory of causation quoted below in 5.7. Her doubts about the Humean theory of causation bore fruit, more than a decade later, in her inaugural lecture, 'Causality and Determination'.

31. Anscombe contrasts mental causes with reasons on p. 10 of *Intention*, with motives on p. 16, and with intentions on p. 17.

32. Anscombe, *Intention*, pp. 17f.

33. Anscombe, *Intention*, pp. 18f & 24.

34. *2 Henry VI*, III.i; *Hebrews* 18.2.

35. Anscombe, *Intention*, p. 21.

36. For a detailed discussion of the causal relevance of dispositions, see MacKitrick, 'Are Dispositions Causally Relevant?'

37. Davidson, *Essays on Actions and Events*, p. 79.

38. On the history of occasionalism, see Fakhry, *Islamic Occasionalism*; Clarke, 'Causal Powers and Occasionalism from Descartes to Malebranche'; Nadler, 'Malebranche on Causation'.

39. Hume, *A Treatise of Human Nature*, 1.3.14.

40. Armstrong, *A World of States of Affairs*, p. 79.

41. Ryle, *The Concept of Mind*, pp. 107f.

42. See especially Molnar, *Powers*, ch.4; Bird, *Nature's Metaphysics*, ch.2. Cross, 'Recent Work on Dispositions' is a good survey and has a useful bibliography.

43. Molnar, *Powers*, p. 86. Both examples are due to Molnar.

44. Strawson, *Analysis and Metaphysics*, p. 120.

45. See Martin, 'Dispositions and Conditionals'.

46. Johnston, 'How to Speak of the Colors'.

47. This example is adapted from one described in Bird, *Nature's Metaphysics*, p. 29.

48. See Molnar, *Powers*, p. 91.

49. Bishop claims that we need to show how to eliminate deviant causal chains in order to defend the idea that intentional acts 'consist in behaviour that is caused by appropriate mental states' (*Natural Agency*, pp. 2 & 148). By contrast, Mayr claims only that we would need to show how to eliminate them in order to defend an 'event-causal' theory of intentional action (*Understanding Human Agency*, ch. 5, esp. p. 104). The argument here supports Mayr's view.

50. The basic point was anticipated by Passmore: 'explanation by reference to a "principle of action" or "a good reason" is not, by itself, explanation at all. [. . .] For a reason may be a "good reason"—in the sense of being a principle to which one *could* appeal in justification of one's action—without having in fact the slightest influence on us' ('Law and Explanation in History', p. 275).

51. Davidson, *Essays on Actions and Events*, pp. 10*f*.

52. See Sehon, 'Teleology and the Nature of Mental States', p. 64; Wilson, 'Reasons as Causes *for* Action', p. 68.

53. Anscombe's solution is defended in Stout, *Things That Happen Because They Should*; Sehon, *Teleological Realism*; Hacker, *Human Nature: The Categorial Framework*.

54. See Anscombe, *Intention*, p. 18; Davidson, *Essays on Actions and Events*, pp. 7*f*.

55. Roth mentions the possibility of a 'composite' view about the explanation of intentional action which 'combines elements of causalism' with the teleological view defended by Wilson, in 'Explanations of Actions: Causal, Singular, and Situational', p. 846, n. 18.

56. See Ginet, *On Action*, ch. 6, and 'Reasons Explanations of Action: Causalist versus Noncausalist Accounts'.

57. Ginet, 'Reasons Explanations of Action: Causalist versus Noncausalist Accounts', p. 166.

58. This point has been argued by several philosophers, e.g. Wilson and Sehon. The main conclusion of Wilson's book *The Intentionality of Human Action* is that 'there is a clear sense in which reason explanations [i.e. explanations of intentional action that refer to desires, beliefs, or intentions] are irreducibly teleological' (p. 17). But Wilson regards this as a vindication of the claim that 'explanations in terms of reasons do *not* purport to identify causal factors of actions' (p. 13, Wilson's italics). Similarly, Sehon argues in *Teleological Realism* that explanations of intentional action are irreducibly teleological and claims that desires are not causal factors (pp. 173*f*), conceding only that 'causal language occasionally enters, metaphorically, into action explanation' (p. 175).

59. Anscombe, *Intention*, p. 16.

CHAPTER SIX: REASON AND KNOWLEDGE

1. Davidson, *Essays on Actions and Events*, p. 12; von Wright, *Practical Reason*, p. 54, but cf. von Wright, *In the Shadow of Descartes*, pp. 10*f*; Audi, *Action, Intention and Reason*, pp. 15*f*; Dancy, *Practical Reality*, pp. 132*f*; Raz, *Practical Reason and Norms*, p. 17.

2. For example, see Raz, *Practical Reason and Norms*, p. 19.

3. Cf. Raz, *From Normativity to Responsibility*, pp. 18*f*.

4. When the terms '*explanans*' and '*explanandum*' were introduced into analytic philosophy by Hempel and Oppenheim in their 'Studies in the Logic of Explanation' (pp. 136*f*), they were meant to refer to sentences. They are

now commonly used to refer to the facts stated rather than the sentences used to state them, so that different sentences can be used (e.g. in different languages) to state the same *explanandum* or *explanans*.

5. Strawson, *Analysis and Metaphysics*, pp. 109*ff*.

6. Geach, *Mental Acts*, p. 8.

7. Davidson, *Essays on Actions and Events*, p. 6. See also Kenny, *The Metaphysics of Mind*, pp. 38*ff*; Stout, *Action*, ch.2.

8. Anscombe, *Intention*, §5.

9. Anscombe, *Intention*, §17.

10. Dancy, 'Two Ways of Explaining Actions', pp. 25*f*; cf. Setiya, *Reasons Without Rationalism*, pp. 29 & 42.

11. Dancy, *Practical Reality*, p. 134.

12. Dancy, 'Acting in Ignorance', p. 350.

13. Either a *that*-clause or a nominal *-ing* clause can be used to express the *explanans*. I have used the latter here because it is more idiomatic. See Quirk et al., *A Comprehensive Grammar of the English Language*, 11.23*f*.

14. Dancy, *Practical Reality*, p.132.

15. See Unger, *Ignorance*, at pp. 206*ff*. Regrettably, I was not aware of this passage in Unger's book when I defended the claim in my article 'How Knowledge Works', so I failed to acknowledge his priority.

16. Prichard, *Moral Obligation*, p. 24.

17. See ch.4, n.8.

18. Dancy, *Introduction to Contemporary Epistemology*, p. 25.

19. Goldman, 'A Causal Theory of Knowing', p. 363. Goldman does not seem to distinguish between events and propositions, but the story could easily be amended to rectify this.

20. Owens, 'Levels of Explanation', p. 76. The detail of Owens's argument, but not the principal point, is challenged in Neander & Menzies, 'David Owens on Levels of Explanation'.

21. Those who have agreed include Williamson, Raz, Hornsby, Alvarez, Neta, and McDowell; those who have disagreed include Dancy, Dustin Locke, and Setiya. See Williamson, *Knowledge and its Limits*, p. 64; Raz, *Engaging Reason*, p. 23; Hornsby, 'A Disjunctive Conception of Acting for Reasons', p. 251; Neta, 'Treating Something as a Reason For Action', p. 690; Alvarez, *Kinds of Reasons*, p. 25; McDowell, 'Acting in the Light of a Fact'; Dancy 'Acting in Ignorance', pp. 346*f*; Locke, 'Knowledge, Explanation and Motivating Reasons'; Setiya, *Reasons Without Rationalism*, p. 29.

22. Dustin Locke may be an exception. He explicitly considers whether one can be guided by a fact one does not know, and concludes that one can, relying on barn-façade cases such as (E). See his 'Knowledge, Explanation and Motivating Reasons'.

CHAPTER SEVEN: KNOWLEDGE AS AN ABILITY

1. See for example Stanley & Williamson, 'Knowing How'; Rumfitt, 'Savoir Faire'; Snowdon, 'Knowing How and Knowing That: A Distinction Reconsidered'; Stanley, *Know How*; Wiggins, 'Practical Knowledge: Knowing How To and Knowing That'; Bengson & Moffett (eds), *Knowing How: Essays on Knowledge, Mind, and Action.*
2. Cassam, 'Can the Concept of Knowledge be Analysed?', p. 27.
3. Ryle, 'Mowgli in Babel', p. 5.
4. The comparison is due to Fine, 'First-Order Modal Theories III: Facts', p. 52. See also Slote, *Metaphysics and Essence*, ch. 6. For the view that facts are simply true propositions, see Carnap, *Meaning and Necessity*, p. 28; Prior, *Objects of Thought*, pp. 4–6; Williamson, *Knowledge and its Limits*, pp. 42f.
5. This argument is expounded in detail in Fine, 'First-Order Modal Theories III: Facts', pp. 46–50.
6. Ryle, *The Concept of Mind*, pp. 116ff.
7. Plato, *Republic* 477d; Wittgenstein, *Philosophical Investigations*, §150; Ryle, *The Concept of Mind*, p. 129.
8. See, for example, Margolis, 'Knowledge, Belief and Thought'; White, *The Nature of Knowledge*, ch. 6; Craig, *Knowledge and the State of Nature*, pp. 11f and passim.
9. White, *The Nature of Knowledge*, p. 119; cf. Wittgenstein, *On Certainty*, §586.
10. White, *The Nature of Knowledge*, p. 121.
11. White, *The Nature of Knowledge*, p. 120.
12. Bernard Williams, 'Knowledge and Reasons', p. 3.
13. Kenny, *The Metaphysics of Mind*, pp. 108f.
14. In 'Knowledge, Explanation and Motivating Reasons', Dustin Locke denies that if one takes a fact into consideration one is thereby guided it, on the dubious ground that a decision to do an act of a certain kind can take reasons *against* doing it into consideration, but cannot be guided by those reasons.
15. Annas & Barnes, *The Modes of Scepticism*, pp. 47–8; cf. Sorabji, *Animal Minds and Human Morals*, ch.7. The story is told by Philo, *On Animals*, 45–6, and by Sextus Empiricus, *Outlines of Pyrrhonism*, I §69.
16. Davidson, 'Thought and Talk', repr. in *Inquiries into Truth and Interpretation*, pp. 155–70.
17. Davidson, 'Thought and Talk', repr. in *Inquiries into Truth and Interpretation*, p. 170.
18. Hacker, *The Intellectual Powers: A Study of Human Nature*, p. 183.
19. Kenny, *Action, Emotion, and Will*, p. 175.
20. Kenny, *Will, Freedom and Power*, p. 132.
21. Hume, *A Treatise of Human Nature*, 2.1.10; Ryle, *The Concept of Mind*, pp. 114f.
22. Kenny, *Will, Freedom and Power*, p. 133.
23. Williamson, *Knowledge and its Limits*, p. 64.

24. Setiya, 'Causality in Action', p. 511.
25. I discuss the identity of acts in 3.2.
26. I discuss colours and appearances in Hyman, *The Objective Eye*, ch.1, and p. 240, n. 6.
27. See Wiggins, *Needs, Values, Truth*, pp. 106f; and cf. Hyman, *The Objective Eye*, pp. 53-6.
28. Wittgenstein, *Philosophical Investigations*, §246.
29. Wittgenstein, *Zettel*, §481.
30. Wittgenstein, *Philosophical Investigations*, §246 & II, p. 221.
31. Ryle, 'Knowing How and Knowing That', in *Collected Essays 1929-1968*, vol.2, p. 224.
32. Wittgenstein, *On Certainty*, §550.
33. Wittgenstein, *Remarks on the Philosophy of Psychology I*, §428.
34. Wittgenstein, *On Certainty*, §504; but cf. *Remarks on the Foundations of Mathematics*, pp. 336-7.
35. Kenny, *Wittgenstein*, p. 201.
36. Wittgenstein, *Philosophical Investigations*, §292; cf. II, p. 189.
37. Wittgenstein, *Remarks on the Foundations of Mathematics*, p. 356.
38. Wittgenstein, *On Certainty*, §563.
39. Vendler, *Res Cogitans*, ch. 5. The argument in 7.2 supports this conclusion, but the conception of facts proposed there is different from Vendler's.
40. Kaplan, 'It's Not What You Know That Counts', pp. 354-6.
41. E.g. Williamson, *Knowledge and Its Limits*, ch.1, s.3; cf. Millar, 'Knowledge in Recent Epistemology: Some Problems', 5.2.
42. I discuss this point in detail in 6.4.

CHAPTER EIGHT: THE ROAD TO LARISSA

1. Daube, *Civil Disobedience in Antiquity*, p. 60.
2. The interpretation, but not the name, derives from *Romans*, 5.12-21.
3. Augustine, *The City of God*, 14.17. Other quotations from *The City of God* are from 14.1 and 14.11-15.
4. Daube, *Civil Disobedience in Antiquity*, p. 60; see also Headlam, 'Prometheus and the Garden of Eden'.
5. Daube, *Civil Disobedience in Antiquity*, pp. 60-1. Kant's interpretation of the story is comparable. See his *Conjectures on the Beginning of Human History*, repr. in Reiss (ed.), *Kant: Political Writings*, esp. p. 226.
6. Arnold, *Genesis*, p. 61.
7. *Rashi: Commmentary on the Torah I, Bereishis/Genesis*, p. 30.
8. Several other implausible interpretations were defended by rabbis anxious to finesse the apparent lie: 'You shall surely be punished', 'You shall surely die within a thousand years', 'You shall be deserving of death', etc. See Linetsky, *Rabbi Saadiah Gaon's Commentary on the Book of Creation*, p. 137.

9. *Julian*, vol.3, p. 327.

10. Daube, *Civil Disobedience in Antiquity*, p. 62.

11. Pritchard ('Knowledge and Understanding', pp. 5–8) distinguishes between the *primary* problem of explaining why knowledge is more valuable than true belief, the *secondary* problem of explaining why knowledge is more valuable than any epistemic standing (such as justified true belief) falling short of knowledge, and the *tertiary* problem of explaining why knowledge has a distinctive kind of value that any epistemic standing falling short of knowledge does not have, and does not merely have the same kind of value to a greater degree. The solution proposed here addresses all three problems.

12. Sosa, 'The Place of Truth in Epistemology', p. 156.

13. Horwich, *Truth-Meaning-Reality*, pp. 58f.

14. I shall not discuss the doctrine of recollection, which Socrates refers to in this passage. See Vlastos, 'Anamnesis in the *Meno*'.

15. Craig, *Knowledge and the State of Nature*, p. 7.

16. Wittgenstein, *On Certainty*, §§6 & 12.

17. See, for example, Stich, *The Fragmentation of Reason*, pp. 122f; Kvanvig, *The Value of Knowledge and the Pursuit of Understanding*; Pritchard, *Knowledge*, ch.7.

18. Gettier, 'Is Justified True Belief Knowledge?'; cf. Kvanvig, *The Value of Knowledge and the Pursuit of Understanding*, p. 139.

19. Wright, 'Scepticism and Dreaming: Imploding the Demon', p. 88.

20. Kaplan, 'It's Not What You Know That Counts', p. 361.

21. Swain, 'Reasons, Causes and Knowledge'.

22. Nozick, *Philosophical Explorations*, pp. 178ff.

23. Cf. Craig, *Knowledge and the State of Nature*, pp. 19ff.

24. Williamson, *Knowledge and its Limits*, p. 40.

25. Attempts to show that knowledge is more valuable than mere true belief because it is acquired through the exercise of intellectual virtues or skills have been criticized on the same grounds. See Haddock et al. (eds), *Epistemic Value*, p. 3; cf. Sosa, *A Virtue Epistemology: Apt Belief and Reflective Knowledge I*, Lecture IV; Riggs, 'Beyond Truth and Falsehood: The Real Value of Knowing that P', pp. 87–108; Zagzebski, 'The Search for the Source of Epistemic Good'; Greco, 'Knowledge as Credit for True Belief', p. 134.

26. Williamson, *Knowledge and its Limits*, p. 78. Williamson's immediate purpose in this passage is to argue that explanations of behaviour referring to knowledge are not equivalent to ones referring to belief. The argument in 6.4 supports this view.

27. Williamson, *Knowledge and its Limits*, p. 101.

28. Williamson, *Knowledge and its Limits*, p. 79.

29. Feldman, 'An Alleged Defect in Gettier Counter-Examples', pp. 68–9; Shope, *The Analysis of Knowing*, chs.1 & 2.

30. A partly similar discussion of Williamson's solution can be found in Kvanvig, *The Value of Knowledge and the Pursuit of Understanding*, pp. 13–19.

31. The sceptics include Kaplan, Kvanvig, and Pritchard; for citations, see notes 17 and 20. The non-sceptics include Zagzebski, Greco, Sosa, and Goldman & Olsson. See Zagzebski, 'The Search for the Source of Epistemic Good', pp. 12–28; Greco, 'Knowledge as Credit for True Belief'; Sosa, *A Virtue Epistemology: Apt Belief and Reflective Knowledge I*, lecture 4; Goldman & Olsson, 'Reliabilism and the Value of Knowledge'.

32. Nozick, *Anarchy, State, and Utopia*, pp. 42*ff.*

Bibliography

Alvarez, Maria, 'Actions and Events: Some Semantical Considerations', *Ratio* 12 (1999), 213–39.

Alvarez, Maria, *Kinds of Reasons* (Oxford: OUP, 2010).

Annas, Julia & Barnes, Jonathan, *The Modes of Scepticism* (Cambridge: CUP, 1985).

Anscombe, G.E.M., *Intention* (Oxford: Blackwell, 1957).

Anscombe, G.E.M., 'Causality and Determination. An Inaugural Lecture', repr. in Sosa, Ernest (ed.), *Causation and Conditionals* (Oxford: OUP, 1975).

Anscombe, G.E.M., 'Under a Description', *Noûs* 13 (1979), 219–33.

Anscombe, G.E.M., *From Parmenides to Wittgenstein* (Oxford: Blackwell, 1981).

Anscombe, G.E.M., 'Von Wright on Practical Inference', in Schilpp, P.A. & Hahn, L.E. (eds), *The Philosophy of Georg Henrik von Wright* (La Salle, Ill.: Open Court, 1989).

Aquinas, Thomas, *Summa Theologiae*, 60 vols. (Cambridge: Blackfriars, 1964–1973).

Aristotle, *Categories and De Interpretatione*, trans. J.L. Ackrill (Oxford: OUP, 1974).

Aristotle, *Nicomachean Ethics*, trans. W.D. Ross, revised edition (Oxford: OUP, 2009).

Aristotle, *Eudemian Ethics*, trans. A. Kenny (Oxford: OUP, 2011).

Armstrong, D.M., 'Beliefs and Desires as Causes of Actions: A Reply to Donald Davidson', *Philosophical Papers* 4 (1975), 1–7.

Armstrong, D.M., *A Materialist Theory of the Mind*, revised edition (London: Routledge, 1993).

Armstrong, D.M., *A World of States of Affairs* (Cambridge: CUP, 1997).

Arnold, Bill T., *Genesis* (Cambridge: CUP, 2009).

Arpaly, Nomy, *Merit, Meaning and Human Bondage* (Princeton, NJ: Princeton UP, 2006).

Atiyah, P.S., 'Economic Duress and the "Overborne Will"', *Law Quarterly Review* 98 (1982), 197–202.

Atiyah, P.S., 'Duress and the Overborne Will Again', *Law Quarterly Review* 99 (1983), 353–6.

Audi, R., *Action, Intention and Reason* (Ithaca, NY: Cornell Univ. Press, 1993).

Augustine, *The City of God*, trans. Henry Bettenson (Harmondsworth: Penguin, 2003).

Aune, Bruce, *Reason and Action* (Dordrecht: Reidel, 1977).

Austin, J.L., *Philosophical Papers* (Oxford: OUP, 1961).

Austin, J.L., *How To Do Things With Words*, second edition (Oxford: OUP, 1975).

Austin, John, *Lectures in Jurisprudence*, fifth edition (London: J. Murray, 1885).

Bach, Kent, 'Refraining, Omitting and Negative Acts', in O'Connor, T. & Sandis, C. (eds), *A Companion to the Philosophy of Action* (Oxford: Wiley-Blackwell, 2013).

Bain, Alexander, *The Emotions and the Will* (London: Longmans & Co., 1865).

Baker, Gordon, *The Voices of Wittgenstein: The Vienna Circle* (London: Routledge, 2003).

Bakhurst, David et al. (eds), *Thinking About Reasons: Themes from the Philosophy of Jonathan Dancy* (Oxford: OUP, 2013).

Bengson, J. & Moffett, M.A. (eds), *Knowing How: Essays on Knowledge, Mind, and Action* (Oxford: OUP, 2012).

Bentham, Jeremy, *An Introduction to the Principles of Morals and Legislation*, ed. J.H. Burns & H.L.A. Hart (Oxford: OUP, 1996).

Berkeley, George, *The Works of George Berkeley*, ed. T.E. Jessop & A.A. Luce, nine vols. (London: Nelson, 1948–57).

Berkeley, George, *The Principles of Human Knowledge & Three Dialogues between Hylas and Philonous*, ed. Roger Woolhouse (London: Penguin, 1988).

Bird, Alexander, *Nature's Metaphysics* (Oxford: OUP, 2007).

Bishop, John, *Natural Agency* (Cambridge: CUP, 1989).

Blackstone, William, *Commentaries on the Laws of England*, third edition, ed. Thomas McIntyre Cooley (Chicago, Ill.: Callahan & Co., 1884).

Bostock, David, *Aristotle's Ethics* (Oxford: OUP, 2000).

Braithwaite, R., 'The Nature of Believing', *Proceedings of the Aristotelian Society* 33 (1932), 129–46.

Broad, C.D., *Ethics and the History of Philosophy* (London: Routledge & Kegan Paul, 1952).

Bronitt, Simon H., 'Rape and Lack of Consent', *Criminal Law Journal* 16 (1992), 289–310.

Brundage, James, *Law, Sex, and Christian Society in Medieval Europe* (Chicago, Ill.: Univ. of Chicago Press, 1987).

Carnap, Rudolf, *Meaning and Necessity* (Chicago, Ill.: Univ. of Chicago Press, 1947).

Cassam, Quassim, 'Can the Concept of Knowledge be Analysed?', in Greenough, P. & Pritchard, D. (eds), *Williamson on Knowledge* (Oxford: OUP, 2009).

Charles, David, *Aristotle's Philosophy of Action* (London: Duckworth, 1984).

Clarke, Desmond, 'Causal Powers and Occasionalism from Descartes to Malebranche', in Gaukroger, S. et al. (eds), *Descartes' Natural Philosophy* (London: Routledge, 2000).

Collingwood, R.G., *The Idea of History* (Oxford: OUP, 1946).

Coope, Ursula, 'Aristotle on Action', *Proceedings of the Aristotelian Society*, suppl. vol. 81 (2007), 109–38.

Craig, Edward, *Knowledge and the State of Nature* (Oxford: OUP, 1990).

Cross, Tory, 'Recent Work on Dispositions', *Analysis* 72 (2012), 115–24.

Dancy, Jonathan, *Introduction to Contemporary Epistemology* (Oxford: Blackwell, 1985).

Dancy, Jonathan, *Practical Reality* (Oxford: OUP, 2000).

Dancy, Jonathan, 'Two Ways of Explaining Actions', in Hyman, J. & Steward, H. (eds), *Agency and Action* (Cambridge: CUP, 2004).

Dancy, Jonathan, 'Acting in Ignorance', *Frontiers of Philosophy in China* 6 (2011), 345–57.

Danto, Arthur, 'Basic Actions', repr. in White, A.R. (ed.), *The Philosophy of Action* (Oxford: OUP, 1968).

Darwin, Charles, *The Expression of the Emotions in Man and Animals*, fourth edition (Oxford: OUP, 2009).

Daube, David, *Civil Disobedience in Antiquity* (Edinburgh: Edinburgh Univ. Press, 1972).

Daube, David, *The Deed and the Doer in the Bible* (West Conshohocken, PA: Templeton, 2008).

Davidson, Donald, *Essays on Actions and Events* (Oxford: OUP, 1980).

Davidson, Donald, *Inquiries into Truth and Interpretation* (Oxford: OUP, 1984).

Davidson, Donald, 'Adverbs of Action', in Vermazen, B. & Hintikka, M.B. (eds), *Essays on Davidson* (Oxford: OUP, 1985).

Davidson, Donald, *Problems of Rationality* (Oxford: OUP, 2004).

Dawson, John P., 'Economic Duress: An Essay in Perspective', *Michigan Law Review* 45 (1947), 253–90.

Day, Jane M. (ed.), *Plato's Meno in Focus* (Abingdon: Routledge, 1994).

Dennett, Daniel, *Elbow Room* (Oxford: OUP, 1984).

DePaul, M. & Zagzebski, L. (eds), *Intellectual Virtue: Perspectives from Ethics and Epistemology* (Oxford: OUP, 2003).

DeRose, Keith, 'Solving the Sceptical Problem', *The Philosophical Review* 104 (1995), 1–52.

Descartes, René, *The Philosophical Writings of Descartes*, trans. John Cottingham et al., three vols. (Cambridge: CUP, 1988).

Dias, R.W.M., *Jurisprudence* (London: Butterworths, 1970).

Dray, W.H., *Laws and Explanation in History* (Oxford: OUP, 1957).

Dray, W.H., *History as Re-Enactment: R.G. Collingwood's Idea of History* (Oxford: OUP, 1995).

du Plessis, J.E., 'Force and Fear', in Reid, K. & Zimmerman, R. (eds), *A History of Private Law in Scotland II: Obligations* (Oxford: OUP, 2000).

Fakhry, M., *Islamic Occasionalism* (London: George Allen & Unwin, 1958).

Feldman, R., 'An Alleged Defect in Gettier Counter-Examples', *Australasian Journal of Philosophy* 52 (1974), 68–9.

Fine, Kit, 'First-Order Modal Theories III: Facts', *Synthese* 53 (1982), 43–122.

Fine, Kit, 'Ontological Dependence', *Proceedings of the Aristotelian Society* 95 (1995), 269–90.

Fine, Kit, 'Neutral Relations', *The Philosophical Review* 109 (2000), 1–33.

Fodor, Jerry, *The Language of Thought* (Cambridge, Mass.: Harvard Univ. Press, 1976).

Frankfurt, Harry, 'Alternate Possibilities and Moral Responsibility', *Journal of Philosophy* 66 (1969), 829–39.

Frankfurt, Harry, *The Importance of What We Care About* (Cambridge: CUP, 1998).

Frankfurt, Harry, 'Disengaging Reason', in Wallace, R. Jay et al. (eds), *Reason and Value: Themes from the Moral Philosophy of Joseph Raz* (Oxford: OUP, 2004).

Frede, Michael, *A Free Will* (Berkeley, Calif.: Univ. of California Press, 2011).

Gardner, John, *Offences and Defences* (Oxford: OUP, 2007).

Gaukroger, S. et al. (eds), *Descartes' Natural Philosophy* (London: Routledge, 2000).

Geach, P.T., *Mental Acts* (London: Routledge & Kegan Paul, 1957).

Geach, P.T., *Reference and Generality*, third edition (Ithaca, NY: Cornell Univ. Press, 1980).

Gettier, Edmund L., 'Is Justified True Belief Knowledge?', *Analysis* 23 (1963), 121–3.

Ginet, Carl, *On Action* (Cambridge: CUP, 1990).

Ginet, Carl, 'Reasons Explanations of Action: Causalist versus Noncausalist Accounts', in Kane, R. (ed.), *The Oxford Handbook of Free Will* (Oxford: OUP, 2002).

Goldman, A.I., 'A Causal Theory of Knowing', *Journal of Philosophy* 64 (1967), 357–72.

Goldman, A.I. & Olsson, E.J., 'Reliabilism and the Value of Knowledge', in Haddock, A. et al. (eds), *Epistemic Value* (Oxford: OUP, 2009).

Greco, John, 'Knowledge as Credit for True Belief', in DePaul, M. & Zagzebski, L. (eds), *Intellectual Virtue: Perspectives from Ethics and Epistemology* (Oxford: OUP, 2003).

Greenough, Patrick & Pritchard, Duncan (eds), *Williamson on Knowledge* (Oxford: OUP, 2009).

Hacker, P.M.S., *Human Nature: The Categorial Framework* (Oxford: Wiley-Blackwell, 2007).

Hacker, P.M.S., *The Intellectual Powers: A Study of Human Nature* (Oxford: Wiley-Blackwell, 2013).

Haddock, A. & Macpherson, F. (eds), *Disjunctivism: Perception, Action, Knowledge* (Oxford: OUP, 2008).

Haddock, Adrian et al. (eds), *Epistemic Value* (Oxford: OUP, 2009).

Hart, H.L.A., *Essays on Bentham* (Oxford: OUP, 1982).

Hart, H.L.A., *Essays in Jurisprudence and Philosophy* (Oxford: OUP, 1983).

Hart, H.L.A., *The Concept of Law*, third edition (Oxford: OUP, 2012).

Hart, H.L.A. & Honoré, A.M., *Causation in the Law*, second edition (Oxford: OUP, 1985).

Headlam, Walter, 'Prometheus and the Garden of Eden', *The Classical Quarterly* 28 (1934), 63–71.

Hempel, Carl, *Aspects of Scientific Explanation and Other Essays in the Philosophy of Science* (New York: The Free Press, 1965).

Hempel, Carl & Oppenheim, Paul, 'Studies in the Logic of Explanation', *Philosophy of Science* 15 (1948), 135–75.

Hobbes, Thomas, *Leviathan*, ed. Edwin Curley (Indianapolis, Ind.: Hackett, 1994).

Holmes, Oliver Wendell, *The Common Law* (London: Macmillan, 1968).

Holmström-Hintikka, G. & Tuomela, R., *Contemporary Action Theory I: Individual Action* (Dordrecht: Kluwer, 1997).

Hornsby, Jennifer, *Actions* (London: Routledge & Kegan Paul, 1980).

Hornsby, Jennifer, *Simplemindedness* (Cambridge, Mass.: Harvard Univ. Press, 1997).

Hornsby, Jennifer, 'A Disjunctive Conception of Acting for Reasons', in Haddock, A. & Macpherson, F. (eds), *Disjunctivism: Perception, Action, Knowledge* (Oxford: OUP, 2008).

Horwich, Paul, *Truth-Meaning-Reality* (Oxford: OUP, 2010).

Hulsewé, A.F.P., *Remnants of Ch'in Law* (Leiden: E.J. Brill, 1985).

Hume, David, *A Treatise of Human Nature*, ed. Ernest Mossner (London: Penguin, 1985).

Hyams, Keith, 'When Consent Doesn't Work: A Rights-Based Case for Limits to Consent's Capacity to Legitimise', *Journal of Moral Philosophy* 8 (2011), 110–38.

Hyman, John, *The Objective Eye* (Chicago, Ill.: Chicago Univ. Press, 2006).

Hyman, John, 'How Knowledge Works', *Philosophical Quarterly* 49 (1999), 433–51.

Hyman, John, '"The Most General Factive Stative Attitude"', *Analysis* 74 (2014), 561–5.

Hyman, John & Steward, Helen (eds), *Agency and Action* (Cambridge: CUP, 2004).

James, William, *The Principles of Psychology* (Cambridge, Mass.: Harvard Univ. Press, 1981).

Johnston, Mark, 'How to Speak of the Colors', *Philosophical Studies* 68 (1992), 221–63.

Julian, *Julian, Volume III*, Loeb Classical Library 157 (Cambridge, Mass.: Harvard Univ. Press, 1989).

Kane, Robert (ed.), *The Oxford Handbook of Free Will* (Oxford: OUP, 2002).

Kant, Immanuel, *Kant: Political Writings*, second edition, ed. H.S. Reiss (Cambridge: CUP, 1991).

Kaplan, Mark, 'It's Not What You Know That Counts', *Journal of Philosophy* 82 (1985), 350–63.

Kenny, Anthony, *Action, Emotion and Will* (London: Routledge & Kegan Paul, 1963).

Kenny, Anthony, *Wittgenstein* (Harmondsworth: Penguin, 1973).

Kenny, Anthony, *Will, Freedom and Power* (Oxford: Blackwell, 1975).

Kenny, Anthony, *Aristotle's Theory of the Will* (New Haven, Conn.: Yale Univ. Press, 1979).

Kenny, Anthony, 'Duress *per minas* as a Defence to Crime II', *Law and Philosophy* 1 (1982), 197–205.

Kenny, Anthony, *The Ivory Tower* (Oxford: Blackwell, 1985).

Kenny, Anthony, *The Metaphysics of Mind* (Oxford: OUP, 1989).

Kilbrandon, 'Duress *per minas* as a Defence to Crime I', *Law and Philosophy* 1 (1982), 185–95.

Kleinig, John, 'The Nature of Consent', in Miller, F.G. & Wertheimer, A. (eds), *The Ethics of Consent* (New York: OUP, 2010).

Kvanvig, Jonathan L., The Value of Knowledge and the Pursuit of Understanding (Cambridge: CUP, 2003).

Leibniz, G.W., *Leibniz: Selections*, trans. P. Wiener (New York: Scribner's, 1951).

Linetsky, Michael, *Rabbi Saadiah Gaon's Commentary on the Book of Creation* (Northvale, NJ: Jason Aronson, 2002).

List, Christian & Pettit, Philip, *Group Agency* (Oxford: OUP, 2011).

Locke, Dustin, 'Knowledge, Explanation and Motivating Reasons', *American Philosophical Quarterly*, forthcoming.

Locke, John, *An Essay Concerning Human Understanding*, ed. R. Woolhouse (London: Penguin, 1997).

Lowe, E.J., *Locke on Human Understanding* (London: Routledge, 1995).

Lowe, E.J., *The Possibility of Metaphysics* (Oxford: OUP, 1998).

Lowe, E.J., 'Free Agency, Causation and Action Explanation', in Sandis, C. (ed.), *New Essays on the Explanation of Action* (London: Palgrave Macmillan, 2009).

MacBride, Fraser, 'Neutral Relations Revisited', *Dialectica* 61 (2007), 25–56.

MacKitrick, J., 'Are Dispositions Causally Relevant', *Synthese* 144 (2005), 357–71.

Margolis, Joseph, 'Knowledge, Belief and Thought', *Ratio* 14 (1972), 74–82.

Martin, C.B., 'Dispositions and Conditionals', *Philosophical Quarterly* 44 (1994), 1–8.

Maynard Smith, John & Szathmáry, Eörs, *The Origins of Life* (Oxford: OUP, 1999).

Mayr, Erasmus, *Understanding Human Agency* (Oxford: OUP, 2011).

McDowell, John, 'Acting in the Light of a Fact', in Bakhurst, D. et al. (eds), *Thinking about Reasons: Themes from the Philosophy of Jonathan Dancy* (Oxford: OUP, 2013).

Melden, A.I., *Free Action* (London: Routledge & Kegan Paul, 1961).

Mele, A.R., *Motivation and Agency* (Oxford: OUP, 2003).

Mele, A.R. & Moser, P.K. 'Intention', *Noûs* 28 (1994), 39–68.

Mill, J.S., *A System of Logic*, second edition (London: John W. Parker, 1846).

Mill, J.S., *Utilitarianism* (New York: Macmillan, 1957).

Millar, Alan, 'Knowledge in Recent Epistemology: Some Problems', in Pritchard, D. et al., *The Nature and Value of Knowledge* (Oxford: OUP, 2010).

Miller, Franklin G. & Wertheimer, Alan (eds), *The Ethics of Consent* (New York: OUP, 2010).

Molnar, George, *Powers* (Oxford: OUP, 2003).

Moore, Michael S., *Act and Crime* (Oxford: OUP, 1993).

Moore, Michael S., *Placing Blame* (Oxford: OUP, 1997).

Nadler, S. (ed.), *The Cambridge Companion to Malebranche* (Cambridge: CUP, 2000).

Nadler, S. 'Malebranche on Causation', in Nadler, S. (ed.), *The Cambridge Companion to Malebranche* (Cambridge: CUP, 2000).

Nagel, Thomas, *The View From Nowhere* (Oxford: OUP, 1986).

Neander, Karen & Menzies, Peter, 'David Owens on Levels of Explanation', *Mind* 99 (1990), 459–66.

Neta, Ram, 'Treating Something as a Reason For Action', *Noûs* 43 (2009), 684–99.

Nozick, Robert, *Anarchy, State, and Utopia* (New York: Basic Books, 1974).

Nozick, Robert, *Philosophical Explorations* (Cambridge, Mass.: Harvard Univ. Press, 1981).

Nozick, Robert, *Socratic Puzzles* (Cambridge, Mass.: Harvard Univ. Press, 1997).

O'Connor, T. & Sandis, C. (eds), *A Companion to the Philosophy of Action* (Oxford: Wiley Blackwell, 2010).

O'Shaughnessy, Brian, *The Will: A Dual Aspect Theory*, second edition, 2 vols. (Cambridge: CUP, 2008).

Oberdiek, Hans, 'The Role of Sanctions and Coercion in Understanding Law and Legal Systems', *American Journal of Jurisprudence* 21 (1976), 71–94.

Olivelle, P. (ed.), *Manu's Code of Law* (Oxford: OUP, 2005).

Owens, David, 'Levels of Explanation', *Mind* 98 (1989), 59–79.

Parsons, Terence, *Events in the Semantics of English* (Cambridge, Mass.: MIT Press, 1990).

Passmore, John, 'Law and Explanation in History', *Australian Journal of Politics and History* 4 (1958), 269–75.

Peels, Rik, 'What Kind of Ignorance Excuses? Two Neglected Issues', *Philosophical Quarterly* 64 (2014), 478–96.

Peterson, Philip L., *Fact Proposition Event* (Dordrecht: Kluwer, 1997).

Plato, *Meno*, trans. W.R.M. Lamb, Loeb Classical Library 165 (Cambridge, Mass.: Harvard Univ. Press, 1989).

Prichard, H.A., *Moral Obligation* (Oxford: OUP, 1949).

Prior, A.N., *Formal Logic* (Oxford: Clarendon Press, 1955).

Prior, A.N., *Objects of Thought* (Oxford: OUP, 1971).

Prior, A.N., *The Doctrine of Propositions and Terms* (London: Duckworth, 1976).

Pritchard, Duncan, *Knowledge* (Houndmills: Palgrave Macmillan, 2009).

Pritchard, Duncan, 'Knowledge and Understanding', in Pritchard, Duncan et al., *The Nature and Value of Knowledge* (Oxford: OUP, 2010).

Pritchard, Duncan et al., *The Nature and Value of Knowledge* (Oxford: OUP, 2010).

Quine, W.V.O., 'Methodological Reflections on Current Linguistic Theory', *Synthese* 21 (1970), 386–98.

Quine, W.V.O., *Theories and Things* (Cambridge, Mass.: Harvard Univ. Press, 1981).

Quirk, Randolph, et al., *A Comprehensive Grammar of the English Language* (Harlow: Longman, 1985).

Rashi (Rabbi Shlomo Yitzchaki), *Rashi: Commmentary on the Torah I, Bereishis/Genesis*, ed. Rabbi Yisrael Isser Zvi Herczeg et al. (Jerusalem: Menorah, 1995).

Raz, Joseph, *The Morality of Freedom* (Oxford: OUP, 1986).

Raz, Joseph, *Practical Reason and Norms* (Princeton, NJ: Princeton Univ. Press, 1990).

Raz, Joseph, *Engaging Reason*, new edition (Oxford: OUP, 2002).

Raz, Joseph, *From Normativity to Responsibility* (Oxford: OUP, 2011).

Reid, K. & Zimmerman, R. (eds), *A History of Private Law in Scotland II: Obligations* (Oxford: OUP, 2000).

Reid, Thomas, *Essays on the Active Powers of Man*, ed. Knud Haakonssen & James A. Harris (Edinburgh: Edinburgh Univ. Press, 2010).

Riggs, Wayne, 'Beyond Truth and Falsehood: The Real Value of Knowing that P', *Philosophical Studies* 107 (2002), 87–108.

Rosen, Gideon, 'Culpability and Ignorance', *Proceedings of the Aristotelian Society* 103 (2003), 61–84.

Roth, Abraham, 'Explanations of Actions: Causal, Singular, and Situational', *Philosophy and Phenomenological Research* 59 (1999), 839–74.

Rumfitt, Ian, 'Savoir Faire', *The Journal of Philosophy* 100 (2003), 158–66.

Russell, Bertrand, *The Analysis of Mind* (London: Allen & Unwin, 1921).

Russell, Bertrand, *An Inquiry into Meaning and Truth* (London: Allen & Unwin, 1940).

Ryle, Gilbert, *The Concept of Mind* (London: Hutchinson, 1949).

Ryle, Gilbert, 'Mowgli in Babel', *Philosophy* 49 (1974), 5–11.

Ryle, Gilbert, *Collected Essays 1929–1968*, two vols. (Abingdon: Routledge, 2009).

Sandis, C. (ed.), *New Essays on the Explanation of Action* (London: Palgrave Macmillan, 2009).

Schilpp, P.A. & Hahn, L.E. (eds), *The Philosophy of Georg Henrik von Wright* (La Salle Ill.: Open Court, 1989).

Schomburg, W. & Peterson, I., 'Genuine Consent to Sexual Violence in International Law', *American Journal of International Law* 101 (2007), 121–40.

Schopenhauer, Arthur, *The World as Will and Representation II*, trans. E.J.F. Payne (Mineola, NY: Dover, 1966).

Schroeder, Timothy, *Three Faces of Desire* (Oxford: OUP, 2004).

Schueler, G.F., *Desire* (Cambridge, Mass.: MIT, 1995).

Sehon, Scott, 'Teleology and the Nature of Mental States', *American Philosophical Quarterly* 31 (1994), 63–72.

Sehon, Scott, *Teleological Realism* (Cambridge, Mass.: MIT Press, 2005).

Setiya, Kieran, *Reasons Without Rationalism* (Princeton, NJ: Princeton Univ. Press, 2007).

Setiya, Kieran, 'Causality in Action', *Analysis* 73 (2013), 501–12.

Shope, R.K., *The Analysis of Knowing* (Princeton NJ: Princeton Univ. Press, 1983).

Simmons, A.J., *Moral Principles and Political Obligations* (Princeton NJ: Princeton Univ. Press, 1979).

Slote, Michael, *Metaphysics and Essence* (Oxford: Blackwell, 1974).

Smith, Michael, *The Moral Problem* (Oxford: Blackwell, 1994).

Snowdon, Paul, 'Knowing How and Knowing That: A Distinction Reconsidered', *Proceedings of The Aristotelian Society* 104 (2003), 1–29.

Sorabji, Richard, *Animal Minds and Human Morals* (Ithaca, NY: Cornell Univ. Press, 1995).

Sosa, Ernest (ed.), *Causation and Conditionals* (Oxford: OUP, 1975).

Sosa, Ernest, 'The Place of Truth in Epistemology', in DePaul, M. & Zagzebski, L. (eds), *Intellectual Virtue: Perspectives from Ethics and Epistemology* (Oxford: OUP, 2003).

Sosa, Ernest, *A Virtue Epistemology: Apt Belief and Reflective Knowledge I* (Oxford: OUP, 2007).

Stanley, Jason, *Know How* (Oxford: OUP, 2011).

Stanley, Jason & Williamson, Timothy, 'Knowing How', *The Journal of Philosophy* 98 (2001), 411–44.

Stephen, J.F., *A History of the Criminal Law of England* (London: Macmillan, 1883).

Steward, Helen, 'Do Actions Occur Inside the Body?', *Mind and Society* 1 (2000).

Stich, Stephen, *The Fragmentation of Reason* (Cambridge, Mass.: MIT Press, 1990).

Stoecker, Ralf, 'Climbers, Pigs and Wiggled Ears: The Problem of Waywardness in Action Theory', in Walter, S. & Heckmann, D. (eds), *Physicalism and Mental Causation* (Exeter: Imprint Academic, 2003).

Stout, Rowland, *Things That Happen Because They Should* (Oxford: OUP, 1996).

Stout, Rowland, *Action* (Durham: Acumen, 2005).

Strawson, P.F., *Individuals* (London: Methuen, 1959).

Strawson, P.F., 'Doers and their Doings', *Times Literary Supplement*, 6 February 1981.

Strawson, P.F., *Analysis and Metaphysics* (Oxford: OUP, 1992).

Stroud, D.A., *Mens Rea* (London: Sweet & Maxwell, 1914).

Swain, Marshall, 'Reasons, Causes and Knowledge', *Journal of Philosophy* 75 (1978), 229–49.

Szabó, Zoltán Gendler, 'On the Progressive and the Perfective', *Noûs* 38 (2004), 29–59.

Tatarkiewicz, Władysław, 'On Perfection', trans. Christopher Kasparek, *Dialectics and Humanism: The Polish Philosophical Quarterly* 4–6 (1979–81).

Thompson, Michael, *Life and Action* (Cambridge, Mass.: Harvard Univ. Press, 2008).

Unger, Peter, *Ignorance* (Oxford: OUP, 1975).

Velleman, J.D., 'What Happens When Someone Acts?', *Mind* 101 (1992), 461–81.

Velleman, J.D., *The Possibility of Practical Reason* (New York: OUP, 2000).

Vendler, Zeno, *Res Cogitans* (Ithaca, NY: Cornell Univ. Press, 1972).

Vermazen, Bruce & Hintikka, Merril (eds), *Essays on Davidson* (Oxford: OUP, 1985).

Vlastos, Gregory, 'Anamnesis in the *Meno*', *Dialogue* 4 (1965), 143–67.

von Wright, G.H., *Norm and Action* (London: Routledge & Kegan Paul, 1963).

von Wright, G.H., *An Essay in Deontic Logic and the General Theory of Action* (Amsterdam: North-Holland, 1968).

von Wright, G.H., *Explanation and Understanding* (London: Routledge & Kegan Paul, 1971).

von Wright, G.H. (ed.), *Problems in the Theory of Knowledge* (The Hague: Martinus Nijhoff, 1972).

von Wright, G.H., *Practical Reason* (Oxford: Blackwell, 1983).

von Wright, G.H., *In the Shadow of Descartes* (Dordrecht: Kluwer, 1998).

von Wright, G.H., 'A Reply to My Critics', in Schilpp, P.A. & Hahn, L.E. (eds), *The Philosophy of Georg Henrik von Wright* (La Salle Ill.: Open Court, 1989).

Waismann, F., *The Principles of Linguistic Philosophy* (London: Macmillan, 1965).

Wallace, R. Jay et al. (eds), *Reason and Value: Themes from the Moral Philosophy of Joseph Raz* (Oxford: OUP, 2004).

Walter, S. & Heckmann, D. (eds), *Physicalism and Mental Causation* (Exeter: Imprint Academic, 2003).

Wegner, Daniel M., *The Illusion of Conscious Will* (Cambridge, Mass.: MIT Press, 2002).

Westen, Peter, *The Logic of Consent* (Aldershot: Ashgate, 2003).

White, A.R., *The Philosophy of Mind* (New York: Random House, 1967).

White, A.R. (ed.), *The Philosophy of Action* (Oxford: OUP, 1968).

White, A.R., *Modal Thinking* (Oxford: Blackwell, 1976).

White, A.R., *The Nature of Knowledge* (Totowa, NJ: Rowman & Littlefield, 1982).

White, A.R., *Grounds of Liability* (Oxford: OUP, 1985).

White, A.R., *Misleading Cases* (Oxford: OUP, 1991).

Wiggins, David, *Needs, Values, Truth*, third edition (Oxford: OUP, 1998).

Wiggins, David, 'Practical Knowledge: Knowing How To and Knowing That', *Mind* 121 (2012), 97–130.

Williams, Bernard, *Moral Luck: Philosophical Papers 1973–1980* (Cambridge: CUP, 1981).

Williams, Bernard, *Shame and Necessity* (Berkeley: University of California Press, 1993).

Williams, Bernard, 'Knowledge and Reasons', in von Wright, G.H. (ed.), *Problems in the Theory of Knowledge* (The Hague: Martinus Nijhoff, 1972).

Williams, Glanville, *Textbook of Criminal Law*, second edition (London: Stevens, 1983).

Williamson, Timothy, 'Converse Relations', *The Philosophical Review* 94 (1985), 249–62.

Williamson, Timothy, *Knowledge and its Limits* (Oxford: OUP, 2000).

Wilson, George, *The Intentionality of Human Action*, revised edition (Stanford, CA: Stanford University Press, 1989).

Wilson, George, 'Reasons as Causes for Action', in Holmström-Hintikka, G. & Tuomela, R. (eds), *Contemporary Action Theory I: Individual Action* (Dordrecht: Kluwer, 1997).

Winch, Peter, *The Idea of a Social Science and Its Relation to Philosophy* (London: Routledge & Kegan Paul, 1958).

Wittgenstein, Ludwig, *The Blue and Brown Books* (Oxford: Blackwell, 1958).

Wittgenstein, Ludwig, *Philosophical Investigations*, trans. G.E.M. Anscombe, second edition (Oxford: Blackwell, 1958).

Wittgenstein, Ludwig, *Tractatus Logico-Philosophicus*, trans. D.F. Pears & B.F. McGuinness (London: Routledge & Kegan Paul, 1961).

Wittgenstein, Ludwig, *Philosophical Remarks*, trans. R. Hargreaves & R. White (Oxford: Blackwell, 1964).

Wittgenstein, Ludwig, *Remarks on the Foundations of Mathematics*, trans. G.E.M. Anscombe (Oxford: Blackwell, 1967).

Wittgenstein, Ludwig, *Zettel*, trans. G.E.M. Anscombe (Oxford: Blackwell, 1967).

Wittgenstein, Ludwig, *On Certainty*, trans. G.E.M. Anscombe & D. Paul (Oxford: Blackwell, 1969).

Wittgenstein, Ludwig, *Notebooks 1914–16*, trans. G.E.M. Anscombe, revised edition (Oxford: Blackwell, 1979).

Wittgenstein, Ludwig, *Remarks on the Philosophy of Psychology I*, trans. G.E.M. Anscombe (Oxford: Blackwell, 1980).

Woodward, James, *Making Things Happen* (Oxford: OUP 2003).

Wright, Crispin, 'Scepticism and Dreaming: Imploding the Demon', *Mind* 100 (1991), 87–116.

Zagzebski, Linda, 'The Search for the Source of Epistemic Good', *Metaphilosophy* 34 (2003), 12–28.

Zimmerman, Michael J., 'Moral Responsibility and Ignorance', *Ethics* 107 (1997), 410–26.

Acknowledgements

The author and publisher gratefully acknowledge permission to reproduce material from previously published articles, in the parts of this book indicated in parenthesis: 'Agents and their Actions', with M. Alvarez, *Philosophy* 73 (1998), 219–245 (§§2.2 and 3.2); 'How Knowledge Works', *Philosophical Quarterly* 49 (1999), 433–451 (§§7.1–7.2); 'The Road to Larissa', *Ratio* 23 (2010), 393–414 (§§8.1–8.5); 'Wittgenstein on Action and the Will', *Grazer Philosophische Studien* 82 (2011), 285–311 (§§1.4 and 2.1); 'Voluntariness and Choice', *Philosophical Quarterly* 63 (2013), 683–708 (§§4.1–4.6); 'Desires, Dispositions and Deviant Causal Chains', *Philosophy* 89 (2014), 83–112 (§§5.2–5.7); 'Acts and Intentions', *Think* 13 (2014), 11–22 (§§2.4–2.5).

Index

du Plessis, J. E. 226 n. 26
duress 80, 81–84, 89, 91, 92–93, 96

Eliezer, Rabbi 194
ellipsis 39–40, 67–68
emotion, expression of 51
eventive object (of a verb) 56
event 41–42, 58, 60, 61, 63–66, 88
exculpation 5, 77, 80, 95
explanans (reason why) 134, 137–139,
    143, 144–146, 148–149, 152–158,
    209, 230 n. 4, 231 n. 13
explanation 41, 106, 128–132, 133–139,
    143–149, 174, 181–183, 230 n. 50
  causal 105, 114, 120–121, 127, 128,
    129, 132, 155–156, 183
  in terms of knowledge or belief 140,
    152–153, 171, 172, 174, 190, 209,
    234 n. 26
  of intentional action 110–121, 131,
    132, 149–152, 155–157, 158, 190,
    228 n. 27, 230 n. 55, 230 n. 58
  and justification 120, 133–136, 139, 145
  teleological 3, 103, 116, 130, 150

fact (*see also* truth) 134, 144–146, 149 n.,
    150, 158, 163, 170, 174, 188
factivity 146–148, 150
Fakhry, M. 229 n. 38
Fall, the 191–196
Feldman, R. 234 n. 29
Fine, K. 71–72, 73, 224 n. 13, 225 n. 26,
    225 n. 27, 225 n. 28, 225 n. 30, 232
    n. 4, 232 n.5
Frankfurt, H. 3, 45–46, 82, 223 n. 9,
    224 n. 25, 227 n. 48
Frede, M. 222 n. 1
Freud, S. 118

Galileo, G. 122
Gardner, J. 38–39
Geach, P. 140
Genesis 42, 58, 121–122, 191, 194–195,
    196, 197
Gettier, E. 154, 189, 201, 203, 204,
    206, 207
Ginet, C. 130–131, 156, 207 n., 225 n. 16
God 42, 58, 121–122, 191–193, 194, 195,
    196, 198, 211, 212

Goddard, R. 90
Goldman, A. I. 155, 231 n. 19,
    235 n. 31
grammar 57–58, 105
Greco, J. 234 n. 25, 235 n. 31
Grice, H. P. 37
grief 52
ground 115, 129, 133, 138–139,
    140–149, 149–158, 172, 174, 208
guilt 76, 77, 78–80

Hacker, P. M. S. 38 n., 176–177,
    223 n. 12, 230 n. 53
Haddock, A. 234 n. 25
Hampshire, S. 115, 128
Hart, H. L. A. 6, 82, 84–85, 90, 92,
    93, 98
Headlam, W. 233 n. 4
Hempel, C. J. 103, 104, 132, 230 n. 4
Hobbes, T. 2, 4, 9 n., 25, 91, 213, 215,
    217, 219
Holmes, O. W. 11
Honoré, A. M. 82, 84–85, 90, 92, 98
Hornsby, J. 23–24, 54 n., 58 n., 59, 66,
    224 n. 10, 231 n. 21
Horwich, P. 198
human sciences vs natural
    sciences 103–104, 105, 106
Hume, D. 4, 27, 66, 102, 111, 122, 123,
    180, 210, 216, 217, 229 n. 30
Hyams, K. 227 n. 32
Hyman, J. 233 n. 26, 233 n. 27

ignorance 5, 11, 18, 77, 78, 225 n. 7
Iliad 78
innocence 76, 77
intention 2, 4, 6, 7–8, 12, 13, 17, 19,
    25, 30–32, 43–44, 45, 46, 48,
    50–53, 74, 76, 78, 91, 97, 100,
    105–107, 114, 115–117, 127,
    128–132, 139, 140–143, 151,
    165, 167, 216–218, 226 n. 8,
    226 n. 24, 227 n. 27, 229 n. 31
'involuntary' 8, 75 n.

James, W. 1, 2, 4, 14, 20, 24, 91,
    219–220, 221
Job 194
Johnson, S. 140, 217

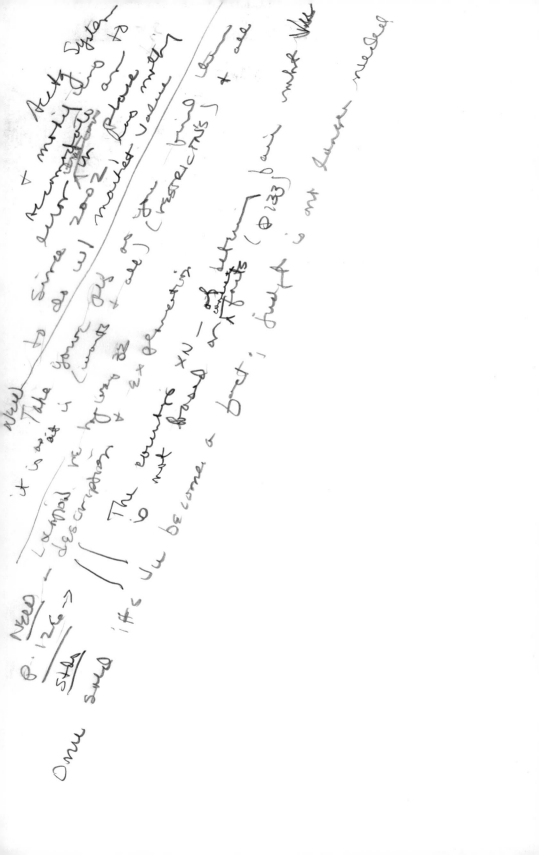

NEED
P.126 → — Legal
STEP   described
it is it

Property System
recommended
∆ since   2002
Take
it is it's

market value

(RESTRICTIONS)

The government
it becomes a ...

(@ 133)

what was
needed